D1238879

HOMELANDS
OF THE
CLANS

HOMELANDS
OF THE
CLANS

GERALD WARNER
O.St.J., M.A., F.S.A.Scot.

COLLINS
LONDON & GLASGOW

First Published 1980
©1980 Gerald Warner
ISBN 0 00 411128 1
Typeset by Bookmag, Inverness
Printed in Spain
by Graficromo, S.A.-Córdoba
for William Collins Sons & Co. Ltd.

To my parents
JAMES and EILEEN WARNER

CONTENTS

INTRODUCTION

WHY DO PEOPLE FIND THE HISTORY OF THE Scottish clans so fascinating? What is it that draws third or fourth generation exiles back to Scotland, from as far away as Canada or Australia, in search of the glen where their remote ancestors eked out a precarious existence? The reasons are complex and varied as the clan system itself, and as enigmatic as the Scottish character. In so far as any one idea can provide an explanation, the essence of this atavistic attraction is probably the search for identity. Amid the turbulence of the twentieth century, men and women gain reassurance from a rediscovery of their origins.

In the succeeding pages, therefore, what has been attempted is to portray the distinctive character of each clan, so far as is possible within the confines of a brief narrative. Too often, people assume that the only thing which distinguishes one clan from another is the pattern of its tartan; it is hoped that this book will go some way towards dispelling that illusion. Another misconception is the notion of the clan system as exclusively Highland. The Lowland and Border clans had as strong a sense of identity as their Highland counterparts, even though they were not so firmly demarcated from the rest of Britain by geography and language. Admittedly, their organization was more feudal than patriarchal, but it should be remembered that Highland chiefs, as time progressed, increasingly held their land by titles such as baronial charters: those who did not (like the MacGregors), found themselves dispossessed. Besides, even if the members of a Border clan did not all claim descent from some mythical patriarch, the intermarriage of neighbours, which was inevitable in a society with limited mobility, soon created a genuine blood-bond. If the blood-feud is any touchstone of clan identity, it is worth recalling that the quarrel between the Johnstones and the Maxwells probably claimed more lives than any Highland vendetta.

What was most important to a clan, however, was its territory or homeland — hence the title of the book. The quality of the land determined the clansmen's standard of living; its geographical situation dictated who were friends and who were enemies and, consequently, which side should be supported during national upheavals; it was for the clan's land that men fought and died, committed atrocities or made heroic sacrifices. In the upper ranks of clan society, chiefs plotted advantageous marriages for their heirs, uncles murdered nephews, and all for one eventual goal: mastery of the land and the power it conferred. The individual clan histories dramatically illustrate this paramount obsession. Though not extensive, the Grahams' lands were rich enough to give them importance; the Camerons' life-or-death struggle to hold Glen Loy and Loch Arkaig was a matter of basic survival; the Campbells' dispossession of the MacGregors created a national problem which endured for three centuries, demonstrating how the fabric of a territorially-based society could be disrupted by a landless clan at large. The land-holdings of many chiefs fully justified the high-sounding titles they bore, especially in an age when sovereign states were geographically smaller than today. The Mackenzie lands traversed Scotland from coast to coast and would have accommodated several of the principalities of the Holy Roman Empire.

It is the diversity of the clans which is their most striking feature. Even in their remote origins they are completely heterogeneous. Clan genealogies claim a rich variety of descents: from Norsemen (for example, the MacLeods), Flemings (the Murrays and Sutherlands), Anglo-Saxons (the Eliotts), Normans and Angevins (the Bruces, Chisholms and Frasers), and even from old Celtic ecclesiastical office-bearers (Clan Chattan and the MacMillans). Any idea that the clans represent a unified ethnic group, therefore, is quite false. Equally misleading is the image of them as an elite of Scottish patriots, a tartan-clad host, uniformly Jacobite in sentiment and always eager to rise against the English yoke. Many clans had consistently Whig loyalties. Of these, the best-known are the Campbells, but the Fergussons, Mackays and Rosses also had a firmly anti-Jacobite tradition. Some clans were divided in their loyalties, the most tragic example being the Chisholms: two of the chief's sons served as officers in Cumberland's army at Culloden, where they found the corpse of their younger brother, killed fighting in the Jacobite army. As regards patriotism, most of the Border clans, with a few honourable exceptions such as the Scotts, were pensioners of England at one time or another and swelled the ranks of English invasions against their countrymen.

In a typically Scottish fashion, the Scottish clans elude any attempt to impose a uniform pattern upon them. They were Presbyterian (like the Campbells), or Catholic (like the Gordons); the Chisholms at one period were a Catholic clan with a chief who was a Covenanter. In their life-styles too, they exhibited an equal diversity. The Gordons were horsemen, the Macleans sailors; the Campbells were lawyers, the MacGregors outlaws. The Johnstones acknowledged their main occupation with disarming frankness in their warcry — 'Light thieves all!' If other clans had been equally honest, they too would have admitted that the economic mainstay of their existence was plunder. Was that a blot on Scotland's escutcheon? Hardly, in a society where the forcible seizure of property enjoyed the sanction of universal practice. Lands or cattle won by the sword were honestly acquired, in contemporary eyes, not to be compared with gains made by such pettifogging devices as lawyers (and Campbells) employed.

There is much in the history of the clans to shock modern morality. Indeed, their behaviour regularly shocked their town-dwelling contemporaries and, occasionally, each other. Yet they had a code of morality and of honour which was both punctilious and generally observed. There were many worse atrocities in Scottish history than the Massacre of Glencoe: what made that incident notorious was not the slaughter of women and children, but the breach of the laws of hospitality. At the same time, there were many occasions in clan history when the murder of enemies was planned to take place during a banquet, or in their beds under the roofs of rival clans. One can only explain this by recognizing that the rules of every society are broken from time to time. The redeeming features of the clansmen were their love of the land they held against all comers, and their devotion to their own kin. In a desperately insecure world, only the ties of kinship could be relied upon. Those were the two keystones of clan civilization: the homeland and the blood-bond. To those outside the clan system, the famous Fraser chief, Simon, 11th Lord Lovat, was a ravisher, a turncoat and a traitor; to the Highlanders, he was the ideal example of a Gaelic patriarch. This was because he understood and adhered to the essential canon of clan morality, and gave it the most perfect expression in a famous remark: 'There is nothing I place in balance with my kindred.' This book is an illustration of that philosophy.

I should like to express my warm thanks to Catriona Montgomery, who kindly corrected the Gaelic in the text; to Jean Robertson of Glasgow University Library; and to Diana Campbell, who typed the manuscript. Finally, I should like to thank Patricia Bascom for invaluable help and guidance.

G.W.

CLAN
ARMSTRONG

Armstrong

MOTTO: _Invictus maneo_ (I remain unvanquished)
ORIGIN OF NAME: Strong arm

THE ARMSTRONGS WERE THE MOST TURBULENT AND feared of the Border clans. Although the clan system in the Borders broke up at the Union of the Crowns in 1603, in the late Middle Ages and the sixteenth century the tribal way of life was as firmly established in the Borders as in the Hebrides. So the Armstrongs were historically as much a clan as, for example, the MacLeods. The name of Armstrong is synonymous with hard-riding 'moss troopers' and daring raids into hostile territory, often at heavy cost; it is appropriate that the first man to set foot on the Moon should have been an Armstrong.

As with most clans, Highland or Lowland, the lack of reliable records as to the Armstrongs' origin is amply compensated by exotic legend. Some traditions claim that the Armstrongs descend from Siward, Earl of Northumberland, the founder of York Minster, who flourished in the eleventh century and who appears as a character in Shakespeare's _Macbeth_. It is said that one of his descendants named Fairbeorn was armour-bearer to a Scots king whose horse was killed under him in battle; Fairbeorn seized him by the thigh and pulled him up onto his own mount, whereupon the king gave him the name of 'Arm Strong'. A more pedestrian theory is that Armstrong is an English version of the Norman name Fortinbras. Whatever the truth may be, it is certain that the Armstrongs lived originally in England and that is where the earliest historical records of them are found. In 1235, Adam Armstrong was pardoned in Carlisle for killing a man and the name appears regularly thereafter in Cumberland until 1342. Between 1361 and 1373 there is mention in the Scots records of one Gilbert Armstrong, a distinguished cleric who became Provost of the Cathedral of St Andrews. In 1376, the name first appeared in Liddesdale, the district that was to be the Armstrongs' clan territory. At that time, Alexandir Armystrand held the lands of Mangerton, which continued to be the chiefly seat until the seventeenth century.

Despite the absence of earlier records, however, it seems likely that the Armstrongs had already been settled in Liddesdale for some time and tradition asserts that Alexander Armstrong, described as 2nd Laird of

'Armstrong's of Gilnockie, Dumfriesshire' — an anonymous drawing of Hollows Tower.

Carlisle Castle. It was from here that Kinmont Willie, a relative of the Armstrong chief, was rescued by a daring raid in 1596.

Mangerton, was murdered about 1320 by his enemies, the Soulis family. According to local legend, young Armstrong was feasting in Lord Soulis's castle of Hermitage when a black bull's head — the symbol of death in ancient Scotland — was placed on the table and he was struck down by his hosts. The nearby fourteenth-century Milnholm Cross marks his grave. Much later, in 1398, Alexander, Geoffrey and David Armstrong were among the knights and gentlemen who became surety for the Earl of Douglas. In 1482, Thomas Armstrong, 5th of Mangerton, surrendered his lands into the hands of the Earl of Angus, in favour of David Scott of Branxholm. Whatever the reason for this transaction, it was either cancelled or short-lived, for the Armstrong chiefs continued to reside at Mangerton. During the civil strife which ended in the Battle of Sauchieburn (1488), the Armstrongs supported the house of Douglas (by now lords of Liddesdale) against James III. Then, in the last decade of the fifteenth century, they were involved, along with the Eliotts, Nixons, Crosiers and other Border clans, in a conspiracy to place the pretender Perkin Warbeck on the English throne. A premature Armstrong raid into Northumberland in 1493, however, spoiled the project. Yet the Armstrongs' star was in the ascendant and the following century was destined to see their power oust that of the king himself in Liddesdale, only to collapse in ruin at the end.

The territory occupied by the Armstrongs was fertile, but not extensive. It comprised the southern half of Liddesdale, a triangular area bounded on the south-east by the English border from Canonbie to Glendhu Hill, on the west by the River Esk and on the north by the Eliott lands. This small homeland was not the source of the Armstrongs' disproportionate power — that was based on their formidable capacity for raiding and carrying off livestock; nor did it represent the full extent of the clan's occupation of territory since, from 1518, they also held the greater part of the Debatable Land, the area between Liddesdale and the Solway Firth, claimed by both Scotland and England. Some of the Armstrong land east of the Esk, in the south-western extremity of the triangle described above, was legally Debatable Land.

As has been mentioned, the principal Armstrong residence was Mangerton, which stood about 1 mile south of Newcastleton (B6357); Whithaugh, the seat of the principal cadet house, stood where Newcastleton now is; Ailmure and the Chingils (also called Raltoun), the next most senior cadet houses, were close to Mangerton. These three main cadets descended from the younger sons of Thomas Armstrong, 5th of Mangerton. The remaining Armstrong fortress of importance was Hollows Tower, or Gilnockie, a strong peel tower, now a ruin, on the west bank of the Esk, near the village of Hollows (on the A7), about 4 miles south of Langholm. This was built by the most famous border reiver of all time, John Armstrong of Gilnockie, younger son of Alexander, 6th of Mangerton.

After the Scots defeat at Flodden in 1513, the English harried Eskdale and Lower Annandale, assisted by the Armstrongs and other Borderers to whom clan politics were more important than patriotism, of which there was little notion on the frontier at that time. By 1524, the Armstrongs had become so troublesome that Archibald Bell-the-Cat, Earl of Angus, who had been appointed Warden of the Middle and East Marches, launched a surprise attack on them. Besides a booty of 3,000 sheep, 600 cattle and 500 goats, Angus captured a dozen Armstrongs, including the Laird of Whithaugh, known as Sym the Larde, and his brother, nicknamed Davy the Lady. No harm came to them, however, for it was Angus's policy generally to favour the Border reivers, much to the disgust of the young James V. During 1527 the Armstrongs gave further cause for concern, having formed an unholy alliance with the Lisles, a family of English outlaws whom Henry VIII was anxious to destroy. The nature of the Armstrongs' activities may be judged from Sym of Whithaugh's boast that he had devastated 60 miles of countryside and 'laide downe thirty parisshe churches'. In 1529 it was recorded that 'the Armestrongges of Liddersdaill had reapoorted presumptuously that thay woode not be ordoured, naither by the king of Scottes, thair soveraine lorde, nor by the king of

Johnnie Armstrong of Gilnockie, one of the most notorious of the Border reivers, romantically conceived by the Victorian painter H.H. Emmerson.

Einglande, but after suche maner as thaire faders had used afore thayme'.

Clearly such anarchy could not be tolerated indefinitely. James V, now freed from the tutelage of the house of Douglas, determined on stern measures. He had to proceed cautiously, for at this period it was estimated that the Armstrongs were capable of raising an army of 3,000 horsemen. Yet, since it was necessary to make an example, the king selected as his victim John Armstrong of Gilnockie, younger son of the 6th Laird of Mangerton. Johnnie Armstrong's career had been the most notorious on the Borders. Between 1526 and 1528 he had colonized the Debatable Land, building peel towers throughout the area. The English Warden, Lord Dacre, retaliated in 1528 by burning Hollows Tower, Johnnie's stronghold on the Esk. In revenge, Armstrong had burned Netherby, in Cumberland. During the same year, he had further contributed to the excitement of life in the Borders by prosecuting a clan feud against the Johnstones. It was understandable, therefore, that James V should regard Johnnie Armstrong as something less than a model subject. In the summer of 1530, the king made a progress to the Borders and halted at Carlanrig, half a mile south-west of Teviothead (on the A7). Johnnie Armstrong came riding confidently to meet him, splendidly dressed and with 50 horsemen in attendance; so secure did he feel that he had not even troubled to obtain a guarantee of safe conduct from the king. The spectacle of

Armstrong's fine clothes and retinue enraged James: 'What wants yon knave that a king should have?' he exclaimed. Then he summarily ordered the hanging of Armstrong and his followers. At first the outlaw tried to bargain for his life, but when he found the king immovable, he resolved to die with dignity, telling James, 'I am but a fool to seek grace at a graceless face'. The outlaws' punishments were made to fit their crimes, so that one of them who had burned a woman and her children alive in their house was himself executed by burning. The episode inspired the most famous of all Border ballads, 'Johnnie Armstrong', composed about 1600 by Ringan's Thom, the last Clan Armstrong bard; it also provides the subject of a modern play, *Armstrong's Last Goodnight*, by John Arden. Johnnie and his men were buried at Carlanrig, at a place now marked by a stone tablet set in the wall of the former churchyard in 1897.

Somehow the Armstrongs never quite recovered the tremendous influence they had had in the heyday of Johnnie of Gilnockie, but they remained a power to be reckoned with in Liddesdale. Sym the Larde, 2nd of Whithaugh, was hanged in 1536, demonstrating that the clan had not changed its ways. In 1541 the Armstrongs challenged the Grahams to mortal combat, but shortly afterwards they were again on friendly terms. After the Rout of Solway Moss in 1542 and the death of their enemy, James V, the Armstrongs became English

Life on the Borders was not all feuding. Alexander Carse's watercolour evokes the more domestic side of Scottish rural life.

pensioners and joined in the harrying of southern Scotland. Throughout 1543, under treaty to England, they burned 124 homesteadings, carried off more than 3,000 cattle, 300 horses and 4,000 sheep and goats, as well as over 400 prisoners and 35 men slain. Then, in 1545, an English garrison was allowed to occupy Langholm Tower, an Armstrong fortress, and the clan fought on the English side at the Battle of Ancrum Moor. Two years later, 300 Armstrongs of Liddesdale were listed among those Scots 'bound by oathe and pledge' to serve the King of England. At this sad period, the Armstrong chief was Thomas the Gude Laird, 7th of Mangerton, who died about 1548 and was succeeded by his eldest son, Archibald.

Archibald, 8th Laird of Mangerton, was an opponent of Mary Queen of Scots, or, more specifically, of her husband Bothwell, in whose castle of Hermitage he was held prisoner in 1567. Yet the Armstrongs' quarrel was not with the Queen herself; the Regent Moray also regarded them as enemies. In 1569, having stayed overnight at Mangerton, the Regent ungraciously ordered the house to be blown up the following morning; Moray's supporters, who signed a bond at Kelso that same year, counted the Armstrongs among their foes. About this time, the defeated Catholic rebels from England, who had risen for Mary Queen of Scots, took refuge in Liddesdale. To the shame of the Armstrongs, Hector of Harelaw, known as Hector with the Griefs and Cuts, betrayed the fugitive Earl of Northumberland to the Regent Moray, who handed him over to Elizabeth of England. After the death of Moray in 1570, the Armstrongs assumed a more patriotic role and devastated the English borders, allegedly to avenge the imprisonment of their Queen. Archibald Armstrong died in 1578, when his son Simon became 9th Laird of Mangerton. He rebuilt Mangerton in 1583, and in the following year suffered the indignity of being captured by the English at his own hearth. In 1596, however, he took part in the famous rescue from Carlisle Castle of his father's second cousin, William Armstrong of Kinmont, celebrated in ballad as Kinmont Willie. He had been treacherously seized by the English on a day of truce, but Scott of Buccleuch led a daring raid which snatched him from the dungeons of Carlisle; as honour demanded, the Armstrong chief and many of his men took part in this exploit.

Kinmont Willie's rescue was the last flicker of Armstrong glory. Simon was killed treacherously by the Douglases and his successor, Archibald, 10th of Mangerton, was destined to be the last chief. In 1603, dismayed by the succession of James VI to the English throne, he led 200 horsemen in an invasion of England in a futile effort to prevent the Union of the Crowns. Inevitably, he failed and James VI took a terrible revenge, razing most of his fortresses in Liddesdale to the very foundations. Archibald, his son and heir, was 'put to the horn' and fled to an unknown refuge. That was the end of what had once been the greatest Border clan of all. Centuries later, however, an Armstrong participated in the most daring expedition ever conceived by men. On 21st July 1969, Neil A. Armstrong stepped out of the Apollo 11 lunar module onto the surface of the Moon, observing, 'That's one small step for a man, one giant leap for mankind'. If the shades of his adventurous forebears were looking on, they must surely have approved. Today there is no officially recognized chief of Clan Armstrong, but the Armstrong baronets of Gallen (later resettled in Rhodesia) would appear to be head of the Irish branch, which migrated to Fermanagh in the seventeenth century. There is an official Armstrong tartan.

CLAN
BRUCE

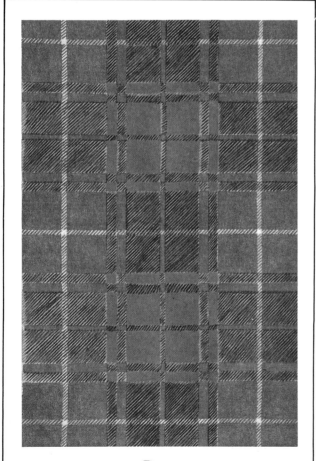

Bruce

MOTTO: *Fuimus* (We have been)
ORIGIN OF NAME: from French town of Brix
PLANT BADGE: Rosemary

THE BRUCES' CLAIM TO FAME IS MORE THAN OBVIOUS. Though other clans, such as the MacDuffs and MacGregors, may rightly boast of royal blood, the Bruces and the Stewarts are unique in having provided Scotland with her two great royal dynasties. In the case of the Bruces, their name will forever be associated with the most glorious episode in Scottish history, the victory of Bannockburn, that triumphant assertion of national independence ending a very bitter and drawn-out war against England.

The remote origins of the Bruces were Norse, but by the eleventh century they were settled in Normandy, whose duke and aristocracy were Christianized Vikings. Adam de Brus is said to have helped William the Conqueror to subdue England, receiving in return huge grants of land in Yorkshire. His son, Robert de Brus, was made lord of Annandale by David I, King of Scots, and this became the inheritance of his younger son, also Robert. Thus, at the Battle of the Standard in 1138, Bruce the elder, fighting in the English army, took his own son prisoner as he fought for David I, his overlord in Annandale. Young Robert left two sons, Robert and William, who became successively lords of Annandale. Robert married the daughter of King William the Lion, but died childless; his brother William died in 1215, when his eldest son Robert succeeded to Annandale. It was this lord, Robert the Noble, who established the royal claims of the family.

In 1209, Robert the Noble married Isabella, second daughter of David, Earl of Huntingdon, the younger brother of Kings Malcolm IV and William the Lion. After the deaths of Alexander III, in 1286, and the Maid of Norway, in 1290, Robert Bruce of Annandale, the son of Robert the Noble and the Lady Isabella, became a claimant to the Scots crown. In strict law, his claim was inferior to that of John Balliol, descended from Isabella's elder sister, but Bruce bolstered his case by emphasizing the fact that Alexander II and his Parliament had nominated him heir and that this had been confirmed verbally by Alexander III. Edward I of England, however, who had been appointed arbiter, found in favour of Balliol in the famous judgement known as the

The statue of King Robert the Bruce stands proudly on the field of Bannockburn.

Stirling Castle, surrendered by the English after Bruce's victory at nearby Bannockburn.

Dunfermline Abbey, the burial place of Robert the Bruce.

Award of Norham. Bruce would not acknowledge Balliol as king, but resigned his own claim to his son Robert, who had become Earl of Carrick through marriage. The earl made his peace with Edward I and died on his English estates in 1304. His son, however, was far from living at peace with England: his extraordinary career brought him to the throne of Scotland and left his name, 'The Bruce', a household word.

He was born in 1274, and at first seemed inclined to follow his father's policy of least resistance. The tyranny of the English, however, changed his attitude dramatically. On 10th February 1306, he killed his enemy the Red Comyn, Balliol's nephew, in the church of the Friars Minor at Dumfries. On 27th March 1306, he was crowned King of Scots at Scone, but was defeated three months later at Methven. While Bruce went into hiding, Edward I took a terrible revenge. Bruce's wife, daughter and sister were imprisoned in England, another sister was confined in a cage at Roxburgh, his brothers, Thomas and Alexander, were beheaded at Carlisle and his youngest brother, Nigel, suffered the same fate at Berwick. The cruelty of the English had the effect of stiffening Scots resistance so that, when Edward was succeeded by his weakling son, Edward II, in 1307, the tide of war began to turn. In 1310, all the clergy of Scotland recognized Bruce as king. One by one the English garrisons surrendered until, by 1314, only Berwick and Stirling held out against Bruce. In an attempt to relieve Stirling, Edward II marched north with an army of 20,000 men. On 24th June 1314, he was routed at Bannockburn by Bruce, commanding an army only one-third as large. A statue of Bruce now dominates the battlefield, which is near the village of Bannockburn, about 2 miles south of Stirling (on the A9). The battlefield is the property of the National Trust for Scotland.

In 1320 the Declaration of Arbroath proclaimed Scotland's sovereign independence before all Christendom. King Robert the Bruce died of leprosy, the most dreaded disease of the Middle Ages, in 1329 and was buried at Dunfermline Abbey. The feelings of the nation he had freed were eloquently expressed by John Barbour in his epic poem *The Brus*, written less than 50 years later:

'"All our defens," tha said, "alas!
And he that all our confort was,
Our wit and all our governing,
Is brocht, alas! her till ending."'

The great King was succeeded by his son, David II, who reigned from 1329 to 1370, when he died childless. Robert II, son of Marjorie Bruce, the daughter of Robert I, and Walter Stewart, then inherited the throne, thus establishing a new dynasty.

Although the direct male line of Bruce was extinct within the royal succession, the Bruce family still flourished. King Robert had an uncle, John Bruce, who appears to have been the progenitor of the senior surviving line, the Bruces of Clackmannan. Thomas, probably his son, received the lands of Clackmannan as a reward for his services against the English in 1334. The head of the family was created Earl of Kincardine in 1647 and this peerage was united with the earldom of Elgin, by inheritance, in 1747. The 3rd Earl of Elgin was a Jacobite, imprisoned in the Tower of London in 1696. From the main line of Clackmannan derived the cadet houses of Airth, Kennet, Rait, Earlshall, Cultmalindie, Auchenbowie, Kinnaird and the Comtes de Brus in France. The present representative of the Bruces of Kennet is Lord Balfour of Burleigh. The Bruces of Stenhouse hold a baronetcy, as do their cadet branch, the Bruces of Downhill in Northern Ireland. The Welsh family of Bruce of Blaen-y-Cwm, in Glamorgan, is an offshoot of the house of Kennet. James Bruce of Kinnaird (1730-94) was a famous explorer who discovered the source of the Blue Nile.

Clackmannan Tower, the ancient Bruce stronghold, still stands on the west side of the town of that name, about 2 miles south-east of Alloa (A907, then B910). Here, on 26th August 1787, Mrs Bruce of Clackmannan knighted the poet Robert Burns with the sword of her great ancestor. The chief of Clan Bruce is the Earl of Elgin and Kincardine. Apart from the archaic form, Brus, there are no sept names of this royal clan. There is a tartan, however, and its plant badge is rosemary.

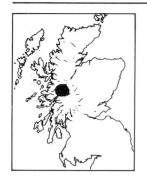

CLAN
CAMERON

AT FIRST GLANCE THE HISTORY OF CLAN CAMERON might be mistaken for an extreme example of Highland lawlessness. By their enemies they were described as 'fiercer than fierceness itself' and for four centuries they were embroiled in possibly the most bitter of all clan feuds because of their illegal occupation of their neighbours' land. This superficial impression, however, is misleading. Their motive was nothing less than a struggle for survival; historians have observed that no other clan, apart from the MacGregors, was so continuously threatened with extinction. The savagery of this fight for life is echoed in the Cameron warcry 'Sons of the hounds, come here and get flesh!' and in the haunting melancholy of their lament 'Lochaber No More', banned in the British Army during the Peninsular War because of its dispiriting effect on Highland soldiers. On occasions when they were sufficiently secure to make a free choice, the Camerons showed themselves scrupulously loyal to legitimate authority, even against their own interests — hence their adherence to the declining cause of the Lord of the Isles, and later to the fallen Stuart kings.

The precise origins of the Camerons are obscure, but it is likely that the majority of them descended from a confederation of three septs who were the original inhabitants of Lochaber: the MacGillonies of Strone, the MacMartins of Letterfinlay and the MacSorleys of Glen Nevis. The first two may have had a Clan Chattan connection, but the MacSorleys appear to have derived from Clan Donald. This confederation was styled Clann Mealanafhaidh (the race of the servant of the prophet), and tradition credits them with an early chief named Angus who married a sister of Banquo, Thane of Lochaber, and who helped save Fleance, Banquo's son, from the tyrant Macbeth.

The original chiefly line, the MacGillonies, intermarried with a knightly family called Cambrun whose principal lands were at Ballegarno in Angus. This junior branch, its name corrupted to Cameron, grew in importance and eventually took over the chiefship of Clan Mealanafhaidh. In the Wars of Independence the Camerons supported Bruce, and a Johannes Cambrun

signed the Declaration of Arbroath. About the same time the seeds of a local feud were sown in Lochaber which was to have far-reaching consequences for the future Clan Cameron.

Lochaber is approximately that area of south Inverness-shire bounded on the north by Loch Arkaig and on the south by Loch Leven, extending as far east as Loch Treig and west to Glenfinnan. The clan's early holdings were on the east shore of Loch Lochy (the MacMartin country), about 8 miles in length, and Glen Nevis (the MacSorley country), south-east of Fort William. Here Ben Nevis, the highest mountain in Britain, towers to a height of 4,406ft. These lands were held of the Lord of the Isles as superior. It was the Camerons' later acquisitions on the western shore of the River Lochy, however, which provoked their bloody feud with the Mackintoshes. In 1291, Angus, 6th Laird of Mackintosh, married the heiress of Clan Chattan and succeeded to the chiefship of that powerful confederation. Through this marriage the Mackintoshes also claimed the lands of Glen Loy and Loch Arkaig. After Bannockburn, however, the Mackintoshes were preoccupied with new territory they had gained in Badenoch. While they were thus distracted, the land-hungry Camerons progressively encroached on Glen Loy and Loch Arkaig. The total area occupied stretched for about 16 miles west of the River Lochy and was bounded on the south by Loch Eil, from which later Cameron chiefs were to take their title.

Throughout the fourteenth century, the Mackintoshes resisted this Cameron intrusion. Besides waging constant war, they employed legal arguments, claiming that the Lord of the Isles had granted them Glen Loy and Loch Arkaig by a charter of 1337, confirmed by King David II in 1359. The first recorded Cameron chief, John Ochtery, who had led the westward expansion of his clan, was succeeded by his equally aggressive son Allan. In 1370, while returning from a raid into the Mackintosh country, he was cut off by a combined army of Mackintoshes, Macphersons and Davidsons. Because of a dispute over the post of honour on the right wing, the Macphersons withdrew and the Camerons routed the remainder of

Inverlochy Castle, by Horatio McCulloch. The ruins of this great Cameron stronghold can still be seen at the head of Loch Linnhe.

their enemies. On the following day, however, the Macphersons vindicated themselves by attacking the Camerons in turn and putting them to flight.

It was in 1396 that the feud between the Camerons and Mackintoshes reached a climax. The Earls of March and Crawford were sent to subdue the north, but, finding their forces inadequate, proposed a settlement which would limit the bloodshed while preserving Highland honour. The Mackintoshes and Camerons were each to provide 30 warriors who would fight a duel to the death on the North Inch of Perth (where the race-course now stands), with King Robert III as adjudicator. The combat features in Scott's *The Fair Maid of Perth*. On the day of the battle, one Mackintosh defected through cowardice; his place was taken by a Perth saddler called Henry Wynd on the promise of half a French crown in gold if his side were victorious. The fight was bloody even by the standards of a clan feud: only the saddler was unhurt on the winning side, his ten surviving Mackintosh comrades dying later from their wounds. Just one of the defeated Camerons saved his life by swimming across the Tay. So far from ending the feud, this duel aggravated it and the Camerons remained in stubborn possession of Glen Loy and Loch Arkaig.

Although the increasingly powerful Camerons had declared their independence of Clan Chattan and were constantly at war with its Mackintosh chiefs, a feudal anomaly sometimes forced them to fight alongside their hereditary enemies. The problem was that they were both vassals of the Lord of the Isles. In 1411, therefore, Donald Dubh (Black Donald), the famous chief from whom descended the house of Lochiel, fought in alliance with the Mackintoshes at the Battle of Harlaw, in the army of Donald, Lord of the Isles, against the Scots crown. It should be noted that the Camerons did not act in a spirit of rebellion, but in conservative-minded fidelity to the ancient authority of the Lord of the Isles. Nevertheless, by 1429 both Camerons and Mackintoshes had recognized the jurisdiction of King James I. Two years later, in 1431, the Camerons suffered for this when a rebel army supporting the Lord of the Isles defeated the royalists at

Inverlochy and ravaged the Cameron country.

Black Donald, however, was a determined warrior who set about the restoration of his clan's fortunes, even though the political situation was unfavourable. James I was reconciled with the Lord of the Isles and recognized him as Earl of Ross in 1436. The following year the king was murdered, and shortly afterwards the Lord of the Isles was made Justiciar during the infancy of James II. Black Donald returned from exile in Ireland to find that his enemy, the Justiciar, had granted the lands of Lochiel to the Macleans. He attacked and defeated them at Corpach (now a village 2½ miles north-west of Fort William on the A830 road) and destroyed the charters which were their title-deeds. Then he turned on the Mackintoshes, who had been granted the Stewardship of Lochaber, and drove them out of the disputed lands of Glen Loy and Loch Arkaig.

Through his military prowess Donald became Captain of Clan Cameron, that is to say senior cadet of the confederation of MacGillonies, MacMartins, MacSorleys and Camerons. He also secured the chiefship to his posterity by marrying the heiress of MacMartin of Letterfinlay, most of whose sept adopted the Cameron name. At the same time the clan spread its influence outside Lochaber: the distinguished Bishop of Glasgow, John Cameron, became Chancellor of Scotland and first minister to James I. In commemoration of their formidable ancestor Black Donald, the successive Lochiel chiefs bore the patronymic Mac-Dhomhnuill Dhuibh.

Donald's son Allan, reckoned as 12th chief in the old genealogies, lived up to his warrior heritage. He is said to have made 35 expeditions against his enemies, one for each of the 32 years of his life and three for the three-quarters of a year in his mother's womb. Not surprisingly, he fell in battle against the Mackintoshes. His son, Ewen, 13th chief, got formal confirmation of all his lands from James IV in 1495, legalizing his clan's position at last. He fought at Flodden and survived to become a trusted ally of the Regent Albany during the minority of James V. In 1528 his services were rewarded

The Jacobite Monument in Glenfinnan. It was here in the heart of Cameron country that the clans gathered at the outset of the 'Forty-five.

Cameron

MOTTO: *Aonaibh ri cheile* (Unite)
OLD MOTTO: *Mo righ's mo dhuchaich* (For king and country)
GAELIC NAME: Clann Chamshron
ORIGIN OF NAME: from Gaelic meaning 'wry-nose'

by the erection of his estates into the feudal barony of Lochiel, which thenceforth became the chief's designation.

In keeping with the new-found stability of his position, Ewen built Tor Castle (whose ruin stands beside the River Lochy 4 miles north of Fort William) and this remained the chiefly residence for more than a century. He even tried to end the ancient clan feud by taking as his second wife the sister of the Mackintosh chief: from this marriage descended the cadet house of Cameron of Erracht. In his last years, heart-broken by the death of his son and heir by his first marriage, Lochiel sought consolation in religion. He built six chapels in honour of different saints, the penance imposed on him for his sins by the Pope. Some of their ruins survive around Lochaber. Despite his marriage to a Mackintosh, Ewen Cameron eventually met his death at the hands of his hereditary foes. On the pretext that Lochiel had supported the Macdonalds in their attack on the Frasers at Blàr-na-Léine in 1544, Mackintosh seized him and handed him over to the Earl of Huntly, who had him beheaded for treason at Elgin in 1547. This intervention by Huntly was an ominous development: secure against the Mackintoshes, the Camerons were now increasingly to find themselves involved in the much more deadly contest between the Gordons of Huntly and the house of Argyll, their lands being uncomfortably situated between the rival factions.

The Camerons' economic existence was also precarious. Red deer from the hills, salmon and trout from the rivers and herring from the lochs ensured a basic food supply, but the land was unsuitable for crops. Horse-breeding and cattle were the main support of life, the cattle stolen as often as honestly traded. There was some rudimentary commerce, with ships sailing up Loch Leven and even Loch Eil, under the protection of Inverlochy Castle, the ruin of which still stands. Fundamentally, however, the Camerons lived by the sword and even sheep farming was a limited and late development. Their one distinctive asset was the rich timber which the chiefs began to exploit commercially in the early eighteenth

Ben Nevis, the highest mountain in the British Isles, stands in the midst of Cameron territory.

century, until disrupted by the 'Forty-five.

The most famous Cameron in the late sixteenth century was not himself a chief, but the natural son of Eòghann Beag, 14th of Lochiel. Christened Donald, he was better known as the Black Tailor of the Axe, so called because he had been fostered by a tailor's wife and the Lochaber axe was his favourite weapon. From this ferocious warrior descended the Taylor family of Stratheachaig. The greatest Cameron of all, however, was undoubtedly Sir Ewen, 17th of Lochiel, the Ulysses of the North, who succeeded to the chiefship in 1647, when Scotland was riven by civil war. After witnessing the execution of his friend Sir Robert Spottiswoode by the Covenanters, young Ewen became an embittered royalist. In 1654 at Achdalieu, on the north bank of Loch Eil, 3 miles west of Corpach (A830), he led a force of 35 Camerons against 300 Cromwellian soldiers who were destroying his woodlands, killing 138 Englishmen for the loss of five of his own men. In personal combat with the English officer, Lochiel sank his teeth in his opponent's throat and 'bitt it quitt throw, and keept such hold of his grip, that he brought away his mouthfull!'

Anxious to establish peace at any price with so formidable an enemy, the English Parliament made an extraordinarily generous treaty with Lochiel, requiring no oath from him beyond his simple word of honour. His warlike career, however, was by no means over. After the Restoration, in 1665, the Mackintoshes made their last attempt to recover Glen Loy and Loch Arkaig, invading the Cameron country with an army 1,500 strong. Lochiel prepared to resist, but Argyll intervened as mediator and a settlement was reached. With money provided by Argyll, Lochiel bought the disputed lands from Mackintosh and agreed to hold them under Argyll's feudal superiority. So, after four centuries, one of the most bitter Highland feuds came to an end. In 1689, the sixty-year-old Lochiel fought for James VII at Killiecrankie, charging barefoot at the head of his clan, half of whom were killed. He was too old to fight in the 'Fifteen Rebellion, but his son John led the clan in the Jacobite army. Sir Ewen built the first Achnacarry Castle on the

south bank of the River Arkaig (off the B8005 road), which replaced Tor Castle as the chief's residence until it was burned after Culloden. Despite his hazardous life, he died at the age of ninety.

Sir Ewen's grandson Donald, 19th chief, known as the Gentle Lochiel, gained a romantic reputation by his part in the 'Forty-five. Though doubting the chances of success, he brought his full fighting strength of 800 men to join Prince Charlie, was wounded at Culloden and escaped to France. His personal intervention saved the Whig city of Glasgow from being sacked by the Highland army; to this day, whenever Cameron of Lochiel pays an official visit to Glasgow, the church bells are rung in his honour. Lochiel's brother, Dr Archibald Cameron, was one of those responsible for burying the prince's treasure on the shore of Loch Arkaig and he was possibly on his way to recover it when captured seven years later, after returning secretly from France. He was hanged at Tyburn on 7th June 1753, the last man in Britain to be executed for Jacobitism; Prince Charlie's gold is rumoured still to lie by the shore of Loch Arkaig.

In 1784, the Lochiel estates were restored to Donald, 22nd chief, who rebuilt Achnacarry in the early nineteenth century. The Camerons' military tradition was revived in 1793 when Major Allan Cameron of Erracht raised the 79th Cameron Highlanders. This regiment gained great distinction and in 1873 was granted the title 'The Queen's Own'.

As well as the MacGillonies, MacMartins and MacSorleys, the names of Chalmers, MacChlery, MacPhail, MacUlric, Paul, Clark and Taylor are associated with Clan Cameron, though, especially in the case of the last three, a Lochaber connection should be established before the relationship is assumed. Cameron of Lochiel still has his seat at Achnacarry Castle; on the hillside to the north, across the River Arkaig, the clan's heritage is as eloquently expressed in the name of a humbler dwelling — Prince Charlie's Cave, where the fugitive Stuart pretender once hid, his person safeguarded by Cameron loyalty. The clan's plant badge is oak or crowberry and its Gaelic name Clann Chamshron.

CLAN
CAMPBELL

NO CLAN HAS EVER AROUSED STRONGER PASSIONS than the Campbells. Around the world, people who have never visited Scotland and are vague about its history always remember one thing: the massacre by the Campbells of the Macdonalds of Glencoe and the resultant hatred between the two names. Again, in the romantic mythology which has grown up around the Jacobite rebellions and the tragedy of Culloden, the Campbells gain no glory. They were on the winning side and winners are not always popular. In general, the controversy surrounding the Campbells arises from the fact that, almost uniquely among Highland clans, they came to an early accommodation with the forces of modernity and centralized government which the rest of Gaelic Scotland resisted. The geographical location of their lands, too, favoured compromise with Lowland institutions. So the Campbells abandoned the sword as a means of expansion in favour of litigation — a device feared and despised by conservative Highlanders — and advanced their fortunes by political acumen. It was inevitable that their sophisticated pursuit of self-interest should be seen as treachery by their less prosperous rivals who envied their success. Undoubtedly they were successful, to a degree that gave them an influence over national politics that was greater than any other clan ever enjoyed. The Campbells might be admired by a few, or hated by many: they could never be ignored.

It has often been claimed that the Campbells are the oldest of the Highland clans, but it would be impossible either to prove or disprove this theory on the slender evidence available. Certainly they are a very ancient house, descended from the Clann Dhuibhne, whose earliest ancestor was called Diarmad. The O'Dhuibhnes were lords of Lochawe in Argyllshire until the eleventh century when the last of the line, Pòl an Sporain (Paul, the king's treasurer) left an heiress, Eva, who married one Gillespic Cam-beul (Crooked Mouth). From Diarmad, progenitor of the O'Dhuibhnes, the Campbells became known as Clann Dhiarmaid; from the Gaelic phrase meaning 'crooked mouth', they acquired their surname. At six generations' descent from Gillespic and Eva was

Sir Colin Campbell, known as Cailein Mór (the Great), who was knighted by Alexander III in 1280. He supported the claims of the house of Bruce to the disputed crown of Scotland, was killed in battle against the Macdougalls at the String of Lorn in 1294, and is buried in the churchyard at Kilchrenan (on the B845 road, about 6 miles south of Taynuilt). From this heroic chief, the real founder of the clan, the Duke of Argyll derives his patronymic Mac-Cailein-Mór.

Sir Colin's son Neil, also knighted by Alexander III, inherited his father's warlike temperament. He was one of Bruce's earliest and staunchest supporters, fighting beside him in every major battle, from Methven to Bannockburn. As a reward, he received the lands belonging to the earldom of Atholl, and the hand of Bruce's sister, the Lady Mary, in marriage. By two earlier marriages he had a son, Colin, who succeeded him, and a younger son, Duncan, who was ancestor of the house of Inverawe. Sir Neil's own brother, Donald, was progenitor of the Campbells of Loudoun. The heir, Sir Colin Campbell, described by King Robert Bruce as 'our beloved and faithful Colin', received the lands of Lochawe as a feudal barony in 1315. He took part in Bruce's disastrous expedition to Ireland in the following year and, in 1334, was instrumental in recovering Dunoon Castle from the English. His son, Sir Archibald, 2nd of Lochawe, received several large land grants before his death, about 1394, and the succeeding chief further increased the family's status by marrying Margaret Drummond, sister of Robert III's queen. It was his son (by a later marriage), Sir Duncan, 4th of Lochawe, who was raised to the peerage by James II in 1445 as Lord Campbell. His first wife was Lady Marjory Stewart, daughter of the Regent Albany, through whom the chiefly line was carried on; by his second wife, also a Stewart, he had a second son, Sir Colin Campbell of Glenorchy, ancestor of the Earls of Breadalbane. Since his elder son predeceased him, Lord Campbell was succeeded by his grandson, Colin, who was created Earl of Argyll in 1457. By that time, the Campbells were established on the lands which were thenceforth to be

Inveraray Castle, the seat of the Campbell Dukes of Argyll, was built in 1746 to replace an older castle.

their patrimony and power base, with the Earls of Argyll exercising a dual role as statesmen involved in national politics and as chiefs of a great Highland clan.

To unravel the innumerable cadet houses of Clan Campbell would be a gargantuan task. Besides the house of Argyll, the most important junior branches were the Campbells of Glenorchy (later Earls of Breadalbane), the Campbells of Loudoun and the Campbells of Calder. Their vast territories, though not concentrated in a single area, probably amounted at one time to the largest land-holding owned by a single clan in Scotland. The Campbell heartland, the adjoining territories of the houses of Argyll and Glenorchy, was bounded on the west by the Firth of Lorn and on the east by the Menzies and Murray lands just east of Loch Tay and Loch Earn in Perthshire; so this broad belt of land reached halfway across Scotland to a length of about 60 miles. Its northern boundary marched with the Stewart enclave of Appin, the Macdonald country of Glencoe and the Robertson lands on the southern shore of Loch Rannoch; to the south it reached as far as the Tarbert Isthmus, just north of Kintyre, and included most of the huge peninsula between Loch Fyne and the Firth of Clyde, after which the boundary meandered north-eastward towards Loch Tay, somewhat eroded by a sizeable area of MacNab country around Glen Dochart. The remaining two territories of significant size held by the Campbells were the Ayrshire lands of the Earls of Loudoun, and a long, thin strip between the Rivers Nairn and Findhorn in the county of Nairn, where the Campbells of Calder held sway.

The great Campbell empire in Argyllshire needed a capital and administrative centre and this requirement was duly supplied by Colin, 1st Earl of Argyll, in 1474, when he obtained a charter erecting the township of Inveraray (on the northern shore of Loch Fyne, A83 road) into a burgh of barony. From here successive Campbell chiefs ruled as absolute princes with power of life and death. The mainstay of the town was its fishing industry, the waters of Loch Fyne abounding in herring and cod. Inveraray, as a modern town, dates from 1742,

when the existing settlement was levelled and a neater township was built in accordance with eighteenth-century taste. Inveraray Castle, the seat of the house of Argyll, stands north-west of the town, on the banks of the River Aray. It is built of local stone and dates from 1746, when it replaced the older castle whose site is nearby. The building, with its four corner towers crowned by French-style extinguisher tops, has become one of the best-known landmarks in Scotland. Recently Inveraray was damaged by a disastrous fire and the Duke of Argyll has had to devote a great amount of time, energy and money to gradual restoration work, hopefully with the help of generous clansmen. The seat of the Campbell chiefs was originally Ardchonnel Castle, now a ruin, on Innischonnel island in Loch Awe (just off Portinnisher-rich, on the B840), but since the fifteenth century the much grander edifice at Inveraray has been the symbol of Campbell power.

Besides establishing Inveraray, the 1st Earl of Argyll had many other claims to distinction. He was made Master of the King's Household in 1464, obtained the lordship of Lorn in 1470 and became Lord High Chancellor of Scotland in 1483. By marriage he acquired Castle Gloom, in Clackmannanshire (now a ruin maintained by the Ministry of Works, just north of the town of Dollar on the A91), whose name he changed to Castle Campbell. His son Archibald, 2nd Earl, was likewise Master of the Household and continued the expansion of the Campbell lands; one of his younger sons was ancestor of the house of Calder. The 2nd Earl of Argyll was killed while in command of the right wing of the Scots army at Flodden (1513). Colin Meallach (the Deceitful), 3rd Earl, was a great soldier who held the hazardous post of Lieutenant of the Borders and Warden of the Marches under James V. Of more significance to the growing power of his house was the grant to him in 1528 of the hereditary offices of Lord Justice-General and Master of the King's Household, the latter post still being held by the Duke of Argyll, who places the sword and baton of these dignities in saltire behind his shield with the modest disclaimer: 'I scarce call these our own.'

Ardchonnel Castle on its island in Loch Awe was the original seat of the Campbell chiefs. The ruin dates from the thirteenth century.

Campbell

MOTTO: *Ne obliviscaris* (Forget not)
ORIGIN OF NAME: Gaelic *cam-beul*, crooked mouth
GAELIC NAME: Clann Dhiarmaid
WARCRY: *Cruachan!*
PLANT BADGE: Wild myrtle, fir club moss
PIPE MUSIC: *Baile Ionaraora* (The Campbells are coming)

Archibald Roy Campbell, 4th Earl of Argyll, fought with distinction at the Battle of Pinkie in 1547. Though a protégé of Cardinal Beaton in early life, he was the first person of note in Scotland to be converted to Protestantism and was a zealous promoter of the Reformation, though he died in 1558, two years before the new religious settlement was finally established. The 5th Earl, also called Archibald, inherited his father's principles and became one of the Protestant Lords of the Congregation. Yet he also enjoyed the favour of Mary Queen of Scots who spent part of the summer of 1563 deer hunting at Inveraray. She addressed Argyll as 'brother' and signed letters to him 'your richt good sister and best friend for ever'. In 1568, while in command of Mary's army at the Battle of Langside, Argyll fainted, an unfortunate accident which helped secure the Queen's defeat. After a complex involvement in the politics of Scotland during Mary's captivity in England, Argyll eventually became Lord High Chancellor in 1572, but died only three years later. Colin, his half-brother, succeeded as 6th Earl of Argyll and similarly held the Chancellorship.

To an even greater extent than is the case with other clans, the history of the Campbells is the story of their chiefs. In the late sixteenth century, however, an attempt was made to alter the chiefly succession by drastic means. On the accession of Archibald, 7th Earl, as a minor, in 1584, the clan was temporarily ruled by the chief's immediate kinsmen. One of them, Campbell of Lochnell, entered into a conspiracy to inherit the earldom by poisoning the young Archibald; this was part of a larger intrigue which actually accomplished the murders of the Bonnie Earl of Moray and Campbell of Calder. The youthful Earl of Argyll survived, however, and in 1594, at the age of 18, he led the royal army which met the rebel Catholic Earls of Huntly and Erroll at Glenlivet. Betrayed by Campbell of Lochnell, who was himself killed in the rout, Argyll's forces fled cravenly from the field while he wept with shame. James VI could not conceal his glee at this humiliation of the haughty Argyll: 'Fair fa' ye, Geordie Gordon,' he exclaimed when his defeated general presented himself, 'for sending him

Kilchurn Castle on Loch Awe was built by the Campbells of Glenorchy in the fifteenth century to hold the lands they had seized from the MacGregors.

Cawdor Castle. In 1510 Sir John Campbell kidnapped and married the heiress to the thaneship of Cawdor, which then passed into the Campbell family.

Campbell of Breadalbane

CREST BADGE: A boar's head, erased, proper
MOTTO: Follow me
PIPE MUSIC: *Bodaich nam Brigisean*
(The Carles with the breeks)

Campbell of Cawdor

CREST BADGE: A swan, proper, crowned, or
MOTTO: Be mindful
PIPE MUSIC: Campbell of Cawdor's Salute

The 'Maiden', the device used to execute the 8th and the 9th Earls of Argyll.

The township of Inveraray, capital of the great Campbell empire in Argyll. In 1742 it was totally rebuilt in accordance with eighteenth-century taste.

back lookin' sae like a subject!' This earl was known as Archibald Gruamach (the Grim), a title he earned by his ruthless hunting down of the MacGregor clan, which ended with the execution of the chief and his right-hand men at Edinburgh in 1604. By a supreme irony, Argyll, who had been humbled by the Catholic rebels at Glenlivet, became converted to Rome in later life and spent much of his time abroad, where he served with the Spanish forces against the Dutch Protestants. He died in London in 1638.

Archibald, the 8th Earl, his son, was the most famous and controversial chief of Clan Campbell. He sided with the Covenant and, in 1640, devastated the lands of the Earl of Atholl and the Ogilvies, who espoused the royal cause. A peace was patched up for the time being and in 1641 Argyll was promoted in the peerage to become a marquess. He was described as 'a man of craft, subtilty, and falsehood, and can love no man'. By this time he was also the most powerful subject in Scotland. That power, however, was soon to be challenged. In 1644, while the Civil War was raging in England, James Graham, Marquess of Montrose, came secretly to Scotland and raised the standard of Charles I. His quick succession of victories threw the Covenanters into confusion. Argyll was commander-in-chief of the Covenanting forces and the war turned into a personal conflict between the two marquesses — Montrose and Argyll. In 1645 Montrose ravaged the Campbell country relentlessly, forcing Argyll to flee before him. Then, on 2nd February 1645, he disgraced Argyll and the whole race of Campbell in

Highland eyes by routing them at Inverlochy, 2 miles north-east of Fort William (on the A82), killing 1,500 of the clan. Argyll himself watched the battle from the safety of his galley, in which he escaped down Loch Linnhe to become an enduring object of Highland ridicule. Later that year he was present at a further defeat inflicted by Montrose on the Covenanting army at Kilsyth, 15th August. After the deaths of both Charles I and Montrose, Argyll continued to play a tortuous role in national politics. When Charles II came to Scotland at the invitation of the Covenanters, Argyll placed the crown on his head at his coronation at Scone on New Year's Day, 1651. Later, after Charles's defeat at the Battle of Worcester, Argyll was present at the ceremony when Cromwell was proclaimed Lord Protector. Eventually his turncoat career caught up with him: at the Restoration he was tried for treason and many other crimes and was sentenced to be executed on the 'Maiden' — the ancient Scots guillotine — at Edinburgh Cross on 27th May 1661. His head was placed on top of the Tolbooth, where the Covenanters had exposed the head of Montrose.

Archibald, 9th Earl of Argyll (the marquessate was lost by his father's treason), was restored to his estates in 1663, but refused the oath prescribed under the Test Act in 1681 and was tried for treason. He was sentenced to death, but escaped disguised as a page in attendance on his step-daughter, Lady Sophia Lindsay. His hiding-place was betrayed to Charles II, but the king generously tore up the informer's letter, exclaiming, 'Pooh, pooh! Hunt a hunted partridge? For shame!' Argyll escaped to Holland, whence he returned in 1685 to lead an abortive rebellion against James VII. This time he was captured and, since he was already under sentence of death, a trial was unnecessary. Like his father, he was executed on the 'Maiden' and his head was placed on the Tolbooth. After the Revolution, however, the fortunes of the Whiggish Campbells were made. In gratitude for his support, William of Orange bestowed a dukedom on the 10th Earl in 1701. The 2nd Duke of Argyll was a great military commander who rose to the rank of field-marshal; at the drawn battle of Sheriffmuir in 1715, he commanded the

Loch Etive, deep in Campbell country, reaching towards the distant Glencoe hills, home of their enemies the Macdonalds.

Hanoverian army. The poet Pope celebrated him in the lines:

> 'Argyll, the State's whole thunder born to wield,
> And shake alike the senate and the field.'

His brother, who became 3rd Duke in 1743, supported the Hanoverian government against the Jacobites, so that the Campbells fought under Cumberland at Culloden. Besides rebuilding Inveraray, the 3rd Duke was also responsible for the policy of recruiting Highland regiments, which was to have a tremendous impact on British military history. After the pacification of the Highlands, the Dukes of Argyll continued to exercise great local power, seated at Inveraray and still very much clan chiefs. The 9th Duke married Princess Louise, a daughter of Queen Victoria, and was Governor-General of Canada from 1878 to 1883.

The most important junior branch of the Campbells was that of Glenorchy. Sir Colin Campbell, 1st of Glenorchy, received this estate in 1432 from his father, Sir Duncan of Lochawe, 1st Lord Campbell, who had driven out its previous occupants, the MacGregors. To hold this territory, he built Kilchurn Castle, now an impressive ruin, at the north-eastern end of Loch Awe (off the A85). Sir Duncan (Black Duncan), 7th of Glenorchy, was created a baronet in 1625 and was the first Highland chief to encourage forestry. His great-grandson, Sir John Campbell, tried to enforce his right to the earldom of Caithness by invading that territory, an episode commemorated by the song 'The Campbells are Coming'. He dropped his claim in 1681 and Charles II, in compensation, created him Earl of Breadalbane, but with precedence dating from 1677. Unlike his cousins of Argyll, Lord Breadalbane was a Jacobite who sent 500 men to fight for the Old Chevalier at Sheriffmuir. For two periods, from 1831 to 1862 and from 1885 to 1922, this branch held a marquessate, but it was twice extinguished and the older title of Earl of Breadalbane is presently borne by its chieftain. The principal cadet houses of Breadalbane were Glenlyon, Aberuchill, Barcaldine and Achallader, the last three of which survive today. It was Campbell of Glenlyon who carried out the massacre of the Macdonalds of Glencoe in 1692.

The Campbells of Calder descend from a younger son of the 2nd Earl of Argyll, Sir John Campbell, who married Muriel, heiress of the ancient Thanes of Cawdor, in 1510, having kidnapped the girl for this purpose. Her Campbell grandson inherited the thaneship of Cawdor from her in 1573. Campbell of Calder conquered Islay in 1612 and his descendants ruled there for more than a century. The 9th Laird of Calder was created Lord Cawdor in 1796 and his son was promoted to be Earl Cawdor in 1827. Cawdor Castle, 6 miles south of Nairn (on the B9090), an imposing fortress with a drawbridge, is still the residence of Lord Cawdor. The castle dates back to 1454 when legend claims that the thane fastened a casket of gold onto a donkey's back and swore to build a castle wherever it came to a halt; the donkey stopped at a hawthorn tree (still protruding from the floor of the vault), around which the castle was duly built. The Campbells of Loudoun descended from the second son of Cailein Mór. They held extensive lands in Ayrshire and became Earls of Loudoun in 1633. In 1804, however, the earldom passed by marriage into the Hastings family. The Campbells of Strachur represent a very old branch of the clan; other surviving cadets are the houses of Kilberry, Inverawe, Inverneill, Jura, Skerrington, Glendaruel, Kilmartin and the Captain of Dunstaffnage.

As Chief of Clan Campbell the Duke of Argyll is styled Mac-Cailein-Mór; the Earl of Breadalbane is Mac-Chailein-'ic Dhonnachaidh and the Captain of Dunstaffnage, from his hereditary office as castellan of that stronghold, is called MacAonghuis an Dùin. The sept names of Campbell of Argyll and Breadalbane are Burnhouse, Burns, Connochie, Denoon, MacConnochie, MacDiarmid, MacDermid, MacGibbon, MacIsaac, MacKellar, MacKessock, MacOran, MacPhedran, MacPhun, MacTause, MacUre, Tawesson and Ure; Caddell is a sept of Calder. Clan Campbell's plant badges are wild myrtle and fir club moss; the warcry is 'Cruachan!' (the name of a mountain overlooking Loch Awe) and its Gaelic name is Clann Dhiarmaid.

CLAN
CHATTAN

Chattan

MOTTO: Touch not a catt but a glove
(Touch not the cat without a glove)
ORIGIN OF NAME: Clan of the Cats
WARCRY: *Clan Chattan*
PLANT BADGE: Red whortleberry

CLAN CHATTAN WAS NOT A CLAN AT ALL, IN THE NORMAL sense of the word, but an exceptionally powerful Highland confederation, some of whose members adhered to the alliance for convenience, others through a genuine blood bond. A full account of Clan Chattan would fill several volumes, so all that can be attempted here is a general outline of the structure and history of this extraordinary clan alliance. The present chiefly family, the Mackintoshes, joined Clan Chattan in the late thirteenth century, when their chief married the heiress of the confederation and ousted the power of the Macphersons who in later generations disputed the chiefship. Clan Mackintosh developed powerful branches of its own, such as the Shaws, Farquharsons, Toshachs and MacCombies (known as Clan Thomas). The ancient generic name for members of Clan Chattan was Cattanach, a surname surviving today. Other old names of the original Clan Chattan line are Macpherson, Davidson, Smith or Gow, MacGillivray, MacBain and Macphail. Associated clans were the Tarrells, the Macleans of the North (see Clan Maclean), Macqueens, MacAndrews, Clarks and the Macintyres of Badenoch.

The progenitor of Clan Chattan was Gillechattan Mór (the Great Servant of St Cattan), who was baillie of the abbey lands of Ardchattan in the second half of the eleventh century. His son Diarmad succeeded as 2nd Captain of Clan Chattan about 1090 and left two sons, a second Gillechattan who in turn inherited the captaincy of the clan, and David of Invernahavon, from whom the Davidsons descended. Gillechattan's younger son Muirach was intended for the church, and actually served as parson of Kingussie until the premature death of his elder brother forced a more worldly destiny on him and he followed his father as 4th chief. He appears to have had at least four sons. They were Gillechattan, 5th Captain of the clan; Ewan, who was known as 'son of the parson' (whence Macpherson); Neil, ancestor of the Smiths or Gows, and Farquhar Gilleriabhach, ancestor of the MacGillivrays. The direct line ended with Eva, granddaughter of Gillechattan, 5th of Clan Chattan. She, as heiress of the clan, married Angus Mackintosh, 6th of

Glen Spean, scene of the Battle of Mulroy where the Macdonells defeated Clan Chattan in 1688, the last clan battle in Scotland.

Mackintosh, in 1291. He accordingly assumed the title of 7th Captain of Clan Chattan; as chief of his own paternal clan he also bore the subordinate style of Mackintosh of Torcastle.

The Mackintoshes claimed descent from Shaw, son of the 3rd Earl of Fife, hence the name Mac-an-Tòisich (son of the thane, or leader). According to tradition, Shaw successfully put down a rebellion in Moray in 1163, on behalf of Malcolm IV, and was rewarded with the lands of Petty, Breachley and Strathdearn, as well as the office of Constable of Inverness Castle. His son, Shaw Mackintosh, 2nd Chief of Mackintosh, was confirmed in these lands, as well as being made Chamberlain of the Crown Revenues in his territory. After his death in 1210, his son Farquhar ruled the clan, becoming also Seneschal of Badenoch, and died without heirs in 1240, when his nephew Shaw Mackintosh became 4th Laird. Shaw had already got a lease of Rothiemurchus in Strathspey in 1236 and he further acquired the lands of Meikle Geddes and the Castle of Rait. His son Farquhar, 5th of Mackintosh, resided at Rothiemurchus and led the men of Badenoch against the Norse invaders in the reign of Alexander III. When he died, the Comyns took advantage of the succession of his son Angus as a minor to seize Inverness Castle, Meikle Geddes and Rait, which remained in their possession for a century.

Angus, 6th Laird of Mackintosh, united his house with Clan Chattan, as already described, by marrying the heiress, Eva. During the War of Independence he supported Bruce, probably because his enemies, the Comyns, were in the Balliol camp. As a reward, in 1319, he received a grant of the Comyns' forfeited lands of Benchar in Badenoch. When Angus died in 1345 he left three sons. The eldest, William, succeeded as 7th Chief of

Mackintosh and 8th Captain of Clan Chattan. The second son, John, was ancestor of the Shaws of Tordarroch and grandfather of the man who led the 30 Clan Chattan men in the famous battle with the Camerons on the North Inch of Perth in 1396. Angus Òg, the third son, was progenitor of the Mackintoshes of Dalmunzie. William, who inherited the double chiefship, soon found himself embroiled in a problem that was to bedevil his successors for generations. In 1336 he received a charter from the Lord of the Isles of the old Clan Chattan lands of Glen Loy and Loch Arkaig. These territories lay between Loch Garry in the north and Loch Eil on the south. While Clan Chattan had been distracted by affairs in Badenoch, this area had been colonized by the land-hungry Camerons. Now the Mackintoshes indignantly attempted to repossess their inheritance, only to be fiercely resisted by the Camerons. In fairness to the latter, their usurpation was not provoked by greed, but by necessity; they had to hold Glen Loy and Loch Arkaig or starve. The situation was still unresolved when William died in 1368 and was buried on the island of Torchionan in Loch Arkaig.

William left a natural son, Adam, from whom descended the important Clan MacThomas of Glenshee, also known as MacCombie. The chiefship, however, passed successively to his two legitimate sons, Lachlan and Malcolm. Lachlan's long rule, from 1368 to 1407, was dominated by the feud with the Camerons. In 1370 the Camerons invaded Badenoch, only to be cut off at Invernahavon, on the south bank of the Spey (about 2 miles east of Cluny Castle on the A86). Despite having the initial advantage, the Clan Chattan camp was divided by a dispute over precedence: both the Davidsons and the Macphersons claimed the post of honour on the right wing. When Lachlan Mackintosh awarded it to the

Balmoral Castle, the Queen's country seat in Scotland, was formerly a Farquharson property.

Davidsons, the Macphersons withdrew from the field in high dudgeon, leaving their confederates in Clan Chattan to be defeated by the Camerons. Next day, however, the Macphersons in their turn attacked the weakened Camerons and carried the day. The feud continued and reached its peak in the famous fight between Clan Chattan and the Camerons on the North Inch at Perth in September 1396, with Robert III adjudicating in person. Although Clan Chattan won the day, the Camerons remained stubbornly entrenched in Glen Loy and Loch Arkaig. In 1407 Lachlan died and was succeeded by his son Farquhar who had a brief reign of only two years before abdicating; it seems he hated the responsibility of the chiefship, an unusual attitude in those days.

So, in 1409, his uncle Malcolm became 11th Captain of Clan Chattan and 10th Laird of Mackintosh. He fought in the royal army at Harlaw in 1411, against the Lord of the Isles, became Steward of Lochaber and, in 1428, Constable of Inverness Castle. The most notable achievement of his reign was his final victory over the Comyns with whom, like his predecessors, he was at feud. The Comyns still held Meikle Geddes and Rait, which the Mackintoshes claimed. In the course of the feud, an army of Comyns was drowned in Loch Moy, whereupon their surviving clansmen devised a stratagem for revenge. Pretending to make overtures for peace, the Comyns invited the Mackintoshes to a banquet in Castle Rait (2½ miles south of Nairn, on the west side of the A939). Their plan was to massacre the Mackintoshes at a given signal, namely the carrying into the hall of a boar's head. This bloodthirsty plan was frustrated by a Comyn who was secretly in love with a Mackintosh girl. He arranged an assignation with her near the church at Croy (7 miles south-west of Nairn, on the B9091), where stood the Grey Stone or Listening Stone (*clach an t-sanais*). Rather than betray his clan directly to a Mackintosh, the young Comyn confessed the plan to the Grey Stone, within hearing of the girl. The Mackintoshes, therefore, went to Rait well prepared and when the boar's head appeared they fell upon their treacherous hosts and slaughtered all of them, with the sole exception of the girl's lover. In 1442

Malcolm Mackintosh at last got a charter from Alexander de Seton, lord of Gordon, recognizing his heritable right to Meikle Geddes and Rait; the power of the Comyns was broken for ever.

By now the lands of Clan Chattan had taken shape, a broad area stretching across parts of Inverness-shire, Nairn and Aberdeenshire. The Mackintosh country was in Inverness-shire and the western fringe of Nairn. It was bounded on the west by a line running roughly from Inverness southwards to the Monadhliath Mountains north of Newtonmore; from there the frontier turned north-eastwards along the eastern bank of the River Findhorn, marching with the Macpherson and Grant lands as far as Carn Glas-choire (2,162ft), thereafter north-westwards to the Moray Firth. Thus, the area occupied by the Mackintoshes was 30 miles long and reached a breadth of 15 miles at its widest point. In the north-western part was the land of the MacBains, whose chief lived at Kinchyle, 5 miles south of Inverness (off the B862); there is a Clan MacBain memorial park there today. Various cadets of MacBain held other lands, reaching as far east as Tomatin (just off the A9). Further south, the MacGillivrays, also members of Clan Chattan, held Dunmaglass in Strathnairn, just to the north-east of Loch Mhor. South of the Mackintosh country lay the great Macpherson territory of Badenoch. Its boundary ran from where the River Spey is only a stream, a few miles east of its source, curving to skirt the south-western extremity of Loch Laggan and down to the slopes of Ben Alder (3,757ft) at the southern end of Loch Ericht; then, from the eastern shore of Loch Ericht, it ran north-east to Glenfeshie Forest at the western end of the Grampians; the northern border reached from there, north-westwards across the Spey, to join up with the Mackintosh country. The chief's seat was at Cluny Castle, 6 miles south-west of Newtonmore (on the A86). The remaining large tract of Clan Chattan land was the area occupied by the Farquharsons, which stretched eastwards along both banks of the River Dee from its source to Ballater, and continued along the north bank as far east as Dinnet. The Farquharsons' main stronghold was

Castle Rait, where the Comyns planned to massacre their Mackintosh guests, but the Mackintoshes got wind of the plot and slaughtered their hosts.

Ben Alder on Loch Ericht marks the southern edge of Macpherson country.

Invercauld, near Braemar, where the chief still resides. Balmoral Castle, the Queen's country seat in Scotland, was formerly a Farquharson property. Finally, on the southern border of the Farquharson lands, the Mac-Thomas lands of Glenshee (on the A93) carried the Clan Chattan presence into northern Perthshire.

Malcolm died in 1464, his reign of 55 years having been a landmark in the history of Clan Chattan which mourned him as one of its greatest chiefs. Duncan, his son, was on good terms with James IV who granted him wide lands in Lochaber on the forfeiture of the Lord of the Isles. Duncan's fiery son Farquhar, however, had actually supported the rebellion by John of the Isles when he attempted to recover the earldom of Ross. As a consequence, Farquhar was imprisoned, though his father's loyalty and friendship with the king saved him from severe punishment. The disastrous outcome of this was that when Duncan died in 1496, the new Captain of Clan Chattan was a prisoner of state whose affairs had to be conducted for him by his cousin William. After the Battle of Flodden in 1513 he was released, only to die the following year. William now became 14th Captain of Clan Chattan; he was an able chief who brought the barony of Dunachton into the clan's land-holding. His brother and successor, Lachlan Beag (the Short), was described as 'an barroun of gude rent, quha keepit hes hole ken, friendes, and tennentis, in honest and guid rewll'. In 1520 he married Jean, daughter of Sir Alexander Gordon of Lochinvar, the 'Young Lochinvar' made famous by Scott's poem. Unfortunately, that same year his cousin Dougal Mór (the Tall) claimed the chiefship, raised a rebellion and seized Inverness Castle. Lachlan Beag took swift action to suppress the uprising, in the course of which Dougal Mór was killed: the short man had cut the giant down to size.

Lachlan Beag did not long survive his triumph: he was murdered while out hunting in 1524. Yet his son William, 16th Captain of Clan Chattan, suffered an even more gruesome fate. In 1550 he was falsely accused of plotting to murder the Earl of Huntly. He was arrested and tried in Aberdeen by a jury composed entirely of Gordons who

duly found him guilty, whereupon Huntly sentenced him to death. To their credit, the provost and citizens of Aberdeen were determined to see fair play and forcibly prevented the execution of Mackintosh. So he was taken instead to Bog-of-Gight Castle where Lady Huntly insultingly received him in the kitchen. She told him that he could only earn her husband's pardon once his head was brought to the block. Interpreting this metaphorically, Mackintosh dramatically laid his head on the block where animals were dismembered, to show his submission. Lady Huntly's cook immediately hacked off his head. Inevitably this sparked off a feud between Clan Chattan and the Gordons. The Mackintoshes had their revenge in 1562 when Lachlan Mór, son of the murdered chief, fought in the royal army which defeated Huntly at Corrichie. Lachlan was a strong Protestant at the Reformation and was also in Argyll's army at Glenlivet in 1594 when it was routed by the Catholic earls led by Huntly. This chief was succeeded in 1606 by his grandson, Sir Lachlan Mackintosh, 17th of Mackintosh and 18th of Clan Chattan, a promising youth who died in his late twenties.

William, 19th Captain of Clan Chattan, was a royalist during the Civil War, and, although he had too feeble a constitution to fight, most of his clan joined Montrose under the command of Mackintosh of Strone. In 1644 Charles I appointed the Laird of Mackintosh lieutenant of Morayshire, being one 'in whom we repose a special trust'. He lived just long enough to see the royal cause triumph, dying shortly after the Restoration, in November 1660. Five years later his successor Lachlan, 20th Chief of Clan Chattan, finally ended the 300-year-old feud with the Camerons, both parties signing a treaty under Campbell mediation. This, however, did not mean an end to feuding for Clan Chattan. In 1688 their quarrel with the Macdonells of Keppoch came to a head at the Battle of Mulroy in Glen Spean, when the Macdonells were victorious. This was notable as being the last clan battle in Scotland; its site is at Coire choille, 2 miles south-east of Spean Bridge, Inverness-shire (access by an unclassified road off the A86). Some months later, at the

Mackintosh

CREST BADGE: A cat, salient, gardant, proper
MOTTO: same as Clan Chattan
GAELIC NAME: Clann-an-Tòisich
ORIGIN OF NAME: Gaelic Mac-an-tòisich, son of the thane
WARCRY: *Loch Mòigh!*
PLANT BADGE: Red whortleberry

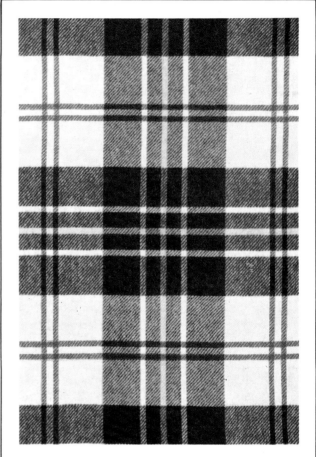

Macpherson, Dress

CREST BADGE: A cat, sejant, proper
MOTTO: same as Clan Chattan
ORIGIN OF NAME: Gaelic Mac-a-Phearsoin, son of the parson
GAELIC NAME: Clann Mhuirich
WARCRY: *Creagan Dubh!*
PLANT BADGE: White heather
PIPE MUSIC: Macpherson's March

Revolution, the Mackintoshes could not bring themselves to join the Jacobite army under Dundee, although they supported James VII, because their enemies the Macdonells of Keppoch were already in that camp. During the 'Fifteen, however, they played a much more glorious part. Some 800 Mackintoshes and Farquharsons, as well as 220 Macphersons, joined the Jacobite forces, in which the main Clan Chattan brigade was commanded by William Mackintosh, younger of Borlum. This contingent of the Jacobite army marched into England where it was defeated at Preston on the same day that the Battle of Sheriffmuir was fought. The chief spent some months in Newgate Prison, but was released the following year.

The last blossoming of Clan Chattan's military glory was in the 'Forty-five Rebellion. Aeneas Mackintosh, 22nd of Mackintosh and 23rd of Clan Chattan, was serving as an officer in the Black Watch at the outbreak of the rising; he thus felt in honour bound not to break his oath to the government. His wife, however, was a fanatical Jacobite who earned the nickname 'Colonel Anne' by raising a Clan Chattan regiment 800 strong and sending it to join Prince Charlie under the command of

MacGillivray of Dunmaglass. This regiment distinguished itself at the Battle of Falkirk. On 16th February 1746, Prince Charlie himself stayed at Moy Hall, the residence of the Mackintosh chief in Strathdearn (beside the village of the same name, about 10 miles south-east of Inverness, on the A9). A force of redcoats advanced from Inverness to seize the prince, but was ambushed in the darkness by Donald Fraser, the blacksmith from Moy, with four other men; imagining themselves to be attacked by a large body of Jacobites, the troops fled back to Inverness, the engagement becoming known as the Rout of Moy. At Culloden, Clan Chattan was the first to charge the Hanoverian army and suffered appalling casualties. 'The brunt of the battle fell on Clan Chattan', wrote a former Provost of Inverness, describing Culloden; Gilleas MacBain, a major in the regiment, killed 13 redcoats before he himself fell. The Clan Chattan colours were saved and carried from the battlefield by a man known ever after as Donald nam Bratach (Donald of the Colours).

The Macphersons, the next most important element in the Clan Chattan confederacy, also had a troubled history. Descended from Muirach, 4th Captain of Clan

Loch Laggan bounds the Macpherson territory on the west.

Chattan, they claimed the chiefship of the whole alliance on occasion. Their chiefs were styled Macpherson of Cluny, from their seat at Cluny Castle, 6 miles south-west of Newtonmore (on the A86), which was sold by them in 1943. The 6th Chief was killed at the Battle of Corrichie (1562), and the 8th Chief held Ruthven Castle against Mackintosh and the Earl of Argyll in 1594, during Huntly's rebellion. (Huntly had cunningly tried to drive a wedge between the Macphersons and the rest of Clan Chattan.) The Macphersons fought under Montrose and, after the Restoration, the 10th Chief matriculated arms in Lyon Court as Chief of Clan Chattan, but, on the objection of Mackintosh, was deprived of this title. James Macpherson, a bastard son of the Laird of Invereshie, was the last man to be executed under the old Heritable Jurisdictions when he was hanged for robbery at Banff in 1700, the episode being commemorated by the song 'Macpherson's Farewell', which the condemned man composed himself. A reprieve was on its way, but the Sheriff of Banff, Dunbar of Castlefield, advanced the time of the execution to frustrate it. Ewan Macpherson of Cluny, 12th Chief, was a famous supporter of Bonnie Prince Charlie. After Culloden, he hid in a cave in the Highlands for nine years, with £1,000 on his head, but was never betrayed; his picturesque existence is portrayed in R. L. Stevenson's *Kidnapped*. In the Macpherson museum at Newtonmore are preserved the clan's legendary Black Chanter and the *Bratach Uaine* (Green Banner) of the ancient chiefs. The principal cadet houses of Macpherson were Dalchully, Blairgowrie, Glentruim, Banchor, Pitmain and Invereshie. Count Axel Fersen, the Swedish admirer of Queen Marie Antoinette, who nearly rescued the French royal family from the Revolution by organizing the 'Flight to Varennes', was descended from a Macpherson who went to Sweden to fight for Gustavus Adolphus in the seventeenth century.

Since 1942 the chiefship of Clan Chattan has been separated from that of Mackintosh, now held by the house of Mackintosh-Torcastle. The Chief of Clan Chattan is styled MacGillechattan Mór; The Mackintosh is Mac-an-Tòisich and Macpherson of Cluny is Mac-Mhuirich. Clan Chattan has a huge variety of septs. The ancient surname Cattanach still survives, while the names Clark, Clarkson, MacChlerich, MacChlery, MacFall, MacNiven, Macphail and Macvail also derive from Clan Chattan. Septs of Mackintosh are Adamson, Ayson, Crerar, Dallas, Doles, Elder, Esson, Glen, Glennie, Hardie, MacAndrew, MacAy, MacCardney, MacHardie, MacKeggie, MacKillican, Macritchie, Noble, Ritchie, Tarrill, Tosh and Toshach. The Clan Shaw and the Clan MacThomas of Glenshee (sept names Combie and MacCombie) are also branches of Mackintosh, as well as the large Clan Farquharson; the Farquharson sept names are Coutts, Farquhar, Findlay, Findlayson, MacCaig, MacEaracher, MacFarquhar, MacKerracher, Reoch and Riach. From the Macphersons descend the families of Currie, Fersen, Gillespie, Gillies, Lees, MacGowan, MacLeish, MacLise, MacMurrich and MacVurrich. Other members of Clan Chattan have a small number of septs. The Davidsons were forebears of the families of Davie, Davis, Dawson, Kay, Macdaid and MacDavid; the MacBains of the names Bean, MacBeath, Macbeth, MacIlvain and MacVean; from the Macqueens derived the septs of MacCunn, MacSwan, MacSween and Swan; the MacGillivray name is also found in the form Macilvrae. As has already been mentioned, the 'Northern Macleans' of Dochgarroch and the Macintyres of Badenoch also belonged to Clan Chattan; another member of the confederation, the Clan Gow, has been anglicized as Smith, but only people with ancestors who lived in the Clan Chattan territory can reasonably assume that this very common surname gives them a clan connection.

The Clan Chattan plant badge is red whortleberry, also borne by the Mackintoshes in their own right; the Macpherson badge is white heather. When fighting as a confederation, the clansmen used the warcry 'Clan Chattan!' The Mackintosh warcry is '*Loch Mòigh!*' (the name of a loch in which stood the chief's castle) and the Macphersons' slogan is '*Creagan Dubh!*' (the Black Rock, near Cluny). In Gaelic the Mackintoshes are called Clann-an-Tòisich and the Macphersons Clann Mhuirich.

CLAN
CHISHOLM

LONG AGO A CHISHOLM CHIEF REMARKED THAT ONLY three individuals in the world were entitled to be described by the definite article: The Pope, The King and The Chisholm. It is a significant story, for it illustrates the pride of this small, but important, clan. The Chisholms have had a contradictory history. One branch was famous for its opposition to the Reformation, another supported the Covenant; the clan even contrived to fight on both sides at Culloden. Altogether, it would be fair to say that the Chisholms have always exhibited a high degree of individuality.

The family is of Norman origin and the name appears as De Cheséholme in early records. A bull of Pope Alexander IV in 1254 mentions John de Chisholme, in Roxburghshire; he married Emma de Vipont who brought him the lands of Paxtoun in Berwickshire. Chisholme is almost 2 miles south of the village of Roberton, 5 miles west of Hawick (on the B711 road). Sir John de Chesholme, grandson of the above, fought for Bruce at Bannockburn and was described by Edward II of England as 'our Scottish enemy and rebel'. He is thought to have been granted land in Nairn by Bruce and was succeeded by his brother Alexander and then by his nephew Sir Robert.

Sir Robert de Chisholme married Anne, the heiress of Sir Robert Lauder, Justiciar of the North and Constable of Castle Urquhart in Inverness-shire. Their son, another Sir Robert, inherited the lands of Quarrelwood, near Elgin, and Cantray, near Nairn, from his mother. In 1359 he succeeded his grandfather as Constable of Castle Urquhart and was appointed Sheriff of Inverness by David II. So, for this one generation, the Chisholm chief possessed land in both the Borders and the Highlands. The inheritance was soon divided, however. Sir Robert's eldest son, Alexander, married an heiress called Margaret del Ard or Margaret of the Aird, and thus acquired the lands of Erchless, Struy and Crochail in Strathglass, Inverness-shire. The local inhabitants of these lands accepted Alexander as chief and took his name; so the Highland clan of Chisholm was born. Alexander's youngest brother, Robert, was ancestor of

the junior line of Chisholme of Stirches, which inherited the old lands in Roxburghshire, and of the Perthshire Chisholms of Cromlix.

The Chisholms' Highland territory consisted of two neighbouring areas. Firstly, the larger portion, bounded on the west by the Mackenzie lands of Kintail, reached from Loch Affric to Comar, 15 miles to the north-east; on the north it was bounded by the Fraser country, on the south-east by Clan Grant. The long expanse of Fraser territory cut across Strathglass, separating the Chisholms' land at Comar from their other holdings around Erchless. This Chisholm country is rich and varied; Strathglass provides good grazing and the River Glass enabled the Chisholms to participate, like the Frasers, in the wool, timber and salmon export trade carried out through Inverness. The chief's residences were Erchless Castle, still standing today (on the A831, 10 miles south-west of Beauly), and Comar House, now the property of the Clan Chisholm Society (on a minor road, half a mile south-west of Cannich, on the A831).

Clan Chisholm (only the Border family continued to spell the name with the final 'e') became an important element in the Highlands. Wiland de Chisholm, on record in 1499, was the first chief to be styled The Chisholm. This form of title was more common in Lowland Scotland among Norman families, for example Le Brus, and in Ireland, though other Highland chiefs, such as The Mackintosh, have on occasion adopted it. From the time of Wiland, however, it came to be particularly associated with the chief of Clan Chisholm. His son, John, had a charter in 1538 erecting the lands of Comar into a barony. John's grandson, also John, became chief in 1590 and had two sons: Alexander, his heir, and Thomas, ancestor of the Chisholms of Kinneries and Lietry. Alexander Chisholm was in rather a quandary during the Wars of the Covenant. Although he helped to defend Inverness against the royalists, the bulk of his clansmen, unlike himself, were Catholics, so that he could not hope to arouse them to very active participation on the Covenanting side. In 1689 his son and namesake had no opportunity to make a move on behalf of James

Culloden, where in 1746 Chisholms found themselves fighting their own brothers.

Chisholm

MOTTO: *Feros ferio* (I am fierce with the fierce)
GAELIC NAME: Clann Siosal
PLANT BADGE: Fern
PIPE MUSIC: Chisholm's March

VII, since Williamite troops were sent to occupy Erchless Castle.

By the eighteenth century, however, the Chisholms had become strong Jacobites. Roderick, grandson of The Chisholm who had remained quiescent in 1689, brought 200 men to fight in the Jacobite army at Sheriffmuir in 1715, when he was 18 years old. In consequence, his property was forfeited, but he was pardoned in 1727; the estates were restored to his son in 1743. In 1745, therefore, the Chisholms were once more in a very embarrassing position, so they adopted a compromise which eventually proved tragic. The old chief stayed at home, while his youngest son, Roderick Òg, with about 100 clansmen, joined the prince; two of Roderick Òg's elder brothers, James and John, were officers in Cumberland's army. At Culloden, they faced each other in their respective front lines; the Hanoverian Chisholms could hear their clan piper playing the legendary ebony chanter 'The Maiden of the Sandal' among the opposing ranks. After the battle they found the body of their younger brother among the Highland dead and kept guard over it to ensure a decent burial. Then the redcoats harried Strathglass, where the impaling of a baby on a bayonet was just one of their recorded atrocities. The brothers Donald, Alexander and Hugh Chisholm were among the Seven Men of Glen Moriston who meanwhile guarded Prince Charlie in hiding.

Clan Chisholm suffered greatly from the Clearances in the nineteenth century, three major emigrations taking place between 1790 and 1840, which amounted to several hundred clansmen. Their places of settlement were Cape Breton, Antigonish in Nova Scotia, and Glengarry, Upper Canada. The Border Chisholmes died out in 1899; their Perthshire cadet house of Cromlix came into prominence during the Reformation, producing no less than three Catholic bishops, all named William, who struggled vainly to preserve the old religious establishment. There are no septs of Clan Chisholm, unless the surname Aird might be considered such. The chief is styled An Siosalach and the Chisholms' plant badge is a fern; their Gaelic name is Clann Siosal.

CLAN
DONALD

CLAN DONALD WAS THE LARGEST AND GREATEST OF the Highland clans. As Kings of Man, Lords of the Isles and Earls of Ross, the Macdonalds were in the fullest sense a royal house, rivals of the Stuarts for the supreme power, at least north of the Highland line. Their territory, the Western Isles, comprised the most beautiful and rugged country in Scotland, and the early history of the Highlands is inseparable from the fortunes of the Macdonalds. Bardic genealogies traced their ancestry back to the ancient Irish High King, Conn of the Hundred Battles, but their first historic forebear was Gillebride, a dispossessed prince who was living in hiding in Morvern in the early twelfth century. His son Somerled organized resistance against the Norsemen whom he eventually expelled from the whole of Argyll, becoming *regulus*, or sub-king, of that district. He married a daughter of the Norse King of Man and was defeated and slain at the Battle of Renfrew in 1164 by an army sent against him by Malcolm IV.

After Somerled's death, the empire he had acquired in the west was divided among his sons Dugall, Ranald and Angus. Dugall received Lorn, Jura, Tiree, Coll and Mull; from him descended the Macdougalls of Lorn. Ranald inherited Islay, Kintyre and part of Arran; he was founder of Clan Donald of Islay. Angus's portion was the remainder of Arran, Bute and the mainland territory of Garmoran, between Ardnamurchan and Glenelg; his line became extinct after a short period. Ranald's son, Donald, was the chief who gave the clan its surname of Macdonald. Of his two grandsons, the elder, Alexander, supported Balliol against Bruce during the War of Independence, so that, after the victory of the latter, he and his seven sons were driven out of their inheritance. The younger grandson, however, Angus Òg, was loyal to Bruce and fought for him at Bannockburn, so that he was granted his brother's forfeited lands, as well as those of Macdougall of Lorn, who had also supported the losing side. Angus died in 1330, leaving two sons, both with the same name: John the elder succeeded to the chiefship, John Òg (the Younger), an illegitimate son, was ancestor of the MacIan Macdonalds of Glencoe. John, the Chief,

was a very successful statesman who enlarged his estates considerably and married a daughter of Robert II. By an earlier marriage with the heiress of the house of Garmoran, he left a son Ranald who was ancestor of the Macdonalds of Clanranald and Glengarry; by his royal consort he begot, with other sons, his successor Donald, John Mór (progenitor of the Macdonells of Antrim) and Alexander (ancestor of the house of Keppoch). Then, in 1354, John took a step which formally proclaimed his independence of the Scots crown and set up a great Highland jurisdiction which endured until 1493: he assumed the title Lord of the Isles.

This act of John was no empty gesture, but the *de facto* establishment of what amounted to an alternative monarchy in Scotland. The Lord of the Isles was inaugurated with a ceremony resembling a coronation, he had a Council of 16 advisers which met at Finlaggan in Islay and a sumptuous court with all the officers pertaining to a royal household — physician, marshal, recorder, purse-bearer, speaker, bard, harper, piper and armourer. There was also a fully-developed system of administering justice, with a judge on every island who received one-eleventh of the property in any action adjudicated — an effective deterrent against frivolous litigation. The 1st Lord of the Isles died in 1387 and was succeeded by Donald, the eldest son of his second (royal) marriage. It was during the reign of Donald that the lordship of the Isles suffered its first serious setback at the hands of the ruling house of Scotland. Donald married the sister of Alexander, Earl of Ross, and when the Earl died, leaving only a daughter, the Lord of the Isles was determined to promote his interest in the succession. The Regent Albany, however, who was the girl's grandfather, incarcerated her in a convent and forced her to transfer her rights to the earldom of Ross to himself. Donald of the Isles, on the other hand, asserted his wife's claim and took up arms in support of it. At 'Bloody Harlaw' in 1411, he led 10,000 men against the royal forces; the carnage was terrible, but neither side had a clear advantage. Donald, however, was forced to fall back and Albany retained possession of the earldom of Ross, so that effectively the

Castle Tioram, situated on its tidal island at the mouth of Loch Moidart, was the seat of the Macdonalds of Clanranald.

house of Donald had been humbled. Donald's successor, Alexander, had to surrender to James I in 1427, but nine years later he had recovered his position and even obtained the earldom of Ross. When he died in 1449, his son John became Earl of Ross and the 4th and last Lord of the Isles. He made a secret pact, the Treaty of Westminster, with the King of England, for which his estates were forfeited in 1475. The following year they were restored to him, but as a fief held of the Scots crown. Inevitably the Macdonalds tried to regain their independence by force, with disastrous consequences. In 1493 the lordship of the Isles was annexed to the crown, being borne thenceforth by the heir to the throne of Scotland (as it is today by the Prince of Wales). The various branches of Clan Donald were declared chiefless and were recognized only as independent clans; the last, dispossessed, Lord of the Isles died in 1503.

So, from the beginning of the sixteenth century, the mighty Clan Donald was no longer unified, but a group of separate clans linked only by the bonds of kinship, fondly preserved by their genealogists and by Highland family pride. The Macdougalls became a completely independent clan, their chief seated at Dunollie Castle, near Oban; before marriage this chief's eldest daughter bears the ancient title of the Maid of Lorn. Clan Donald proper was divided into eight major banches. These were: Clan Alister of Kintyre, the MacIans of Ardnamurchan, the MacIan Macdonalds of Glencoe, the Clan Ranald of Garmoran (including Glengarry, Knoydart and Morar), the Clan Donald of Islay and Kintyre (also known as Clan Donald South), the Macdonells of Keppoch, the Macdonalds of Lochalsh and the Macdonalds of Sleat (also known as Clan Donald North). Of these eight, however, the house of Lochalsh became extinct as early as 1527, when it was absorbed into Glengarry, so that in relatively modern times there were just seven significant branches of Clan Donald. The most important of these were the Clan Ranald of Garmoran and its offshoot the house of Glengarry, the Clan Donald South in Islay and Kintyre, and the Clan Donald North in Sleat.

As has already been indicated, the progenitor of the Clan Ranald of Garmoran was Ranald, son of John, 1st Lord of the Isles. His son Allan, 2nd Chief of Clanranald, found his property of Uist usurped by his uncle, whose line held it until 1460 when it reverted to Clanranald. At its full extent, the Clanranald territory consisted of the islands of Uist, Rhum, Eigg and Muck, with Garmoran and Moidart on the mainland. These coastal areas were bounded on the south by Loch Shiel, on the east by Glenfinnan and the Glengarry lands and on the north by Loch Hourn; the two most northerly areas were held by the Clanranald cadet houses of Knoydart and Morar. The chief's residence was Castle Tioram, an impressive fortress standing on a tidal island at the mouth of Loch Moidart, 3 miles north of Acharacle, and now a ruin (access by an unclassified road off the A861). The 4th Captain of Clanranald, Allan, fought for Angus, Master of the Isles, at the Battle of Bloody Bay; he was recognized in 1502 as heir to the lands of Sleat which passed after his death to his kinsman Donald, 3rd of Sleat. Dugall, 6th of Clanranald, made himself so unpopular by his cruelties that he was murdered by his own people in 1520, and his sons were excluded from the succession, which passed to his uncle, Alexander, who ruled for the next 10 years. None of this chief's eight sons were the fruit of canonical marriage, but the eldest, John of Moidart, was legitimized by James V in 1531 and succeeded as 8th Captain of Clanranald. Subsequently he was kidnapped and imprisoned in Edinburgh while the Frasers of Lovat imposed his uncle, Ranald Gallda, as Chief of Clanranald. John of Moidart, however, escaped from prison and, with the help of the Camerons, defeated the usurper and his Fraser allies at the battle known as Blàr-na-Léine (The Field of the Shirts) on Loch Lochy, 15th July 1544.

Sir Donald Macdonald, 11th of Clanranald, received a charter erecting Castle Tioram into a feudal barony in 1610 and was knighted by James VI in 1617. Both his son John and grandson Donald fought under Montrose in the Civil War. Donald's son Allan, 14th Captain of Clanranald, fought with Dundee at Killiecrankie and commanded the right wing of the Jacobite army at the Battle of Sheriffmuir in 1715, where he was killed. On his

Doom-laden Glencoe, sight of the massacre of the MacIan Macdonalds in 1692 by government troops under Campbell of Glenlyon.

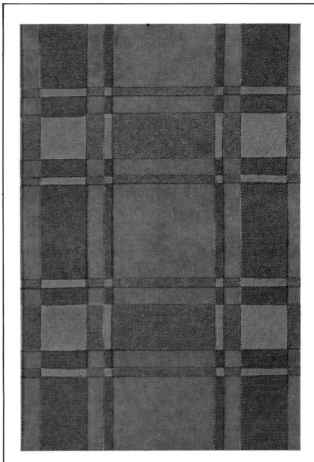

Macdonald of Sleat

CREST BADGE: Out of a coronet a hand in armour fessways, holding by its point a cross crosslet fitchy, gules.
MOTTO: *Per mare per terras* (By sea and by land)
PLANT BADGE: Heather

Macdonald

ORIGIN OF NAME: Gaelic *Domhnull*, world ruler
GAELIC NAME: Clann Dhòmhnuill
WARCRY: *Fraoch Eilean!* (The Heathery Isle)
PLANT BADGE: Heather
PIPE MUSIC: March of the Macdonalds

orders, Castle Tioram was burned to prevent it falling into the hands of the Hanoverians. Yet the most famous chief was Ranald Macdonald, 18th of Clanranald, the famous Jacobite who met Bonnie Prince Charlie on board the *Doutelle*, on his arrival in Moidart in 1745. He brought 250 men to the Jacobite army and his regiment was given the honour of fighting in the front line of the right wing at Prestonpans. Clanranald impoverished himself by giving a substantial bond to enable the prince's army to march south, was wounded in the head at Culloden and hunted through Moidart by the redcoats. Despite these difficulties, he contrived to marry the lady of his choice at a secret ceremony in Brahan Castle, the seat of the Seaforths, before escaping to France. Later he entered the French army and was aide-de-camp to the famous Marshal de Saxe.

A branch of Clanranald almost important enough to be considered a separate clan was the house of Macdonell of Glengarry. Donald, second son of the 1st Captain of Clanranald, inherited the lands of Glengarry in Inverness-shire from his father and became 2nd Laird of Glengarry. This was a territory some 26 miles long, bounded on the south by the Cameron country north of

Eigg and Rhum seen from Ardnamurchan. Both islands were part of Clanranald territory.

The castellated ridge of An Teallach rears above the northern lands of the Macdonells of Glengarry.

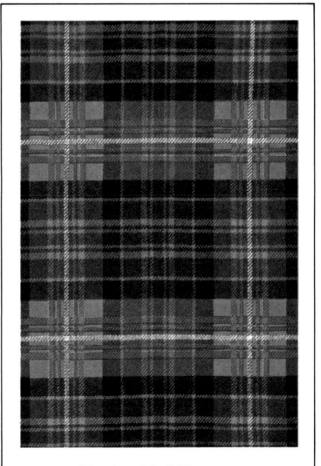

Macdonald of Clanranald

CREST BADGE: On a castle triple towered, an arm in armour, embowed, holding a sword, proper
MOTTO: My hope is constant in thee
WARCRY: *Dh'aindeòin có theireadh e!* (Gainsay who dare)
PIPE MUSIC: *Spaidsearachd Mhic Mhic Ailein*
(Clanranald's March)

Macdonald of Glengarry

CREST BADGE: A raven, proper, perched on a rock, azure
MOTTO AND WARCRY: *Creagan-an-Fhithich!*
(The Raven's Rock)
PIPE MUSIC: Glengarry's March

The Paps of Jura overlook the southern dominions of the Lord of the Isles.

Loch Arkaig, on the east by Loch Oich and the river of the same name; it reached as far north as Glen Affric where it marched with the Chisholm and Grant lands; on the west it merged with the Clanranald country of Knoydart. These lands of Glengarry were watered by Loch Quoich, Loch Garry and Loch Cluanie. The chiefly seat was Invergarry Castle on the western shore of Loch Oich, just south-east of Invergarry village (on the A82); its ruin is imposing rather than picturesque. Aeneas Macdonell, 9th of Glengarry, was one of Montrose's most faithful adherents during the Civil War and noted for his resistance to Cromwell. At the Restoration he was created Lord Macdonell and Aros and recognized by Charles II as principal chief of Clan Donald. The title died with him, however, and the chiefship passed to his cousin, Macdonell of Scotus. Alastair Macdonell, 11th of Glengarry, rallied the Clan Donald contingent in the Jacobite army at the Battle of Sheriffmuir: when the clansmen were dismayed to see the Captain of Clanranald fall, the Laird of Glengarry exclaimed, 'Revenge today and mourning tomorrow!' He was created Lord Macdonell by the exiled James VIII in 1716. The Macdonells of Glengarry had a fighting strength of 600 men during the 'Forty-five, in which they rose for Prince Charlie. Their service was rendered less valuable, however, by their reluctance to fight at Culloden because of the insult afforded them by being positioned on the left wing instead of the place of honour. Too proud to leave the field, they were mown down uselessly by the redcoat musketry as they taunted the Hanoverian troops to break ranks and fight with cold steel. Alastair Macdonell, 15th of Glengarry, was the last Highland chief to live flamboyantly in the old style. He killed a Black Watch officer in a duel in 1798, lived with a full household of Gaelic courtiers and was accompanied everywhere by a 'tail' of retainers in Highland costume. This chief was the original of the character Fergus MacIvor in Scott's *Waverley*.

The Clan Donald South (the Macdonalds in Islay and Kintyre) were descended from John Mór, second son of John, Lord of the Isles, and the Princess Margaret, daughter of Robert II. John Mór married the heiress of the Bissets of the Glens, in Antrim, and so acquired estates in Ireland; he was murdered by a Campbell about 1427. His son, Sir Donald Ballach (the Freckled), joined the rebellion of the Islesmen in 1431, ravaged Lochaber, then withdrew to his lands in Ulster. Besides these Antrim estates, this branch of Clan Donald held the island of Islay, the southern half of Jura and all of Kintyre south of Loch Ciaran. In Scotland the chief was styled lord of Dunyveg, from his principal residence at Dunyveg Castle in the south-east of Islay; in Antrim he was lord of the Glens. Sir John, 4th of Dunyveg, led his clan in battle against the king's forces in 1493, at the time of the forfeiture of the lordship of the Isles. The following year he hanged the royalist governor of Dunaverty Castle in South Kintyre within sight of the king and his fleet. Shortly afterwards he was betrayed by one of his Clan Donald kinsmen of Ardnamurchan and executed for treason in Edinburgh. After the eclipse of the lordship of the Isles, the fortunes of Clan Donald South revived somewhat, so that they were the most powerful branch of the Macdonalds in the sixteenth century. They fell victim to the powerful Clan Campbell's greed for land, however, and were progressively dispossessed, finally losing Islay in 1615. Although the Dunyveg branch became extinct, the Irish line continued: Sir Randal Macdonell was created Earl of Antrim in 1620 and his son was advanced to a marquessate. Montrose's much-feared lieutenant Sir Alasdair Macdonell — Colkitto — belonged to the Clan Donald South. The Irish Macdonells still hold the earldom of Antrim.

The remaining powerful branch, which eventually inherited the chiefship of all Clan Donald, was the house of Sleat, also called Clan Donald North. These Macdonalds descended from Hugh, son of Alexander, 3rd Lord of the Isles, hence their Gaelic name Clann Uisdein (Children of Hugh). Their territory consisted of North Uist, the Trotternish peninsula in Skye and the lands of Sleat in the south-east of the same island, with a settlement reaching as far west as the eastern slopes of the Cuillin Hills. Their strongholds in Skye were Dunscaith

Colonel Alastair Macdonell of Glengarry, the last clan chief to live flamboyantly in the old style.

Flora Macdonald, the Jacobite heroine who helped Prince Charlie to escape after the 'Forty-five.

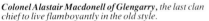

Donollie Castle, near Oban, seat of the Macdougalls, a clan once closely linked to Clan Donald.

Castle, now a ruin (on the unclassified road between Ord and Tarskavaig) on the shore of Loch Eishort; Duntulm Castle, also ruined, on a cliff-top site at the northern extremity of the island, about 3 miles north of Kilmuir (on the A855); and Armadale Castle on the Sound of Sleat. Donald Gruamach (the Grim), 4th of Sleat, claimed the lordship of the Isles and was killed in 1539 while besieging Eilean Donan Castle. The 8th Laird of Sleat was created a baronet in 1625 and his son Sir James Macdonald joined the army of Montrose. Sir Donald, 4th baronet and 11th Laird of Sleat, fought in the Jacobite army at Killiecrankie and was 'out' in the 'Fifteen. Nevertheless, his nephew Alexander, 7th baronet, refused to support Prince Charlie in 1745, believing that the absence of French troops foredoomed the rebellion to failure. In 1776, Sir Alexander Macdonald, 9th baronet of Sleat, was created Lord Macdonald. His line had already been recognized as overall chiefs of Clan Donald. The chiefship of Sleat and the chiefship of Clan Donald became separated, however, in the nineteenth century, due to complex matrimonial arrangements reflecting the differences between Scots and English law, so that the family of Bosville Macdonald inherited the baronetcy and chiefship of Sleat, while Lord Macdonald remained chief of the whole name.

The Macdonells of Keppoch were staunch Jacobites and noted for having won the last clan battle in Scottish history, against the Mackintoshes at Mulroy in 1688. Of the lesser Macdonald houses, the MacIans of Ardnamurchan suffered greatly from a feud with the powerful Macleans and, later, from despoliation by the Campbells who finally dispossessed them in the early seventeenth century. The MacIan Macdonalds of Glencoe have become a byword for human suffering. Their chief having been a few days late in taking the oath of allegiance to William of Orange, soldiers of the Argyll regiment under Campbell of Glenlyon were quartered on them. After 10 days as guests of the Macdonalds, they rose in the night and defiled the most sacred law of Highland hospitality by slaughtering their hosts in their beds, on 13th February 1692. Even today visitors frequently remark on the eerie atmosphere which still envelops Glencoe. The MacAlisters of Kintyre, whose chief was styled MacAlister of the Loup, are possibly the most senior of all branches of Clan Donald, genealogically speaking, but they remained dependents of the more important lords of Dunyveg. Among the famous members of this clan were Flora Macdonald, who helped Prince Charlie in his wanderings; Marshal Macdonald, Duke of Taranto, one of Napoleon's generals; and Alexander Macdonald, the great Gaelic poet — all, coincidentally, from the Clanranald line.

As Chief of Clan Donald, Lord Macdonald is styled MacDhòmhnuill. Macdonald of Clanranald is Mac-'ic-Ailein and Macdonell of Glengarry Mac-'ic-Alasdair. The sept names of Clan Donald are Beath, Beaton, Bethune, Bowie, Colson, Connall, Darroch, Donald, Donaldson, Drain, Galbraith, Gilbride, Gorrie, Hawthorn, Hewison, Houston, Howison, Hughson, Hutcheson, Hutchinson, Isles, Kellie, Kinnell, MacBride, MacCaishe, MacCash, MacCodrum, MacConnell, MacCook, MacCrain, MacCuish, MacDaniell, Macdrain, MacEachern, MacElfrish, MacElheran, MacGorry, MacHugh, MacHutcheon, Macilreach, Macilrevie, Macilvride, Macilwraith, MacKellachie, MacKelloch, MacLardie, MacQuistan, MacRory, MacRuer, MacSporran, MacWhannell, May, O'Drain, O'May, Purcell, Revie, Shannon, Train and Whannell. Clanranald septs are Allan, Allanson, MacAllan, MacEachin, MacGeachie, MacKeachan, Mackechnie, MacKeochan and MacKichan; Macdonald of Glencoe names are Henderson, Kean, MacHenry, MacIan and MacKean; Glengarry names are Alexander and Sanderson. The Clan Donald plant badge is heather and the general warcry is *'Fraoch Eilean!'* (The Heathery Isle!). The particular warcries of different branches are: *'Dh'aindeòin có theireadh e!'* (Gainsay who dare!) for Clanranald; *'Creagan-an-Fhithich!'* (The Raven's Rock!) for Glengarry; *'Dia's Naomh Aindrea!'* (God and St Andrew!) for Keppoch. Each major branch has a distinctive tartan and Gaelic title; the overall name is Clann Dhòmhnuill.

CLAN
DOUGLAS

Douglas

MOTTO: *Jamais arrière* (Never behind)
ORIGIN OF NAME: Place name, Lanarkshire,
meaning 'black water'
WARCRY: *A Douglas! A Douglas!*

NOBODY COULD ACQUIRE EVEN A SUPERFICIAL knowledge of Scots history without discovering the importance of the house of Douglas. On every page of Scotland's story the Douglases feature grandly — Black and Red, heroes and villains, they are always there. The list of peerages accumulated by them is longer than the tally of sept names attached to most of the larger clans! As late as the second half of the twentieth century, a Douglas chief became the Queen's prime minister; it was by no means the first time that one of his family had exercised the supreme power in the state, short of the crown itself.

The name Douglas derives from the Border dale owned by William de Douglas who lived there at the end of the twelfth century. His son, Sir Archibald, left two offspring: Sir William, who carried on the main Douglas line, and Sir Andrew of Hermiston, who was ancestor of the Earls of Morton. Sir William de Douglas, nicknamed 'Long-leg', adhered to the pro-English faction among the Scots nobility, probably because he held lands in Northumberland as well as Douglasdale, and died about 1274. His son and heir, Sir William le Hardi, provoked the rage of Edward I of England by abducting an English heiress, Eleanor de Ferrers, whom he married. For this crime he underwent a brief imprisonment in Leeds Castle. Soon afterwards, he became embroiled with Edward in a more serious quarrel: Douglas supported Wallace in his struggle against English domination and ended his days a prisoner again, dying in the Tower of London in 1298.

It was the eldest son of Sir William le Hardi who first made the Douglas name glorious in the annals of Scotland. Known as 'The Good Sir James', his story is inseparable from that of Bruce, whose faithful lieutenant he became. After fighting under Bruce at the Battle of Methven in 1306, James Douglas made a daring raid the following year on his confiscated estate in Douglasdale. Disguised as peasants, he and his men surprised and massacred the English garrison as they attended the Palm Sunday Mass; then Douglas's band calmly ate the Englishmen's dinner before destroying their supplies, beheading the prisoners and burning Douglas Castle.

Tantallon Castle, *perched on a cliff east of North Berwick, was a stronghold of the Earls of Angus — the Red Douglases.*

The Pass of Brander, *where the Black Douglas defeated a Highland army in the early fourteenth century.*

This bloodthirsty revenge was called the 'Douglas Larder'. Other exploits in which Sir James Douglas played a notable part were the defeat of a Highland army at the Pass of Brander, the capture of Roxburgh Castle and, of course, Bannockburn. By now 'The Good Sir James' was more commonly nicknamed 'The Black Douglas'. In 1316 he defeated an English force which had ridden across the border, hoping to surprise Douglas at Lintalee, near Jedburgh, where he was building a castle; it was Douglas, however, who ambushed the English and routed them. After the victory of the Scots in the War of Independence, Douglas not only recovered his father's estates, but was also given Balliol's lands in Galloway. The Black Douglas's last adventure, however, was his most famous. King Robert Bruce, who died of leprosy in 1329, charged him to remove his heart from his body after death and carry it to Jerusalem, since he had never had

time to redeem his vow to go on a crusade. Douglas got as far as Granada, in Spain, where he died in battle against the Moors, his king's heart hung round his neck in a silver casket. Bruce's heart was brought back home and buried in Melrose Abbey; the body of Douglas was interred beneath a splendid tomb in the church of St Bride at Douglas, in Lanarkshire (on the A70, about 2 miles south-west of its junction with the A74).

William, son of The Black Douglas, did not long survive his father; he fell at Halidon Hill in 1333 and was succeeded by his uncle, Hugh the Dull, who bemused his contemporaries by preferring scholarship to warfare. Hugh's younger brother, Sir Archibald Douglas, who had just been made Regent of Scotland, was also killed at Halidon Hill. In 1342, Hugh the Dull resigned his rights and the Regent's son, Sir William, became lord of Douglas. Like his forebears, he too made war on the

Loch Leven, in Kinrosshire, is surrounded by Douglas lands.

English for much of his life, even fighting in the French army at the Battle of Poitiers (1356). In 1358 he was created Earl of Douglas and, by his marriage with the heiress of Mar, he acquired that earldom too. He was involved in a minor rebellion against David II in 1363, but after the accession of Robert II, the first Stewart king, in 1371, he was appointed Justiciar of Scotland south of the Forth. By the time of his death in 1384 he had become the most powerful subject in the kingdom. James, 2nd Earl of Douglas, married Isabel, daughter of Robert II, and gained immortality at the Battle of Otterburn in 1388. In that year Douglas led a famous raid into England, as the old ballad records:

'It fell about the Lammastide,
　When the muir men win their hay,
The doughty Douglas boun' him ride
　Into England to drive a prey.'

Duelling in single combat with the great Percy, nicknamed Hotspur, Douglas captured the English knight's pennon and boasted that he would place it as a trophy on the battlements of his castle, unless Percy retrieved it by force. Three days later Hotspur surprised the Scots at Otterburn on a moonlit night. He was defeated and taken prisoner, but Douglas was mortally wounded:

'Last night I dreamed a dreary dream,
　Beyond the Isle of Sky
I saw a dead man win a field,
　And I wot that man was I.'

So the earl died, but the name of Douglas gained a further hold on the hearts of Scotsmen and he provided the original for Sir Walter Scott's *Marmion*.

By now the Douglases were a great family, possibly the greatest in Scotland, with extensive lands and formidable political power. They were divided into three principal branches. First was the senior line, the Earls of Douglas; then there were the Douglases of Dalkeith, later Earls of Morton, descended from Sir Andrew of Hermiston, younger son of Sir Archibald Douglas, the second recorded chief of the name; finally there were the Earls of Angus, the first of whom was the illegitimate half-brother of the hero of Otterburn. The latter left no legitimate issue, but his two bastard sons, William and Archibald, were ancestors respectively of the Marquesses of Queensberry and the house of Cavers.

Throughout Lowland Scotland there were impressive pockets of Douglas territory. Their original stronghold was Douglas Castle, now a ruin (to the north-east of the town of Douglas, on the A70), the original of Sir Walter Scott's Castle Dangerous. From this base the Douglases' territory stretched south-east to the Lowther Hills and, further west, Drumlanrig, a barony they owned from at least 1356. The source of the Clyde lay in Douglas land. Their next largest land-holding was in Teviotdale, reaching from just south of the source of the Ettrick Water, eastward to beyond Hawick. Then there were the lands around Dalkeith and, north of the River Forth, the district surrounding Loch Leven (through which the M90 now passes). Tantallon Castle, whose awesome ruin stands on the coast 3 miles east of North Berwick (beside the A198), was a stronghold of the Earls of Angus. Douglas in Lanarkshire, however, remains the place most associated with the ancient Douglas chiefs, who were generally laid to rest there in the church of St Bride, or at Melrose Abbey, further east (on the A6091). In all these lands, dependents adopted the Douglas surname and became 'spears' or retainers of their chief; 2,000 armed men was considered quite a normal retinue for a Douglas earl.

After his death at Otterburn, the 2nd Earl was succeeded by a bastard son of The Good Sir James who 'was callit Archibald Grym be the Englismen, becaus of his terrible countenance in weirfair'. Archibald the Grim was already Constable of Edinburgh Castle, Warden of the West Marches and lord of Galloway, where he had been granted all the land between the Rivers Nith and Cree 'becaus he tuke grit trawell to purge the countrey of Englis blude'. He built Threave Castle, whose ruin stands on an island in the River Dee, 1 mile west of Castle Douglas (on the A713) in Dumfries-shire. His daughter Marjory married the Duke of Rothesay, heir apparent to the throne of Scotland. The 4th Earl of Douglas, who

Threave Castle, on an island in the River Dee in Galloway, was built by a bastard son of the Black Douglas known as 'Archibald the Grim'.

The escape of Mary Queen of Scots from Lochleven Castle, where her gaoler had been the Earl of Morton, a Douglas of Dalkeith.

succeeded his father in 1400, was suspected of having a hand in the murder by starvation of his brother-in-law, Rothesay, two years later. He fought at Homildon Hill (1402), was a prisoner in England, and later entered the service of the French king. In 1424 Charles VII of France created him Duke of Touraine and lieutenant-general of his forces. Only four months later he was killed fighting the English at Verneuil. His grandson, William, 6th Earl of Douglas, died without issue in 1440, whereupon the earldom reverted to the brother of the 1st Duke of Touraine, James the Gross. He survived for just three years, dying in 1443, when his son William became 8th Earl.

Earl William's accession marked the beginning of the end for the old line of Douglas. At first he was a great favourite of James II, but he became involved in a deadly feud with the Chancellor Crichton, in which the latter was supported by the junior Douglas line, the Earls of Angus, known as the Red Douglases, to distinguish them from the senior branch who were called the Black Douglases. At last, in 1452, the Earl of Douglas was summoned, under safe conduct, to Stirling Castle, where he supped with the king. After supper, the king demanded that Douglas dissolve his potentially treasonable alliance with the Earl of Crawford. Douglas refused. 'Then if you will not, this shall!' exclaimed James II, drawing a dagger and stabbing him; his courtiers finished the work. Eager for revenge, the murdered man's brother, James, now 9th Earl of Douglas, rode into Stirling at the head of 600 men. Publicly denouncing James, who had by now absented himself, 'they gaif the King uncomlie wordis' and dragged the dishonoured document of safe conduct through the streets, tied to a horse's tail. Although a reconciliation was patched up, it was only superficial. Soon after, in 1455, the entire Black Douglas clan, in arms against the king, was defeated at Arkinholm by a royal army commanded by the Earl of Angus, chief of the Red Douglases. The Black Douglases were forfeited and Threave Castle was bombarded by the famous cannon Mons Meg. After various vicissitudes, the 9th Earl died a prisoner at Lindores Abbey in 1488 and the Black Douglases appeared no more in Scottish history.

George, 4th Earl of Angus, chief of the Red Douglases, now became head of the whole clan. His son, Archibald Bell-the-Cat, led the nobles' rebellion against James III which ended in the defeat and death of the king at the Battle of Sauchieburn (1488). Bell-the-Cat also fought at Flodden, where he was one of the few Scots of any note to survive. His grandson, also Archibald, became 6th Earl of Angus and married Queen Margaret Tudor, widow of James IV who had fallen at Flodden; he conducted a fierce feud with the Hamiltons. Since he left no issue, the earldom of Angus passed to the Douglases of Pittendriech. After the death of the 8th Earl, the peerage went next to the Douglases of Glenbervie. As the 10th Earl became converted to Catholicism, he eventually had to emigrate to France, where he died in 1611. The 11th Earl of Angus was promoted by Charles I to be Marquess of Douglas and later served under Montrose. The 3rd Marquess was created Duke of Douglas in 1703; he fought on the Hanoverian side at the Battle of Sheriffmuir (1715), and during the 'Forty-five he again supported the government. When he died in 1774 his dukedom became extinct, his marquessate was inherited by the Duke of Hamilton and his estates by his nephew Archibald Steuart Douglas of Douglas. The famous lawsuit which determined this was known as 'The Douglas Cause'.

Of the ancient line of Douglas of Dalkeith, the 1st Lord Dalkeith married a daughter of Robert III, the 1st Earl of Morton married the deaf and dumb daughter of James I and the 3rd Earl married a natural daughter of James IV. The 4th Earl of Morton was Regent of Scotland, the 6th Earl was gaoler to Mary Queen of Scots in Lochleven Castle, and the 7th Earl was a zealous supporter of Charles I in the Civil War. The earldom of Morton is still held by this family today. It would appear that the senior representative of the house of Douglas at present is Lord Home, but he cannot exercise this chiefship while he is also Chief of Home; the heir male is the Duke of Hamilton. Sept names of Douglas are Morton and Drysdale. The clan slogan is 'A Douglas! A Douglas!' and there is an official Douglas tartan.

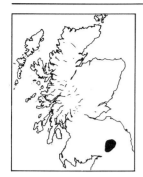

CLAN
ELIOTT

Eliott
MOTTO: *Fortiter et recte* (With strength and right)
OLD MOTTO: *Soyez sage* (Be wise)
ORIGIN OF NAME: Elwald, old Saxon Christian name

THE ELIOTTS WERE AN IMPORTANT BORDER CLAN, closely allied with the Armstrongs, and constantly to the fore in all the strife that made Scotland's only land frontier one of the most unruly areas of Europe. Since Liddesdale, where the Eliotts had their territory, was just east of the 'Debatable Land' — the stretch of country claimed by both Scotland and England — their history was inevitably violent, even by the standards of the Border clans.

The name Eliott derives from Elwald, an old Saxon Christian name, by which the clan was known for much of its history. Early records are scarce and the first mention of the name occurs in 1357, when Henry Elwald was owner of a small property in Bamburgh, on the English side of the Border. The first appearance of the name in Scotland was in Teviotdale in 1426, when John Elwalde was one of 19 gentlemen who held an inquisition into an alleged death from leprosy. Proper records of the clan's history begin in 1476 when Robert Elwald of the Redheugh, in Liddesdale, was 'velbelufyt fameliar squiar' to Archibald Bell-the-Cat, Earl of Angus. This Robert was the first known chief of Clan Eliott. He acquired the lands of Larriston in 1484 and died in 1497, being succeeded by his grandson and namesake.

Robert Elwald, 2nd of Redheugh, was an important enough chief to be sent for, under safe conduct, to negotiate with James IV a truce in the Borders, giving surety for good behaviour in return for immunity from punishment for 19 years. His heir was killed at Flodden in 1513, but the chief survived until 1526, though the last years of his life were particularly disturbed. After Flodden the English ravaged Scotland at will: 'There never was so mekill myschiefe, robbry, spoiling and vengeance in Scotland than there is nowe, without hope of remedye; which I pray our Lord God to continewe,' the English commander, Lord Dacre, reported jubilantly. The Eliotts were among those Scots who decided that reprisals were called for. In 1516 they made several raids into Northumberland and they even burned the town of Hexham, the property of the English chancellor, Cardinal Wolsey. The Regent Albany took an indulgent

Hermitage Castle, Liddesdale. In the sixteenth century, Robert Eliott was Captain of this impregnable fortress.

view of these activities; after all, some other Scots Border clans were helping the English for private gain, so that the Eliotts' behaviour contrasted favourably with their unpatriotic neighbours. In the period 1523-24 there was so heavy an invasion from England that the Eliotts had to leave their home in Liddesdale and take refuge further north among the Scotts in Teviotdale. Thereafter the Eliotts were frequently in alliance with Clan Scott.

Shortly after the Eliotts returned to Liddesdale, the chief died. His grandson, Robert Elwald, 3rd of Redheugh, had only just inherited when the clan was involved in a serious incident. The Eliotts followed Scott of Buccleuch in his attempt to seize the person of the young James V from the Douglases at Melrose in 1526. The coup was beaten off and, in the fight, Kerr of Cessford was killed by an Eliott. In revenge, the Earl of Angus raided Liddesdale the following year and reduced the Eliotts to submission. Fortunately for them, in 1528 the king escaped from the tutelage of the Douglases, confiscated their estates and gave the overlordship of Liddesdale to the Earl of Bothwell. Two years later, however, there occurred an episode which alienated the Borderers from James V and gave birth to one of their most famous ballads. In July 1530, the king met Johnnie Armstrong of Gilnockie, the most notorious Border reiver of all, at Carlanrig, near Hawick, and summarily hanged him and his followers. There were a number of Eliotts among Armstrong's men.

Bothwell, who had been thrown into prison at the time of Armstrong's execution, was now desperate for revenge on the king. Accordingly, on 21st December 1531, he and the Eliott chief secretly met the English Lord

Warden, the Earl of Northumberland, at Dilston. There they agreed to allow safe passage through Liddesdale for an English force which was to raid Buccleuch's lands. In the changing alliances of Border politics, however, such occasional treason counted for little. Robert Eliott does not seem to have been punished and for years he held the important post of Captain of Hermitage Castle, the impregnable fortress which commanded Liddesdale. The 3rd Chief's reign covered some of the best years in Liddesdale, for there was virtual peace from 1534 to 1541, under the unusually effective Keepership of Lord Maxwell. For a brief respite, the Eliotts had leisure to turn their attention to more peaceful concerns.

As has been said, the Eliott country was Liddesdale, at the south-western corner of the Scots Middle March. Its southern boundary ran along the border with England, from where the Liddel Water crosses the frontier near Kershopefoot to where Peel Fell rises 1,975 ft; some land east of the Liddel, however, belonged to the Armstrongs, whose stronghold of Mangerton was situated there. To the north lay the Douglas territory in Teviotdale, but a north-eastern peninsula of Eliott land reached as far north as Stobs, only about 3 miles south-east of the Scott fortress of Branxholm. To the west were the Maxwells, to the east the Kerrs. The Eliotts' chief houses were Redheugh, near Newcastleton, 11 miles north-east of Canonbie (on the B6357), Stobs Castle, 4 miles south of Hawick (off the B6399), and of course Hermitage Castle which they held as captains under the Keeper of Liddesdale for part of the sixteenth century. Hermitage, now a ruin in the care of the Ministry of Works, stands 14 miles south of Hawick (off the B6399).

'Return from the Foray' by Sir John Watson Gordon. The Eliotts were frequently involved in raids across the Border into England.

Essentially, the Eliotts' territory centred on the Liddel Water and its tributaries. Although the ground was only rough pasture near the source of the river, from the ford at Riccarton to Kershopefoot there was rich land. In 1514 the English Lord Dacre reported that there were 100 ploughs on the 12 mile stretch of the Liddel Water and 40 in the township of Carlanrig. This was a considerable cultivation and, when one remembers that the Borderers never fully exploited agricultural land, preferring to herd cattle and sheep which could be driven to safety during enemy raids, it is a clear indication of the richness of the Eliotts' holdings. Much of the south-western area was in fact occupied by the Armstrongs, who were the principal clan of Liddesdale; the two smaller clans, called Nixon and Croser, or Crosier, were dependents of the Eliotts.

On 4th November 1542, the Rout of Solway Moss once more brought war and insecurity to the Borders, besides breaking the heart of James V and leaving Scotland with an infant sovereign. Robert Eliott soon took the offensive; he raised a formidable force which amounted to some 400 men, including his Crosier dependents. As the situation grew more desperate, the Eliotts alone in Liddesdale refused to put on the red cross of England as their defeated neighbours did. In 1545 they had the satisfaction of helping to defeat the English at Ancrum Moor. Robert, 3rd of Redheugh, died about 1563 and his son, also Robert, became chief, but lived only for three more years. Since his son was a minor, the clan was led by Martin Eliot of Braidley. This cunning chief quickly settled a brief feud which had flared up with the clan's old allies, the Scotts, then turned his attention to some double-dealing with the English government. In October 1566, the Earl of Bothwell (soon to become the husband of Mary Queen of Scots) tried to put down the Eliotts. He was seriously wounded for his pains by John Eliott of the Park and the inevitable ballad celebrating the event gave rise to a well-known Scots saying:

'My name is little Jock Eliott,
And wha daur meddle wi' me?'

Martin of Braidley seems to have acted as chief during most of the latter part of the sixteenth century and little is known of his nephew, the chief of line, except that he married Lady Jean Stewart and had two daughters, but no sons. One of the chief's younger brothers, however, Gilbert Eliott of Stobs, earned celebrity as 'Gibbie wi' the gowden gartens', often referred to in Border ballads; his fourth son, Gavin, was ancestor to the Earls of Minto. During the chiefship of Robert, 5th of Redheugh, the Borders were finally pacified by the succession of James VI to the English throne. Yet such Eliott names as Jock Half-lug and Archie Fire-the-Braes still preserve the flavour of Border forays.

In the seventeenth century the chiefly line was styled 'of Larriston'. Robert, 5th of Redheugh and Larriston, was accused of conspiring to murder Buccleuch and spent a period in prison. He died some time after 1643 and was succeeded by his daughter Margaret who, in 1637, married her cousin James, sixth son of 'Gibbie wi' the gowden gartens'. Their son, Robert Eliott of Larriston, was chief of the name during the second half of the seventeenth century and was succeeded in 1712 by his son Robert. This heir dissipated his fortune and the estate was sold. His grandson, Major-General William Eliott, who had been assisted in his career by his cousin the Laird of Stobs, succeeded in repurchasing Larriston, where he lived until his death without legitimate issue in 1803.

The house of Stobs then became the chiefly line. They had been Covenanters, but had also opposed Cromwell in

Gilbert Elliot, 1st Earl of Minto, politician, diplomat, and governor-general of Bengal from 1806 to 1813.

George Augustus Eliott, who defended Gibraltar against the French from 1779 to 1783, and was subsequently made Lord Heathfield.

the later stages of the Civil War. In 1666 Gilbert Eliott of Stobs was created a baronet by Charles II. His grandson, Sir Gilbert Eliott, 3rd baronet, had several sons. John, the eldest, succeeded him as 4th baronet; the eighth son, George Augustus Eliott, defended Gibraltar against the French from 1779 to 1783, received the thanks of Parliament and was created Lord Heathfield in 1787. Sir William Eliott of Stobs, 6th baronet, became 11th chief of Clan Eliott in 1803 and the chiefship remains in his line today.

The principal cadet house is that of the Earls of Minto. Gilbert of Minto, grandson of 'Gibbie wi' the gowden gartens', was a strong Presbyterian who joined in Argyll's rebellion against James VII in 1685. After two years' exile in Holland he received a pardon, returned to Scotland and was an active supporter of William of Orange during the Revolution. He subsequently became Clerk of the Privy Council, was knighted in 1692 and created a baronet in 1700. In 1703 he was elected to Parliament and in 1705 was appointed a judge under the title of Lord Minto. He died in 1718 at the age of 67, when his son Gilbert succeeded him in the baronetcy. Sir Gilbert Elliot (the single *l* spelling is used by the house of Stobs, the double *l* by Minto) followed in his father's footsteps, sitting in Parliament for Roxburgh and becoming Lord Justice Clerk, also under the style of Lord Minto. His grandson, Sir Gilbert Elliot, 4th baronet, was Viceroy of Corsica and was raised to the peerage as Earl of Minto in 1813.

The earl's great-grandson, the 4th Earl of Minto, ruled much larger territories as Governor-General of Canada from 1898 to 1904 and Viceroy of India from 1905 to 1910.

Other cadet houses of Eliott were Thorlieshope, Arkleton, Falnash, Phillop and Harwood. Today the chief still resides at Redheugh and the Earl of Minto likewise has his country seat in Roxburghshire. The peculiarities of spelling can give a clue to the origins of various families called Eliott, as the old rhyme indicates:

'The double L and single T
Descend from Minto and Wolflee,
The double T and single L
Mark the old race in Stobs that dwell,
The single L and single T
The Eliots of St Germains be,
But double T and double L
Who they are, nobody can tell.'

Apart from discrepancies in spelling, there are literally dozens of variations of the name, the modern form of Eliott dating only from the seventeenth century. The versions possibly surviving today include: Allat, Aylewood, Dalliot, Eliot, Eliott, Ellat, Elliot, Elliswood, Ellot, Ellwood, Elwaird and Elwald (the original form of the name). Since the Nixons and Crosiers, or Crosers, had a permanent dependence on the Eliotts, they might be considered as septs, along with the Nixons' own subordinates, the Glendinnings, Hunters and Thomsons. Clan Eliott has a recognized tartan.

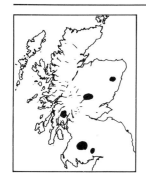

CLAN
FERGUSSON

IT IS UNLIKELY THAT CLAN FERGUSSON IS GENEALOGIcally one family. Most probably, different individuals named Fergus gave their origins to separate tribes in areas remote from each other and their descendants inherited the same patronymic. On the other hand, the scarcity of early records makes it difficult to discount certain claims to kinship, such as the tradition among the Balquhidder Fergussons that they derived from the house of Craigdarroch, so that while it is unconvincing to regard all Fergussons as related by blood, it is equally impossible to segregate them into rigid tribal groups. For practical purposes today they are a single clan, with Fergusson of Kilkerran as chief of the name. Historically, they may be divided into five main branches settled respectively in Ayrshire, Dumfries and Galloway, Perthshire, Argyll and Aberdeenshire.

The chiefly house of Fergusson of Kilkerran, in Ayrshire, is apparently descended from Fergus, Prince of Galloway, who died in 1161. Fergus, son of Fergus, is mentioned in an Ayrshire charter of the time of Bruce. In 1464 there is record of a John Fergusson of Kilkerran, who died in 1483 and was succeeded by his son Fergus. William, grandson of Fergus, was killed at the Battle of Pinkie in 1547. The first notable chief was Sir John Fergusson of Kilkerran, a cavalier who followed Montrose, though the other Ayrshire Fergussons were Covenanters. He was ruined in the service of Charles I, who knighted him in 1641, and he died in exile. His grandson, Alexander, inherited his debts and had to sell Kilkerran to his cousin, John Fergusson, who restored the family fortunes and was created a baronet in 1703. Sir John Fergusson was a distinguished advocate and many of his descendants were also prominent in the legal profession. In modern times, both the 6th and 7th baronets of Kilkerran were Governors-General of New Zealand; the 8th baronet was Keeper of the Records of Scotland from 1949 to 1969 and one of his brothers, Sir Bernard Fergusson, created Lord Ballantrae, was Lord High Commissioner to the General Assembly of the Church of Scotland, 1973-74. The principal cadet houses of Kilkerran were Auchinsoull (whose laird retired to

Ireland for 22 years after being excommunicated by the Kirk in 1689 for keeping a mistress), Threave and Dalduff.

Nearest geographically, and almost certainly related to the chiefly house, were the Fergussons in Dumfries and Galloway. Fergus of Glencairn appears as a witness to early thirteenth-century charters of the abbeys of Melrose and Dryburgh. The main family in this area was Fergusson of Craigdarroch, 2 miles west of Moniaive (B729), mentioned in records of 1398 and 1484. Like their Ayrshire cousins, these Fergussons became Whigs; William of Craigdarroch signed the Covenant in 1638 and his grandson, John, was killed fighting on the Williamite side at Killiecrankie. Alexander Fergusson, 10th of Craigdarroch, married Bonnie Annie Laurie of Maxwelton in 1709. Most important among the cadet houses were the Fergussons of Isle and of Caitloch, though there were a dozen lesser lairds. The house of Isle descended from John Fergusson, who had a charter in 1580 and who built the stronghold of Isle Tower, 5 miles north of Dumfries (on the east side of the A76 road). The Fergussons of Caitloch were also leading Covenanters. In the mid-seventeenth century the Fergussons owned 'the whole lands between the Dalwhat and Castlefairn waters, besides the lands of Jedburgh', but the main line of these Dumfries and Galloway families lapsed early in this century.

The Highland Fergussons were settled in Perthshire under the superiority of the Murrays of Atholl. Their earliest land-holding was Derculich on the north bank of the Tay, about 3 miles north-east of Aberfeldy. They descended from Adam, son of Fergus, a thirteenth-century chief who murdered his neighbour, the Bald Baron of Dunfallandy, and annexed his estate by marrying his son to the orphaned heiress. The Fergussons of Derculich and Dunfallandy, therefore, lived in the area bounded by the confluence of the rivers Tay and Tummel, just south-west of Pitlochry. Traditionally the chief of Dunfallandy was known as Baron Fergusson, though he did not in fact become a feudal baron until 1510 when John of Dunfallandy acquired the barony of

'Covenanters' Communion' by Sir George Harvey. Most of the Lowland Fergussons were ardent Covenanters.

Loch Faskally lies in the Highland territory of the Fergussons.

Fergusson of Atholl

MOTTO: *Dulcius ex asperis* (Sweeter after difficulties)
ORIGIN OF NAME: Gaelic *Fearghas,* first choice
GAELIC NAME: Clann Fhearghuis
WARCRY: *Clann Fhearghuis gu bràth!* (Clan Fergus for ever!)
PLANT BADGE: Poplar, pine

Douny; his chiefly title was MacFhearghuis. The clan spread eastward across the Tummel, settling in Strathardle and Glenshee and establishing cadet houses of Muling, Middlehaugh, Baledmund, Ballyoukan and about 10 smaller branches.

In a report dated 1587, the Atholl Fergussons were described as an 'unruly clan'. Later, they supported Montrose and were to become well-known Jacobites. Finlay Fergusson, 5th of Baledmund, was 'out' in the 'Fifteen, tried for treason and fortunately acquitted; the same befell James Fergusson of Dunfallandy in the 'Forty-five. Captain Thomas Fergusson of Ballyoukan was wounded at Culloden. The families of Dunfallandy and Baledmund are extant today and still possess their original lands. Fergussons have also been settled around Balquhidder, Loch Earn and Comrie for six centuries and the oldest graves in Balquhidder churchyard bear their names.

Clan Fergus of Argyll claims descent from the royal house of Dalriada and the chiefs held the hereditary office of *Maor* of Strachur, on Loch Fyne, with the lands of Glenshellich (3 miles south of Strachur, A815). A tombstone dated 1774 in Strachur churchyard bears the same coat of arms as the Kilkerran Fergussons, who may originally have migrated from Argyll. The chief of Clan Fergus of Strachur now lives in the United States of America.

In Aberdeenshire (where the name is spelled with a single *s*) the Fergusons have held land since 1364. Their chief house was Badifurrow, near Inverurie, acquired in 1655 by William Ferguson, a royalist, and member of the Scots Parliament after the Restoration. One of his sons, Robert the Plotter, was a churchman and notorious political turncoat. The main cadets of Badifurrow were Pitfour and Kinmundy. James Ferguson, Lord Pitfour (1700-77) was a famous judge; the Lairds of Kinmundy were staunch Whigs, so that the Jacobite army despoiled the estate in 1745.

Besides these five distinct branches, Fergusons were to be found in Banffshire, Angus, Kincardineshire and Peebles. The Fergusons of Raith, in Fife, produced several distinguished soldiers and politicians, including Sir Ronald Ferguson, Viscount Novar, who was Governor-General of Australia from 1914 to 1920. Fergusson sept names are Fergus, Fergie, Ferrie, Ferries, Ferris, MacAdie (from the Perthshire branch), MacKerras and MacKersey (both from the Argyll branch). The badge of the Kilkerran and Dunfallandy families is poplar; for Fergusson of Strachur it is pine. In Gaelic the name is Clann Fhearghuis and the warcry '*Clann Fhearghuis gu bràth!*' (Clan Fergus for ever!).

CLAN
FRASER

THE FRASERS PROVIDE A STRIKING ILLUSTRATION of the great variety of experiences which can be found within the history of a single Scottish clan. At different times they have lived in the Borders, the Lowlands and the Highlands; they have been Covenanters and Jacobites, fishermen and farmers, and most notably soldiers. Even by the standards of the Highland clans they have always preserved an exceptionally strong sense of blood-ties. As their most famous chief, Simon, 11th Lord Lovat expressed it: 'There is nothing I place in balance with my kindred'.

Legend traces their origin to Jules de Berry, a tenth-century French gentleman who served a plate of delicious strawberries to King Charles the Simple who gratefully knighted him and gave him the name Fraiseur, from the French word for a strawberry. In allusion to this fable the Frasers have always borne strawberry flowers in their coat of arms. Sober history records a family in Anjou called Frezel, which gave its name to the lordship of La Frézelière, and it is thought a cadet of this house came to southern Scotland in the twelfth century when the Kings of Scots encouraged Frankish nobles to settle and keep order in their turbulent kingdom. In 1109 Gilbert de Fraser witnessed a charter to the monastery at Coldstream and in 1160 Simon Fraser held lands at Keith in East Lothian. Through marriage, the Frasers acquired Castle Oliver on the Tweed and became Sheriffs of Peebles. Sir Simon Fraser of Castle Oliver was a staunch supporter of William Wallace in the Wars of Independence and gained renown by defeating the English three times in one day, at Rosslyn on 25th February 1303. He was captured in 1306 and taken to London where he was hanged, drawn and quartered.

The family's patriotism, however, did not go unrewarded. Sir Alexander Fraser of Touch became Chamberlain of Scotland and married Lady Mary, sister of King Robert Bruce, thus founding the fortunes of his house. His grandson Alexander obtained the estates of Philorth in Buchan by another judicious marriage in 1375 and his descendants grew into a powerful Aberdeenshire clan. About 1570, Alexander, 8th Laird of Philorth, founded the town of Fraserburgh where, by charters of 1st July 1592 and 4th April 1601, King James VI granted the Frasers the unusual privilege of establishing a university. This project was short-lived, its only surviving relics being a street in Fraserburgh called College Bounds and a slab of stone carved with the Ten Commandments, once part of the college wall, now built into the rear of the South Church. In 1670, the 10th Laird of Philorth inherited the Saltoun peerage through his mother and the chiefs of the name of Fraser have since then been Lords Saltoun.

Yet it was a junior branch of the family which was destined to found one of the great Highland clans and attain major political importance. Sir Alexander, the Chamberlain, had a younger brother Simon who fought at Bannockburn and was later killed at the Battle of Halidon Hill (1333). His descendants, whose chief was always styled Mac Shimidh (Son of Simon), also made profitable marriages and so acquired vast lands in Inverness-shire, around the districts of the Aird and Stratherrick. From their property in the Aird this branch became known as Fraser of Lovat and recognized as an independent clan, with Mac Shimidh as chief. About 1460, Mac Shimidh was created Lord Lovat.

The extent and richness of their lands gave the Lovat Frasers considerable importance. Their territory is divided in two by the River Ness and the Glen of Albyn. The northern portion, the Aird, stretches for about 30 miles westward from Inverness along the southern shore of the Beauly Firth. Stratherrick, their less fertile land, reaches a similar distance from Inverness down the southern bank of Loch Ness to just below Fort Augustus. These two tracts of land unite several miles south-west of Inverness, but there was always a segment of Chisholm and Grant country separating their western extremities. Though peaceably acquired through marriage, the defence of this territory was an endless struggle for the Frasers and their attitude even to national issues was dictated by local clan politics. In the fourteenth century they formed an alliance with the Mackays to resist the encroachments of the Lords of the Isles, but the threat from Clan Donald continued into the next century. In

Rosslyn in Midlothian, where Sir Simon Fraser defeated the English three times in one day in 1303.

Simon Fraser, 11th Lord Lovat, after Hogarth. Soon after the portrait was made he was beheaded for his part in the 'Forty-five.

1461 the Macdonald chief, Angus Òg, invaded Inverness and defeated the Frasers and their allies — the Mackenzies on this occasion. Despite such setbacks, the Frasers grew in strength, building up their clan organization by establishing cadet branches which in turn leased out land to tacksmen, those principal tenants who were the backbone of the clan in war and peace.

Though the Frasers fought at Flodden in 1513, this national disaster did less damage to their fortunes than their terrible defeat by the Macdonalds some thirty years later. Mac Shimidh supported the claim of his nephew Ranald, who had been fostered in the Lovat country, to the chiefship of Clan Ranald against John of Moidart. Ranald's claim was good, but he was unpopular among his Macdonald kin. So John of Moidart swept into Stratherrick and 'herrit, reft and spulziet the haill country'. On 15th July 1544, by the shore of Loch Lochy, on a site now under water, a furious battle was fought, known as Blàr-na-Léine (the Field of the Shirts), because the combatants stripped to their shirts for the bloody work.

About 260 Frasers were killed and it is claimed that only four Frasers and ten Macdonalds survived the battle. Among the dead were Mac Shimidh and his heir, the Master of Lovat, a mere boy who had disobediently rushed to the battlefield after being taunted with cowardice by his stepmother. But for the exceptional number of posthumous children born to Fraser widows, said to number 80, the clan might never have recovered from this massacre.

In times of peace, however, life could be good for the Frasers. From their early days on the Aberdeenshire coast they had learned to harvest the sea as well as the land and the Lovat Frasers carried on this tradition. Their boats landed catches of herring and cod which were bartered in Inverness for wine and foodstuffs. The Beauly River was so bountiful in salmon that a Lovat chief is said once to have lit a fire under a cauldron on the rock beside the Beauly falls, whereupon within minutes a salmon obligingly leapt out of the river and landed in the pot where it was quickly cooked! Beauly salmon, salted or smoked, was being exported as far afield as Italy by the eighteenth century, one of the many cargoes carried by locally-built ships from Inverness, whose Provost also rejoiced in the title of Admiral of the Moray Firth. When the Inverness magistrates ordered the price of salmon to be raised to twopence per pound, the citizens were furious at this extortionate increase.

At first the Lovat chiefs were seated at Beauly, where many of them are buried near the ruins of the old Valliscaulian Priory founded in 1223 by the Bissets, whose heirs they were. Mac Shimidh held his Court at Tomnahurich (the Hill of the Yew-wood), now an Inverness cemetery. Here the Frasers of the Aird used to pluck sprigs of yew, the clan emblem, for their bonnets in time of war. The Stratherrick Frasers took their sprigs from a famous old yew tree still standing on the western slope of Beinn a' Bhacaidh (the Hill of the Hindrance). It is situated on the southern bank of Loch Ness, but visible from the main Fort Augustus-Inverness road (A82) on the northern shore, from a point 3 miles out from Fort Augustus.

In 1511 the Fraser chiefs moved some 4 miles upstream on the Beauly River to Castle Dounie, on whose site Beaufort Castle now stands and from which they took their warcry 'Caisteal Dhunaidh!'. In each generation their dependents grew in number, as lesser tribes adopted the Fraser name and married into the clan. During the wars of the Covenant they fought against Montrose, not out of hostility to the King, but from fear of their powerful enemy, Gordon of Huntly, who took the royalist side. Dread of Huntly was so widespread in the eastern Highlands that the Frasers were joined not only by the Mackays, Munros and Forbeses, but even by Huntly's own kinsmen the Gordons of Sutherland. Montrose punished the Frasers by harrying their lands, so that after the victory of the Covenant, compensation was awarded to Lord Lovat out of fines levied on royalists. When Charles II landed in Scotland and subscribed to the Covenant, 800 Frasers commanded by Lovat's uncle marched south with him to fight against Cromwell at the Battle of Worcester.

Loch Lochy now covers the site of the Field of the Shirts battle, fought in 1544 between the Frasers and Macdonalds.

At the Revolution in 1689, national issues were again blurred by clan politics. Hugh, Lord Lovat, was married to Lady Amelia Murray, a daughter of the Marquess of Atholl. When the Murrays mustered a force of Atholl Highlanders at Blair Castle, Lovat joined them with 300 men. On being told that they were to fight for William of Orange, however, and not, as they had thought, for King James, the Fraser clansmen rushed to a nearby burn, filled their bonnets with water and drank the health of James VII. Then they marched off to join the Jacobite army. The humiliated Mac Shimidh had no alternative but to accept this democratic decision and follow his men into the Jacobite camp.

After the death of this chief a bitter dispute arose over the succession, with both Murrays and Mackenzies as interested parties. By marrying a Fraser heiress, one of the Mackenzies temporarily gained control of the Lovat inheritance, but he miscalculated by joining the 1715 Rebellion while his rival, Simon, Master of Lovat, prudently sided with the government. In reward, George I reinstated Simon as 11th Lord Lovat. It was under the leadership of this most celebrated of all Fraser chiefs that the clan's fortunes reached their zenith, only to sink in ruin.

Simon, 11th Lord Lovat, was one of the outstanding figures of eighteenth-century Scotland, a devious politician and an accomplished courtier. During his exile in France he had impressed Louis XIV by the eloquence of an extempore address in French which he delivered in private audience; Madame de Maintenon described him as 'ravishing', an unfortunate choice of phrase since one of the crimes which had made necessary his flight overseas was his forcible 'marriage' to his cousin's widow. His manners were cosmopolitan and he renewed links with the French branch of his family, entering into a formal bond of friendship with the Marquis de la Frézelière. In fact the Frasers had never lost sight of their continental origins: the young Master of Lovat killed at Blàr-na-Léine in 1544 had just returned from being educated at the University of Paris. Yet, above all, the 11th Lord Lovat was a great Gaelic chief. At Castle

Dounie he lived like a king, entertaining hundreds of guests, his hospitality strictly graded according to social precedence. French cuisine, accompanied by champagne and claret, was served to his most important visitors; the lesser lairds and tacksmen ate beef and mutton, washed down with port, whisky or ale. Salmon, being little regarded since it was in plentiful supply, was the portion of his 'faithful commons', as many as 400 of whom might be bedded down on straw in the castle after a large feast.

Despite his notorious cunning, this strain of Celtic romanticism eventually caused Mac Shimidh's heart to overrule his head. He entered into correspondence with the exiled Stuarts and in 1740 the Old Chevalier secretly created him Duke of Fraser. When Prince Charles Edward landed, Lovat mustered 750 of his clan on the Field of Dounie, just west of where Beaufort Castle now stands. Then, while still publicly protesting his loyalty to the Hanoverian government, he sent his son, the Master of Lovat, with 500 men to join the Prince. Half of them were killed at Culloden, including their lieutenant-colonel, Charles Fraser, younger of Inverallochy. While lying wounded, he was shot dead on the orders of General Hawley whose A.D.C., the future General Wolfe of Quebec fame, had refused to carry out this command. On the evening of the battle, Prince Charlie fled to Gorthleck House, a Fraser property on the shore of Loch Mhor (also called Loch Garth) about 18 miles south-west of Inverness (B862). Here he met Lovat for the first time.

After the ruin of the Stuart cause, Mac Shimidh could not escape the penalties of his double-dealing. Castle Dounie was razed to the ground by Cumberland's army and Lovat was later captured in hiding and taken to London. He remained defiant to the end. As his coach left Westminster Hall, where he had just been sentenced to death, a cockney woman screeched at him: 'You'll get that nasty head of yours chopped off, you ugly old Scotch dog!'. 'I believe I shall, you ugly old English bitch', replied Mac Shimidh imperturbably. After being painted in captivity by Hogarth, he was executed on Tower Hill on 9th April 1747, the last death by beheading in Britain.

The Lovat peerage and estates were forfeited, but

The Beauly Firth. *The southern shore is known as the Aird, and comprises the Fraser territory west of Inverness.*

Fraser

MOTTO: *Je suis prest* (I am ready)
GAELIC NAME: Clann Fhriseal
WARCRY: *Caisteal Dhunaidh!* (Castle Dounie)
PLANT BADGE: Yew
PIPE MUSIC: Lovat's March

Simon's son was pardoned and later raised two regiments for the Crown, the 78th (Fraser's Highlanders) which served from 1757 to 1763 and the 71st Regiment, 1775 to 1783. The 78th helped General Wolfe to take Quebec in 1759 and there is a tradition that Wolfe, who had refused to kill Young Inverallochy at Culloden, died in the arms of a Fraser on the Heights of Abraham. For his services, General Simon Fraser had the forfeited Lovat estates restored to him in 1774. Both he and his brother, Colonel Archibald Fraser, who succeeded him as M.P. for Inverness, supported the campaign by the Marquess of Graham to abolish the Act (19 George II, cap. 39) which had prohibited Highland dress after Culloden. In 1782 their efforts secured the repeal of the Unclothing Act and the clan tartans again appeared in the Highlands.

Appropriately, it was in the Fraser country, in the nineteenth century, that a curious epilogue to the Jacobite Movement was enacted which gave impetus to the revival of Highland dress. The Sobieski-Stuarts, two brothers who claimed to be grandsons of the Young Pretender, gained the patronage of Lord Lovat (a new peerage had been created by William IV in 1837). Mac Shimidh gave them Eilean Aigas, an island in the Beauly River, upstream from Beaufort Castle, where he built a hunting lodge. Here the Sobieski-Stuarts lived in regal state and were eventually buried at the Catholic Chapel of Eskadale on the south bank, where the later Lovat chiefs also have their tombs. Despite their eccentricities, the Sobieski-Stuarts' work *Vestiarium Scoticum* was an important influence in popularizing the Scottish national dress once more.

The original Scots peerage of Lovat was restored in 1857 and the Fraser chiefs bear it to this day, still seated at Beaufort Castle on the site of Dounie, the old fortress burned in 1746. During the Boer War and both World Wars, the Lovat Scouts continued the Fraser military tradition, serving with distinction. Frizell is an alternative form of the Fraser name; its septs are the Tweedies, the MacGruers and most surnames derived from Simon, for example Sime or Simpson. In Gaelic they are known as Clann Fhriseal.

CLAN
GORDON

It should perhaps be explained at the outset that the 'Gay Gordons' were not so called because of any hereditary cheerfulness of disposition. The Scots word *gey*, almost untranslatable, means 'overwhelming' or 'self-important', with undertones of hostility; it is a reminder of the power which the Gordons once enjoyed and the fear which they provoked. At the height of their fortunes they ruled what was virtually an independent kingdom in the north-east of Scotland. The Gordons possessed many unique characteristics, two of the most notable being their stubborn championship of Roman Catholicism and their mastery of horse-breeding, which provided them with the only effective cavalry force north of the Highland line.

According to early records, the family was of French origin. Adam Gordon was granted the lands of Long-Gordon in Berwickshire by Malcolm III and died alongside that king at the siege of Alnwick in 1093. His great-great-grandson Richard, Baron of Gordon, gave land grants to the monks of Kelso in 1150 and 1160; Bertram de Gordoun who slew Richard Coeur de Lion at Chalus in 1199 was said to be his kinsman. Richard Gordon's son, Sir Alexander, earned the favour of Alexander I by killing or capturing a band of traitors who had tried to murder the king. For this service Sir Alexander received the lands of Stitchel in the Merse. His eldest son, William, died while commanding the Scots contingent on crusade with St Louis IX of France in 1270; the second son, Adam, inherited the estate which he passed on to his son and namesake. This Sir Adam Gordon won fame during the wars between Henry III of England and his barons by fighting a single combat against Prince Edward (later Edward I, Hammer of the Scots) which ended honourably in a draw.

His grandson, yet another Sir Adam Gordon, began as a supporter of Balliol, serving under Edward I as Justiciary of Lothian in 1305 and taking a seat in the English council at Westminster. Later he changed sides and joined Bruce, so that in 1320 he was one of the Scots ambassadors who laid the Declaration of Arbroath before the Pope. Bruce rewarded him with a grant of the lordship of Strathbogie, a large territory straddling Banffshire and Aberdeenshire, forfeited by the Earl of Atholl. Henceforth, while retaining his Berwickshire lands, the chief of the Gordon family lived in Strathbogie, whose capital was renamed Huntly by its new lords. Sir Adam was killed at Halidon Hill in 1333.

Of his two sons, Adam, the heir, succeeded to the Huntly estate; William, the younger, inherited the lands of Stitchel and was ancestor of the Viscounts of Kenmure. Adam Gordon of Huntly had two grandsons, John and Adam. John, the elder, contracted a handfast marriage and had two sons: John Gordon of Scurdargue, known as Jock, and Thomas Gordon of Ruthven, known as Tam. Since the marriage had not been blessed by the Church, Jock and Tam were illegitimate and could not inherit the Huntly lands. Both left many descendants, however, including the Marquesses of Aberdeen, who derive from the disinherited Jock. In the meantime, Adam Gordon, the uncle of Jock and Tam, became lord of Huntly and increased the family's importance by marrying Elizabeth Keith, an heiress who brought him the lands of Aboyne, Glentanar and Glenmuick in Aberdeenshire. Yet no sooner had the two great estates of Huntly and Aboyne been united than the Gordon succession faltered: Adam was killed at the Battle of Homildon Hill in 1402, leaving an only child, Elizabeth.

When, in 1408, Elizabeth married Alexander, second son of Sir William Seton of Seton, the cadet house of Gordon of Lochinvar became senior male representatives of the blood line, but the Seton Gordons remained chiefs of the clan and inherited the vast Huntly estates. Elizabeth's husband was created Lord Gordon, but the crowning recognition of the family's status came in 1445 when his son was made Earl of Huntly. Simultaneously, rival houses declined. Early in the fifteenth century, the earldom of Mar lapsed, leaving a power vacuum in north-eastern Scotland which the Gordons rapidly filled. Then, in 1451, as part of his policy of undermining the house of Douglas, James II gave Huntly the lordship of Badenoch, as well as other grants of land in Inverness-shire and Moray. In the following year, Huntly earned his

Huntly Castle, the ancient northern seat of the Gordons.

The Duchess of Gordon's House, Castle Hill, Edinburgh, in the early nineteenth century.

new honours by coming to the assistance of King James, whose murder of the Earl of Douglas at Stirling Castle had provoked a rebellion led by the Earls of Crawford and March. Huntly defeated the rebels at Brechin, though two of his brothers were killed in the battle. James II was suitably grateful and gave his sister, the Lady Annabella, in marriage to Huntly's son, who succeeded to the earldom in 1470.

George, 2nd Earl of Huntly, was one of the most powerful nobles in Scotland. Lord of Huntly and Aboyne and intermarried with the royal family, his position was further strengthened in 1476 when he was appointed the King's Lieutenant in the North. His residence was Huntly Castle, now a picturesque ruin beside the town of the same name (on the A96 road, 40 miles north-west of Aberdeen), where the rivers Bogie and Deveron unite. This was the ancient northern seat of the Gordons, but the 2nd Earl built another stronghold at the Bog of Gight, 1 mile north-east of Fochabers (A98 road). Since Bog-of-Gight Castle was held in feu from the earldom of Moray, Huntly was sometimes derisively called 'the Gudeman of the Bog' ('gudeman' meaning a tenant-farmer). From the seventeenth century, the Bog of Gight was known more elegantly as Gordon Castle; only a portion of it survives today. The Earls of Huntly had other castles at Aboyne and Drumin (in Glenlivet), besides frequently holding royal fortresses as King's Lieutenants in succeeding generations.

The Gordons' territory was divided into three main parts. The oldest, most westerly area was Huntly (formerly called Strathbogie). It had a natural defensive frontier in the Grampians which kept it remote from the south, the three highest mountains in Scotland, after Ben Nevis, forming part of this barrier. While effectively a Highland clan, the Gordons held prime farming land between the Grampians and the Moray Firth which gave them great economic advantages. To the south, on Royal Deeside, their second tract of territory centred on Aboyne (32 miles west-by-south of Aberdeen on the A93). Here the land was less hospitable to crops, but rich in pine forests. The modern royal residence of Balmoral is

nearby. A third sphere of Gordon influence formed a patchwork of lesser estates belonging to cadet houses in the areas west and north of the city of Aberdeen. These junior branches were exceptionally prolific: of the bastard brothers Jock and Tam, one alone was progenitor of 30 lairdly families.

More important still was the connection with Aberdeen. In 1462, the burghers entered into a 'bond of manrent' with the 1st Earl of Huntly, whereby he promised to protect the city in return for hospitality whenever he visited it, and a contribution to the Gordons' fighting forces when required. The port of Aberdeen also offered profitable trading opportunities. It had especially close links with the Baltic, so that salmon from Huntly's rivers could be exported to Danzig (the herring trade scarcely existed before the nineteenth century). The flat lands of Aberdeenshire enabled the Gordons to engage in large-scale horse-breeding which was both commercially rewarding and militarily useful, providing them with a cavalry force, unlike other Highland clans. Besides taking an interest in the banking, woollen exports and fishing trade of Aberdeen, the Gordons found the port a convenient gateway to the continent, particularly after the Reformation when their support for the Catholic cause alienated them from most of Scotland. The Baltic connection even caused a number of the clan to make careers in the service of the Russian Czars, most notably General Patrick Gordon of Auchleuchries (1635-99), Governor of Kiev.

At home the Gey Gordons went from strength to strength. The 2nd Earl of Huntly was Chancellor of Scotland from 1498 to 1500. His son Alexander, who became 3rd Earl in 1502, commanded one wing of the Scots army at Flodden, but survived the battle; a younger son, Adam, married the Sutherland heiress, so that the Gordons thenceforth held that earldom too. Even more ambitious was the match made by their sister, Lady Catherine Gordon, who in 1496 married Perkin Warbeck, pretender to the English throne. Warbeck claimed to be Richard, Duke of York, one of the young princes murdered by their uncle Gloucester in the Tower of

The Grampians form a natural barrier protecting the Gordon lands in Aberdeen-shire.

London. His marriage to Lady Catherine — 'the highest ornament in Scotland', as he called her — was a love match and she accompanied him into England the following year when he raised a rebellion. The uprising was a failure and Warbeck was hanged at Tyburn, 23rd November 1499. Lady Catherine survived her grief and, having charmed the victorious Henry VII, lived to enjoy three more marriages and the romantic title of 'The White Rose'.

The 3rd Earl died in 1523 and was succeeded by his grandson, George, under whom the Gordon power reached its peak, only to be irreversibly humbled. This 4th Earl of Huntly began promisingly enough. He too was made Lieutenant of the North, became Chancellor in 1547 and got a grant of the earldom of Moray the following year. It was while visiting him at Huntly Castle that the Queen Regent, Mary of Guise, coined the name 'Cock o' the North' by which the Gordon chiefs were known ever after. The Reformation, however, brought about a dramatic reversal of fortune. Huntly resisted the reformed religion and soon became identified as leader of the Catholic party. This might have been expected to earn him the favour of Mary Queen of Scots, newly arrived from France, but the Queen's bastard brother, Lord James Stewart, poisoned her mind against Huntly and persuaded her to deprive him of the earldom of Moray and transfer it to himself.

Shortly afterwards, a quarrel between one of Huntly's sons and the Ogilvies further estranged the Gordons from Queen Mary. When Huntly's followers refused to surrender the castles of Inverness and Findlater to the Queen, the Gordons were 'put to the horn', meaning their outlawry was proclaimed with three blasts of the horn at the Market Cross. So, in 1562, Huntly rose in open rebellion. On 28th October, with only 500 men, he was overwhelmed by a royalist army numbering 2,000 at Corrichie, on the eastern side of the Hill of Fare, 15 miles west of Aberdeen (just north of the junction of the A980 and B977 roads). Though taken alive, Huntly cheated his captors by dying of apoplexy on the battlefield: 'The Earl suddenly fell from his horse stark ded', reported the English ambassador. His embalmed corpse was brought to Edinburgh seven months later and publicly disgraced. The Cock o' the North had had his wings clipped, as his enemies gleefully observed.

The 5th Earl, also George, made his peace with Mary and became Chancellor in 1565. Despite the triumph of Protestantism, he retained his inheritance until his sudden death while playing football in 1576. His brother was the famous Edom o' Gordon celebrated in ballad. George, 6th Earl of Huntly, the next chief, had been educated in France and consequently involved himself in conspiracies to restore Catholicism. Yet it was an ordinary clan feud which brought his affairs to a crisis. He alarmed the Mackintoshes by building a castle at Ruthven in Badenoch, while simultaneously quarrelling with the Grants of Ballindalloch. The two clans united against him and gained the support of the Bonnie Earl of Moray, son-in-law of Huntly's grandfather's enemy. In 1592 Huntly provoked public outrage by murdering the Earl of Moray — the theme of the well-known song. Since Huntly was also accused of involvement in a Jesuit plot, the Earl of Argyll with 10,000 men marched against him and the Earl of Erroll, whose forces were only one-third that strength. On 4th October 1594, Huntly destroyed Argyll's army at Glenlivet; the site of the battle is on the right bank of Allt a' Choileachan burn (south of the B9009 road, just before its junction with the B9008). Argyll lost 500 men, including two of his own cousins and Macneill of Barra; Huntly's casualties amounted to only 14 gentlemen. In spite of this victory, Huntly wisely surrendered on favourable terms to James VI and was pardoned soon afterwards. By 1599 he was sufficiently restored to the king's confidence to be created Marquess of Huntly and, a little later, Lieutenant of the North.

His son George, 2nd Marquess, succeeded in 1636 and served Charles I staunchly during the wars of the Covenant. The famous Gordon cavalry provided a vital arm to Montrose's ragged force of Highland infantry, distinguishing themselves at the battles of Auldearn and Alford, where the Gordon heir was killed. A few weeks after the execution of Charles I, Huntly too was

Old Aberdeen. In 1462 the Earl of Huntly agreed to protect the city in return for its hospitality and its support in time of war.

Edinburgh Castle. At the Revolution of 1688-9 it was held for a year against the army of William of Orange by the Duke of Gordon.

beheaded, fulfilling his proud boast: 'You may take my head from my shoulders, but not my heart from my sovereign'. His daughter Catherine married Count Andreas Morsztyn, Grand Treasurer of Poland, and was the great-grandmother of Stanislas Poniatowski, the last Polish king.

The Restoration revived the Gordon fortunes. Lord Charles Gordon, a younger son of the executed marquess, was created Earl of Aboyne in 1660 and the present Marquess of Huntly descends from this line. In 1682, Sir George Gordon of Haddo (a descendant of Jock of Scurdargue) was made Earl of Aberdeen and two years later the 4th Marquess of Huntly became Duke of Gordon. At the Revolution he held Edinburgh Castle against the Williamites for a year, until starved into surrender.

During the 'Fifteen Rebellion, the Duke of Gordon was imprisoned by the government, but his son Lord Huntly, with Gordon of Glenbucket and General Gordon of Auchintoul, brought 500 horse and 2,500 foot into the Jacobite army. William, Viscount of Kenmure, head of the Border family of Gordon, was Jacobite commander in southern Scotland till defeated at Preston and executed on Tower Hill, the subject of the song 'Kenmure's on and awa', Willie!' The remaining Gordons were leniently treated, but remained firmly Jacobite, though the 3rd Duke, who succeeded in 1728, was the first chief to be brought up as a Protestant. He took no part in the 'Forty-five, but his uncle, Lord Lewis Gordon, with old Glenbucket and Gordon of Park, led the clan 'out' for Prince Charlie. They defeated a government force at Inverurie in December 1745, and fought at Culloden, but again suffered only relatively mild reprisals when the rising was put down.

Later in the eighteenth century, several regiments of Fencibles were raised among the Gordons. Finally, in 1794, the 4th Duchess of Gordon raised and recruited the 92nd (Gordon) Highlanders, choosing for the regimental tartan the Black Watch pattern with a distinctive yellow stripe added for the Gey Gordons. The 92nd earned immortality by their famous charge at Waterloo, hanging

Gordon

MOTTO: Bydand (Remaining)
OLD MOTTO: *Animo non astutia* (By courage not craft)
GAELIC NAME: Clann Ghòrdan
WARCRY: *A Gordon! A Gordon!*
PLANT BADGE: Ivy
PIPE MUSIC: The Gordon's March

onto the stirrups of the Scots Greys for greater impetus.

It should be noted that the surname of the poet, George Gordon, 6th Lord Byron (1788-1824), was Byron, not Gordon—he was a Gordon of Gight on his mother's side.

The dukedom became extinct in 1836, but the Huntly marquessate passed to the Earls of Aboyne, along with the clan chiefship. The present Marquess of Huntly still holds the title Coileach an Taobh-tuath (Cock o' the North) and the chiefly seat of Aboyne Castle, Aberdeenshire. Sept names of Clan Gordon are Adam, Adie, Crombie, Edie, Huntly, Milne and Todd. Its warcry is 'A Gordon! A Gordon!' and its plant badge ivy. The Gaelic name is Clann Ghòrdan.

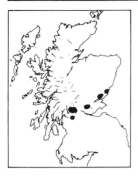

CLAN
GRAHAM

THERE IS NO DIFFICULTY ABOUT DETERMINING the Grahams' niche in Scottish history. Although one of the clan was guilty of murdering an early Stuart king, the family that produced both the Great Montrose and Bonnie Dundee must surely take pride of place in devotion to the royal house of Scotland. It is as royalists that the Grahams are remembered: the fact that their quixotic attachment to the crown led to death and disaster only sheds a more romantic lustre around their name.

Legend has it that the first of the line was one Gramus who forced a great breach in Antonine's Wall, the northern frontier of the Roman Empire between the Clyde and the Forth. It is true that part of the ruin of this famous Wall is known as Graeme's Dyke, but any connection with Clan Graham would seem to be tenuous. Historians generally have favoured the theory that the Grahams were a Norman family who came to Scotland in the reign of David I. William de Graham was granted the lands of Abercorn and Dalkeith by that king and in 1128 he was a witness to the charter establishing the Abbey of Holyrood. His elder son founded the house of Graham of Dalkeith; his younger son was ancestor of the eventual chiefly line of Montrose. David de Graham, third generation of the Montrose branch, was granted the lordship of Kinnabar in Forfarshire by William the Lion; his grandson, Sir David Graham of Dundaff, married Annabella, daughter of the 4th Earl of Strathearn, thus acquiring the barony of Kincardine in Perthshire. Of the sons of this marriage, Sir Patrick, the eldest, succeeded to the chiefship about 1270; Sir John, the second son, described as 'Richt hand of Wallace', was killed fighting in the cause of Scots independence at the Battle of Falkirk (1298). Sir Patrick's descendants were also patriotic Scots: his son Sir David received the lands of Old Montrose for faithful service to King Robert Bruce and signed the Declaration of Arbroath in 1320, while his grandson, also Sir David, was taken prisoner by the English at the Battle of Durham in 1346. This Sir David died about 1376 and was succeeded by his son Patrick. The three sons of Patrick had very interesting careers. Sir William, the eldest, married Mariota Oliphant and,

secondly, Lady Mary Stewart, a daughter of Robert III; from these two marriages descended the principal cadet houses of Graham. The second son, Sir Patrick, married the Countess Palatine of Strathearn and was ancestor of the Earls of Menteith. The third son, Sir Robert Graham of Kilpont, murdered King James I at the Blackfriars in Perth on 21st February 1437. His quarrel with the king was a result of the latter's refusal to confirm the earldom of Strathearn in the house of Graham, substituting for it the inferior earldom of Menteith. The episode is famous for the attempt of Katherine Douglas — known thereafter as 'Kate Barlass' — to keep out the murderers by placing her arm in the bolt-sockets of the door, as well as for the refinements of cruelty with which Graham of Kilpont was later tortured to death for regicide.

This disgrace, however, does not seem to have impeded the fortunes of the Grahams. The junior line held the Menteith earldom until 1694, while the chiefly branch also flourished. Sir William, the chief, had several sons who were ancestors of the cadet houses of Fintry, Claverhouse, Duntrune, Garvock and Knockdolian; he was succeeded by his grandson Patrick, created Lord Graham about 1445. His grandson William was in turn created Earl of Montrose in 1505 and was killed at Flodden (1513). The 2nd Earl of Montrose was a friend of Cardinal Beaton and was reputed to have remained a Catholic at the time of the Reformation. He behaved so discreetly, however, that he made few enemies, despite remaining loyal to Mary Queen of Scots throughout her turbulent reign and opposing her dethronement. On the other hand, his grandson John, who succeeded him as 3rd Earl of Montrose in 1571, was a zealous Protestant reformer. He fought against Queen Mary at Langside in 1567, was prominently involved in the confused politics of late sixteenth-century Scotland and was Lord Chancellor from 1599 to 1604, when he was appointed Viceroy of the kingdom, a post he held until his death in 1608. This was one of the most distinguished chiefs of Clan Graham, yet his achievements were destined soon to be eclipsed by the meteoric career of his grandson, James, 5th Earl and 1st Marquess of Montrose.

Mugdock Castle, north of Glasgow, a residence of the Grahams in the seventeenth century.

James Graham, Marquess of Montrose, one of the most brilliant and romantic soldiers Scotland has ever known.

The circumstances into which the Great Montrose was born were those of a small but important clan, living on the fringe of the Highlands and owning a chain of separate properties, not vast in extent, but richer than many larger holdings. Looking from south to north, the geographic settlement of the Grahams was as follows. First, they held the barony of Mugdock, north of Glasgow. Here their seat was Mugdock Castle, now a sadly neglected ruin (access by an unclassified road off the A81, near Mugdock Reservoir), which in 1646 briefly became their chief residence. Further north were the Graham lands of Menteith, the largest single area held by the clan. It covered most of the north and south shores of Loch Katrine, including the famous beauty spot called The Trossachs, and reached as far east as Callander; it was further watered by Loch Venachar, Loch Ard, the Lake of Menteith and the upper reaches of the Forth. On the south it was bordered by the Buchanan country to the east of Loch Lomond. Altogether this territory was about 15 miles long by 8 miles broad. Graham strongholds in this area were Talla Castle in the Lake of Menteith (the only Scottish lake, as distinct from loch), Kilbride Castle and Ruskie Tower, whose site was on an islet in Loch Ruskie (beside the A81, 3 miles north-east of Port of Menteith). Then there was the ancient Graham land-holding around Kincardine Castle in Perthshire. The castle is now a ruin, having been demolished by Argyll in 1645, standing a short distance south of Auchterarder (on the A9). The remaining Graham enclaves were around Dundee (where cadet houses were established at Claverhouse, Duntrune and Fintry) and at Old Montrose, just south-west of the town of the same name on the east coast.

This, then, was the heritage of Montrose, the greatest of Scotland's heroes after Bruce and Bonnie Prince Charlie. Like all clan chiefs, he was sustained in his military adventures by his numerous kinsmen. James, 5th Earl of Montrose, was born in 1612 and succeeded his father in 1627. A promising youth, he was sent to St Leonard's College, St Andrews, where he won the silver arrow for archery. In the religious conflict between Charles I and the Kirk he was a zealous supporter of the Covenant, whose armies he successfully commanded until 1641. When he realized that the Covenanters under Argyll were aiming at the destruction of the monarchy, however, he broke with them and retired to his estates where he lived privately for two years. After various negotiations, Montrose joined the king in 1644 and received a commission as Lieutenant-General in Scotland; he was also raised in the peerage to be Marquess of Montrose. What followed was more like some extravagant romance than sober history. Travelling to Scotland in disguise, Montrose met his kinsman Black Pate Graeme, younger of Inchbrakie, and raised the royal standard at Blair Atholl in August 1644. The only troops in his command were 1,200 Irishmen under Alasdair Macdonald (known as Colkitto) and various Graham dependents, amounting altogether to 3,000 men. On 1st September he defeated a well-equipped Covenanting army twice as large at Tippermuir, outside Perth. Thereafter followed a dazzling series of victories: Aberdeen (13th September), Inverlochy (2nd February 1645), Auldearn (9th May), Alford (2nd July) and Kilsyth (15th August). After the Battle of Kilsyth, Montrose was master of Scotland, of which Charles I appointed him Lieutenant-Governor and Captain-General. He was in the precarious position, however, of one who has only to lose a single battle to lose the war. His Highland levies melted away, as so often happened with clansmen after a successful campaign, and the Irish were pursuing their own ends in Argyllshire. Thus, on 13th September 1645, Montrose was overwhelmed at Philiphaugh by a Covenanting army which outnumbered his own by ten to one. For almost a year he struggled on, trying to raise a new army in the king's cause, but without success. In August 1646 he escaped overseas.

Yet such a spirit could not languish indefinitely in exile. Early in 1650 he landed with 200 men at Kirkwall in the Orkneys and made his way south to the Scottish mainland. Fate was against him and on 27th April he was defeated at Carbisdale, on the south bank of the Kyle of Sutherland, where he was wounded, but escaped from the battlefield. He then made the mistake of seeking

Loch Katrine. In the Graham lands in the Trossachs, mountains and lochs combine to create an area of outstanding natural beauty.

Graham of Montrose

MOTTO: *Ne oublie* (Do not forget)
GAELIC NAME: Clann Ghreum
PLANT BADGE: Laurel
PIPE MUSIC: Killiecrankie

Loch Achray.

shelter from MacLeod of Assynt, who betrayed him to his enemies. Argyll and the Covenanting party could not contain their joy at his capture. Every possible humiliation was inflicted upon him by the mean spirits who had so often fled before him in battle. Denied even the privilege of beheading, he was hanged as a common criminal in the Grassmarket of Edinburgh on 21st May 1650; his head was displayed on the Tolbooth and his quartered limbs were exposed in the four chief towns of Scotland. After the Restoration his remains were reinterred with great pomp in St Giles' Cathedral. Montrose himself, a poet as well as a soldier, wrote the most fitting epitaph on his gallant career:

'He either fears his fate too much,
Or his deserts are small,
Who dares not put it to the touch,
To win or lose it all.'

The great-grandson of the cavalier hero was created Duke of Montrose in 1707, but the chiefly line forsook its allegiance to the Stuarts and supported the Hanoverian government during the Jacobite rebellions. One of the cadet houses, however, produced another champion of the Stuart cause in John Graham of Claverhouse, better known as Bonnie Dundee. During the reign of Charles II

Loch Ard.

Loch Venachar.

he was a fierce enemy of the Covenanters, being defeated by them at Drumclog in 1679, but turning the tables with a victory shortly afterwards at Bothwell Brig. It was at the Revolution in 1689 that he emerged as a major supporter of James VII, who had created him Viscount of Dundee just before he escaped to France in 1688. Dundee raised the Highland clans to fight against the usurping William of Orange. On 17th July 1689, he ambushed a superior Williamite army under General Hugh Mackay in the Pass of Killiecrankie, a spectacular gorge about 4 miles south-east of Blair Atholl (the route of the A9 now runs through it). The Jacobites won a famous victory, but Dundee was mortally wounded. As he was carried from the field he asked a soldier, 'How goes the day?' 'Well for King James,' the man replied, 'but I am sorry for your lordship.' 'If it goes well for him,' said Dundee, 'it matters the less for me.' He was taken to Blair Castle where he died soon after the battle; he was buried in the parish church at Blair Atholl.

The Border Grahams, allegedly descended from one William Graham and his numerous sons who settled on the English side of the Border in the early sixteenth century, must be reckoned an English family and so separate from the main Graham tradition. Thomas Graham, 7th of Garvock, was a famous general who defeated the French at Barossa in 1811 and was created Lord Lynedoch in 1814. Technically, the 7th Duke of Montrose was the last clan chief to rebel against a London government, having signed the Rhodesian Declaration of Independence in 1965. As Chief of Clan Graham, the Duke of Montrose is styled An Greumach Mór. Sept names of Graham are Allardice, Bontein, Bontine, MacGilvernock, MacGrime and Monteith. The clan's plant badge is laurel and its Gaelic name Clann Ghreum.

CLAN
GRANT

THE GRANTS MIGHT BE TAKEN AS REPRESENTA-tive of the history, organization and life-style of an average Highland clan, always provided that the term 'average' is on no account to be confused with 'mediocre'. Their lands were extensive, but not massive; they had a number of cadet houses, but not on such a scale as to defy comprehension; and they had both a Whig and a Jacobite branch of the clan. Add to this a rich heritage of legend and poetry and Clan Grant emerges as a fairly accurate reflection of Highland society and the clan system generally.

There is confusion regarding the origin of the Grants. The most generally accepted theory derives them from a family of Norman adventurers, the first of whom, Laurence le Grant, was Sheriff of Inverness by 1263. His son, John le Grant, was taken prisoner by the English at the Battle of Dunbar (1296), and received a charter of the lands of Inverallan in Strathspey in 1316. This branch soon became extinct in the male line, but a collateral branch prospered and one Robert Grant became Scots ambassador to France and was famous for fighting a duel with an English knight, Thomas de l'Strother, at Liliot Cross in the Borders on St Martin's Day 1380. Possibly this diplomat and duellist was father of John Ruadh Grant, Sheriff of Inverness in 1434, who married the heiress of Glencharnie, whose lands included half of the barony of Freuchie in Strathspey. The son of this union, Sir Duncan Grant, was 1st Laird of Freuchie and chief of the clan. Sir Duncan's son predeceased him, so, at his death in 1495, he was succeeded by his grandson, John Grant, 2nd of Freuchie.

The 2nd Laird of Freuchie married the daughter of Sir James Ogilvy of Deskford, by whom he had two sons: James, his heir, and John, ancestor of the Grants of Corriemony. The Laird, who was nicknamed 'Am Bard Ruadh' ('The Red Bard'), had his lands erected into the barony of Freuchie in 1494 and he obtained a further charter of the barony of Urquhart in 1509. This chief also had a natural son Iain Mór (Big John), so called because of his height, who received a charter of the barony of Glenmoriston and became founder of the secondary branch of Clan Grant. By the death of the 2nd Laird of Freuchie in 1528, therefore, the clan organization had taken shape and the Grants were established in their two distinct land-holdings.

The principal territory of Clan Grant, occupied by the chiefly family, was Strathspey. This is the fertile valley of the River Spey, flowing north-eastwards from Inverness-shire along the border between Elgin and Banffshire. That part occupied by the Grants reached from Aviemore to Craigellachie, but, as there is also a Craigellachie just south of Aviemore, it is sometimes claimed that the northern and southern limits of the Grant country were marked by places of the same name. This area of Grant occupation was about 33 miles long and varied in breadth from about 18 miles in the south to 10 miles at its northern extremity. The chief's stronghold of Freuchie was converted into a proper castle, called the Balla-Chaisteil, in 1536; later it was known as Castle Grant. It stands 1 mile north of Grantown-on-Spey (off the A939). The Grants of Ballindalloch held the castle of that name, at the confluence of the Rivers Spey and Avon, 15 miles north-east of Grantown (on the A95). Another important cadet branch was established at Rothiemurchus House on the south bank of the Spey, 1 mile south-east of Aviemore.

The secondary territory held by the Grants was loosely called Glenmoriston, an area bounded on the west by Strathglass (the narrow strip along the eastern bank of the River Glass occupied by the Chisholms) and on the east by Loch Ness; its southern boundary reached from the slopes of Aonach Shasuinn to Fort Augustus and its most northerly point was near Balchraggan, about 10 miles south-west of Inverness. Today the road from Inverness to Fort Augustus (A82) runs down its eastern border, while other roads lead through Glen Moriston (A887) and Glen Urquhart (A831), the two straths inhabited by this western branch of Clan Grant. Castle Urquhart, whose extensive ruins stand on the west bank of Loch Ness (A82), was held by the Grants from 1509. An expanse of Fraser and Clan Chattan territory in Stratherrick and the Monadh Liath separated the Grants

Inverness. Laurence le Grant, a Norman adventurer and forefather of Clan Grant, was Sheriff of Inverness in the thirteenth century.

of Glenmoriston from their kinsmen in Strathspey.

James Grant, who became 3rd Laird of Freuchie in Strathspey and chief of the name in 1528, was nicknamed 'Seumas nan Creach' ('James of the Forays') because of his warlike character. He built the fortress at Freuchie which later became known as Castle Grant and he adhered to the cause of Mary of Guise. In 1543 he signed a bond with Cardinal Beaton and other noblemen against 'our awld enymyis of Ingland'. When he died in 1553 his eldest son, John the Gentle, became chief; an order signed by Mary Queen of Scots in 1562 is the first official document in which the title Laird of Grant is used. Despite close links with the Earl of Huntly, John Grant took no part in the rebellion raised by the earl in 1562. Four years later, however, he was in Huntly's train at Holyrood and was present on the night when Rizzio was murdered. Despite the dangerous times through which he lived, John the Gentle died peacefully at Freuchie in 1585.

The grandson and heir of John the Gentle, another John, was famous for his pawky retort on being offered a peerage by James VI: 'And wha'll be Laird o' Grant?' Although, after the outlawing of Clan Gregor, he was sometimes forced by the government to go through the motions of persecuting the MacGregors, he covertly did all he could to help them; some genealogists believe the MacGregors to be of the same stock as Clan Grant, though this would conflict with the theory of the latter's Norman origin. In 1590, the Earl of Huntly, using his official powers in prosecution of a clan feud, besieged and captured the Grant house of Ballindalloch. The Laird of Grant was already attached to the Protestant party and had recently signed a bond to that effect. This outrage by Huntly now gave him a personal interest in the quarrel and, at the Battle of Glenlivet in 1594, Clan Grant fought on the left wing of Argyll's defeated Protestant army. Such a setback meant little to a clan so well entrenched as the Grants, and their power continued to grow.

During the Civil War in the seventeenth century, James Grant, 7th of Freuchie, supported the Covenant, but had to submit to Montrose after the Battle of Inverlochy in 1645 and send him 300 clansmen to serve in the royal army; these recruits made the looting of Elgin their first duty, when they eagerly 'brak doun bedis, burdis, insicht, and plenishing'. The Covenanting forces later reciprocated by plundering Strathspey.

It was after the Revolution of 1689 that the Grants' fortunes rose to their zenith. As a reward for serving the cause of William of Orange, the barony of Freuchie was erected into the regality of Grant for Ludovic, 8th Laird, in 1694. This charter conferred semi-royal rights and privileges, including power of life and death, and cemented the loyalty of the Grants to the Whig party. In 1715 they were in arms for George I and in 1745 they raised 400 men in the Hanoverian cause. Many of the clansmen had Jacobite leanings, however, and the Grant Independent Company easily surrendered Inverness Castle to Prince Charlie's army, whereupon some of the Grants went over to the prince. The chief at this time married the heiress of Colquhoun of Luss, who brought a baronetcy into the family. Sir James Grant, his grandson, known as 'The Good Sir James', founded Grantown-on-Spey in 1766. In 1812 Sir Lewis Grant of Grant inherited the earldom of Seafield and the chiefs bore this title until 1915 when it was separated from the chiefship, leaving the lesser peerage of Strathspey to be borne by the Laird of Grant. The principal cadet houses of the Strathspey Grants were Ballindalloch (senior and junior), Tulloch-gorm, Corriemony, Elchies, Monymusk (in Aberdeen-shire) and Rothiemurchus.

The Grants of Glenmoriston, descended from Iain Mór, natural son of the 2nd Laird of Freuchie, had a rather different history from their cousins in Strathspey. Iain Mór's grandson, Iain Mór a' Chaisteil, built a house at Invermoriston and was appointed chamberlain of the lordship of Urquhart. His descendant, John, 6th of Glenmoriston, while still a minor, fought for James VII at Killiecrankie. In 1715 he was 'out' for James VIII, fought at Sheriffmuir and had his estates sequestrated. His son recovered them in 1734 and the Glenmoriston Grants fought for Prince Charlie in the 'Forty-five, though their chieftain stayed at home. Patrick Grant of Crasky was

Castle Urquhart on Loch Ness, held by the Grants from 1509.

Grant

MOTTO: Stand fast
GAELIC NAME: Clann Ghrannda
WARCRY: *Creag Eileachaidh!* (Stand fast, Craigellachie!)
PLANT BADGE: Pine
PIPE MUSIC: Stand fast, Craigellachie

A view of the high Cairngorms from near Grantown-on-Spey.

Loch Morlich, deep in the Rothiemurchus Forest. The Grants of Rothiemurchus were an important cadet branch of Clan Grant.

one of the 'Seven Men of Glen Moriston' who guarded the prince during his flight after Culloden. The principal cadets of Glenmoriston were the houses of Carron and Wester Elchies.

Lord Strathspey, as Chief of Clan Grant, is styled An Granndach; Grant of Glenmoriston is Mac-'ic-Phàdruig. Sept names of Grant are Alanach, Gilroy, Kearns, Kerrons, MacGilroy, MacIlroy, MacKerron, MacKiaran and Patrick. The clan plant badge is the pine and its warcry is '*Creag Eileachaidh!*' (most commonly rendered in English as 'Stand fast, Craigellachie!'). Its Gaelic name is Clann Ghrannda.

CLAN
HAMILTON

THE HAMILTONS WERE THE MOST IMPORTANT OF the Lowland clans. Their chief is still Premier Duke of Scotland and at one time they aspired to the crown itself, as serious rivals to the Stuarts. Although they did not lead the same style of life as the Highland clans, their hereditary chiefship, network of cadet houses with dependents, and their distinctive tartan make it clear that they were truly a Scottish clan, with the sense of blood kinship and family loyalties which are inseparable from this concept.

It is generally believed that they originated in Northumberland, where they were settled on the lands of Hameldone. The first of the line in Scotland was Walter FitzGilbert of Cadzow, who witnessed a charter to the monks of Paisley in 1295. He fought at the Battle of Halidon Hill in 1333 and died before 1346, leaving two sons: David, who succeeded him, and John, ancestor of the house of Innerwick and the Earls of Haddington. David FitzWalter, 2nd of Cadzow, was taken prisoner by the English at the Battle of Nevill's Cross (also called the Battle of Durham) in 1346 and sat in various Scottish parliaments between 1368 and 1373; he died about 1375. David Hamilton, 3rd of Cadzow, was next chief of the family until about 1392 when his son, Sir John Hamilton, succeeded as 4th Laird. Sir John added the lands of Kinneill on the south bank of the River Forth to his estates and led an adventurous life, being taken prisoner twice by the English, first in 1396 and again in 1398. His son, Sir James, was a hostage for the ransom of James I in 1426; he married a daughter of Livingstone of Callendar and had, besides James his heir, several younger sons from whom descended the baronets of Silvertonhill and the Lords Hamilton of Dalzell.

So far the story of the Hamiltons had been the typical progress of a family of Lowland lairds, preoccupied with the consolidation of their estates and doing military service when the occasion arose. In the time of Sir James Hamilton, 6th Laird of Cadzow, however, a great change took place in the family's fortunes. Sir James was born about 1415 and inherited the chiefship in 1440. Five years later he was created Lord Hamilton and was confirmed in

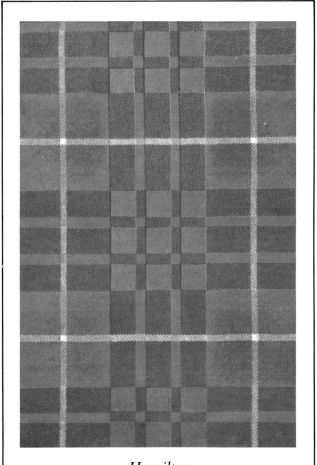

Hamilton
MOTTO: Through
ORIGIN OF NAME: Hameldone, place-name in Northumberland

Cadzow Forest, *painted by Alexander Fraser in the nineteenth century. Cadzow was the first land owned by the Hamiltons in Scotland.*

the feudal baronies of Cadzow, Mauchan and Kinneill. He was attached to the house of Douglas and sided with them in their rebellion against James II until 1455, when he changed sides and joined the king. For this politic move he was well rewarded; not only did he receive confirmation of all his lands, but after the death of his first wife he was given the hand of James II's daughter, the Princess Mary, in 1474, by which time her brother was reigning as James III. Thus, in the course of one lifetime, the Hamiltons became a peerage family with eventual rights of succession to the throne of Scotland. Yet more dazzling success was to follow. James, 2nd Lord Hamilton, who inherited the title in 1479, was a nobleman of great accomplishments. He took part in a naval expedition against the Swedes in 1502 and in the following year was created Earl of Arran, with a grant of that island to augment his already large estates. At a tournament held in 1508 he was champion archer on horse or foot in all Scotland. In 1517, during the minority of James V, he was one of the six regents appointed to deputize for the Duke of Albany, who was absent in France. His growing power, however, provoked the jealousy of the Earl of Angus and a feud erupted between the two great lords. On 30th April 1520, the followers of Arran and Angus met in a deadly brawl in the streets of Edinburgh — known as 'Cleanse the Causeway' — in which the Hamiltons were defeated and one of their leaders, the Laird of Kincavil, was killed. Later, Arran made common cause with Angus against their enemy the Duke of Albany, whom they defeated and slew at Linlithgow, 4th September 1526. Lord Arran died in 1529 and was succeeded by his son James.

The 2nd Earl of Arran lived in insecurity all his life because of certain legal doubts surrounding the validity of his parents' marriage. Since his whole inheritance could have been called in question if the matter had been investigated from a hostile viewpoint, the Earl was understandably fearful of making enemies and tried to tread a neutral path, an impossible ambition in sixteenth-century Scotland. He became Regent of the kingdom in 1542 and on 13th March 1543, an Act of State declared him heir to the throne after the infant Mary

Queen of Scots. In 1549 the King of France created him Duke of Châtelherault, as a bribe for his consent to Queen Mary's marriage to the Dauphin and in the hope that he would resign the regency in favour of the Queen Mother, Mary of Guise. He did not do so until 1554, after which he retired into private life for a while. At the Reformation, however, he was active in the Protestant cause and came into conflict with Mary Queen of Scots, whose marriage to Darnley he opposed. Eventually he was forced into exile in France and by the time of his return, in 1569, Mary had lost her throne. Claiming the regency as his own right, he became an opponent of the Regent Moray and headed Mary's faction until 1573 when the rival parties came to an accommodation. Châtelherault (as he was known from his French dukedom) died in January 1575.

Since the heir, James, 3rd Earl of Arran, had become insane, it was a younger son, John, who inherited the Hamilton estates. He had the misfortune to become embroiled in a dispute with the Douglases over the abbey lands of Arbroath, which forced him to subsidize the Ogilvies to occupy the property forcibly on his behalf. In 1579 the Hamiltons' estates were forfeited when the Regent Morton denounced them for the murder of the Earls of Lennox and Moray and razed their castles of Hamilton and Draffen (later known as Craignethan). The insane lord's earldom of Arran was given to James Stewart and the Hamiltons fled into exile. In 1585, however, they returned to Scotland, took Stirling, along with the person of James VI, and assumed the reins of government. Lord John, the acting chief, became successively Captain of Dumbarton Castle, Lord Lieutenant of the West March and, in 1590, Lieutenant of the Kingdom during the king's absence to fetch his bride, Anne of Denmark. Finally, in 1599, Lord John was created Marquess of Hamilton; he died in 1604, when his son James became chief of his name.

Although, as has been said, the Hamiltons did not lead a patriarchal clan life like their Highland counterparts, their feudal organization was very similar in effect and they held extensive lands. The island of Arran was their

William, 2nd Duke of Hamilton, who was fatally wounded while fighting for Charles II at Worcester.

The fatal duel of 1712 between the 4th Duke of Hamilton and Lord Mohun.

Kinneill House, south of the River Forth. Sir John Hamilton succeeded to the chiefship in 1392 and added the lands of Kinneill to his estates.

only Highland property; their stronghold there was Brodick Castle (now in the hands of the National Trust for Scotland), overlooking Brodick Bay. On the mainland their largest tract of land was on the south bank of the Clyde, from about Carmunnock to Lanark, and stretching south-westwards beyond Strathaven; this area was roughly 20 miles long and 10 miles broad on average. The ancient family seat was Cadzow Castle, beside the modern town of Hamilton, where Mary Queen of Scots held a court before the Battle of Langside, in 1568, but it was superseded by Hamilton Palace, whose building was begun in the sixteenth century. The ruin of Cadzow Castle stands in a park famous for its herd of white cattle; the Palace was demolished because of subsidence from mineworkings and all that survives is the striking family mausoleum. Craignethan Castle, a picturesque ruin about 10 miles south-east of Hamilton (on the A72) was built by the gifted architect Sir James Hamilton of Fynnart, commonly called the Bastard of Arran. This castle also has literary associations, being the original of Tillietudlem in Scott's *Old Mortality*. In the county of Linlithgow, another Hamilton estate was centred on Kinneill House, about 1 mile south-west of Bo'ness, and there were other lands a little further south.

James, 2nd Marquess of Hamilton, was made a Lord of the Privy Council and Steward of the Royal Household by James VI, who also created him a peer of England as Earl of Cambridge in 1619 and a Knight of the Garter in 1621. He died, possibly from poisoning, in 1624. The 3rd Marquess was created Duke of Hamilton in 1643, but, having been slandered to Charles I, was later imprisoned and only released in 1646. Thereafter he tried to promote the king's interests, but Charles's refusal to sign the Covenant made his negotiations vain. Hamilton, therefore, embarked on a ploy known as 'The Engagement' and invaded England with a Scots army, committed to rescuing the king from the hands of the Parliamentarians. He was defeated and forced to surrender at Uttoxeter, 25th August 1648. After a trial at Westminster, he was beheaded like his royal master, in Palace Yard, on 9th March 1649. Two years later his brother William, 2nd

Duke of Hamilton, was fatally wounded while fighting for Charles II at the Battle of Worcester. The dukedom then passed to Anne, daughter of the 1st Duke, who had a regrant of all the family lands and baronies after the Restoration. She married the Earl of Selkirk, who was then created Duke of Hamilton for life; at the Revolution he supported William of Orange and died shortly afterwards, in 1694. James, the eldest son of this marriage, succeeded as Duke of Hamilton in 1698, on his mother's resignation of the dignity. The 4th Duke won great popularity by his stubborn resistance to the Act of Union in 1707, though he faltered at the crucial moment and the measure was passed. He also attained the unusual distinction of being invested with both the Order of the Thistle and the Garter; he was killed in a duel with Lord Mohun in 1712. Though sometimes credited with Jacobite sentiments, neither of the succeeding dukes rose for the Stuarts in 1715 and 1745. From the eighteenth century, therefore, their roles were those of great nobles and statesmen, rather than clan chiefs.

Since 1868 a junior branch of the Hamiltons has held the dukedom of Abercorn. By an historical curiosity, both Hamilton dukes also hold the French title of Duke of Châtelherault. The peerages of Boyne, Belhaven and Stenton, Hamilton of Dalzell and Holm Patrick are also held by members of the clan. The Barons Hamilton in Sweden are of Scots extraction, while some Hamiltons who emigrated to Ireland (probably of the cadet house of Killenure, in Donegal) became Counts of the Holy Roman Empire in Austria. Count Anthony Hamilton (1646-1720), son of Sir George Hamilton, baronet, of Donalong (Co. Tyrone), was a lieutenant-general in the French service and author of the famous *Memoirs of the Count de Grammont*.

The cadet houses of Clan Hamilton, amounting to several hundred families, are too numerous to mention. Besides being chief of the clan, the Duke of Hamilton and Brandon is also Premier Peer of Scotland, heir male of the House of Douglas and hereditary Keeper of the Palace of Holyroodhouse. Cadzow and Dalserf are said to be sept names of Hamilton and there is an official clan tartan.

Brodick Castle, the Hamilton seat in Arran.

The splendid interior of Brodick Castle.

Holyrood Palace, of which the Duke of Hamilton is hereditary Keeper.

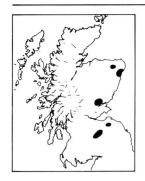

CLAN
HAY

CLAN HAY IS NOTABLE FOR THE FACT THAT ITS CHIEF, the Earl of Erroll, by virtue of his hereditary office of Lord High Constable, is the highest-ranking individual in Scotland after the royal family. Their close connection with the Crown since the days of Bruce has brought the Hays' name into prominence in every generation and they have also distinguished themselves in France, their country of origin.

If one discounts the early mythical Hay ancestors — including one Kenneth who was supposed to have married the daughter of an implausibly named baron, Giles Fitzboot — the clan's first historically recorded forebear was William de la Haye, a Norman who was cupbearer to Malcolm IV and William the Lion. He was granted the feudal barony of Erroll, on the north bank of the Tay, 12 miles south-west of Dundee, about 1180. His eldest son, David, succeeded him in the early thirteenth century; his youngest son, Robert, was most likely ancestor to the Hays of Yester, now represented by the Marquess of Tweeddale. David's son, Gilbert de la Haye, 3rd of Erroll, was a regent of Scotland during the minority of Alexander III, in 1255. Gilbert's younger brother, William, was ancestor of the Hays of Leys, now represented by the Earls of Kinnoull.

It was Gilbert's grandson and namesake, the 5th Laird of Erroll, who established the family's fortunes. One of Bruce's earliest and most trusted followers, he fought through all the campaigns of the War of Independence and was appointed Constable of Scotland. After Bannockburn, the office was made hereditary in his family and he was sent as ambassador to England to negotiate the truce. He also signed the Declaration of Arbroath in 1320. In reward for his services, King Robert the Bruce granted him the lands of Slains in Aberdeenshire. He died in 1333 and his grandson, Sir David, who succeeded him, was killed at the Battle of Nevill's Cross (1346). In 1372 the next Laird of Erroll, Sir Thomas, married Elizabeth, daughter of King Robert II, by whom he had two sons, William and Gilbert.

William became 1st Lord Hay and was joint Lord Warden of the Marches in 1430. His younger brother, Sir

Hay
MOTTO: *Serva jugum* (Keep the yoke)
GAELIC NAME: Clann Chuidh
WARCRY: *A Hay, A Hay, A Hay!*
PLANT BADGE: Mistletoe

'The Yester Lords', a seventeenth-century portrait of Hay of Yester, 2nd Marquess of Tweeddale, and his brother, Hay of Belton.

Gilbert of Dronlaw, served with Joan of Arc's forces in France and was ancestor of the cadet houses of Delgatie and Park. The grandson of the 1st Lord Hay, William, 9th chief, was created Earl of Erroll in 1452. His lands were by then a regality, conferring on him extraordinary authority, virtually independent of the Crown.

The centre of Hay power was Slains Castle, now ruinous, at Collieston on the Aberdeenshire coast (at the termination of the B9003, which branches off the A975 about 5 miles north of Newburgh). The immediate Hay territory stretched along the coast from Newburgh to Buchan Ness and inland to a depth of 10 miles, bounded on the south by the River Ythan. There were other Hay enclaves around the Loch of Strathbeg and at Lochloy on the Moray Firth, near Auldearn. More important was the cadet house established at Delgatie, 2 miles north-east of Turriff (access by a minor road off the A947); the castle there was made the headquarters of the Clan Hay Society about 1950. Further south, the Earls of Erroll acquired the baronial lands of Logiealmond in central Perthshire through the marriage of the 4th Earl's brother with the Logie heiress. The Hays of Megginch and Kinfauns (later Earls of Kinnoull) held the land between Perth and the Carse of Gowrie, on the north bank of the Firth of Tay; there were also Hay land-holdings on the south bank of the Firth, around Tayport. The Hays of Locherworth and Yester (now Marquesses of Tweeddale) held lands around Yester Castle, built over the strange cavern known as 'Goblin Ha'', near Gifford, 4 miles south of Haddington. This family's settlement in Tweeddale, stretching from Peebles to the source of the Tweed, was the largest single area of Hay territory.

The Hays retained their French connection more tenaciously than most families of Norman descent. Besides Sir Gilbert of Dronlaw, the supporter of Joan of Arc, another Sir Gilbert Hay in the fifteenth century was a chamberlain to Charles VII of France. He was a priest and a poet who, on his return to Scotland, translated three medieval 'best sellers' into his native tongue in 1456. After his death, Dunbar mourned him in the 'Lament for the Makaris':

'Schir Gilbert Hay endit has he;
Timor Mortis conturbat me.'

These French associations were strengthened after the Reformation when the Hays took the Catholic side. Francis, 9th Earl of Erroll, was joint leader with Huntly of the Catholic rebellion of 1594, when Argyll's government forces were defeated at Glenlivet. In revenge, James VI blew up Slains Castle the following year. Thereafter the Earls of Erroll lived at the Tower of Bowness, renamed Slains, and converted it into a great castle in succeeding generations; the ruins stand at Port Erroll on Cruden Bay (just off the A975 road, 3 miles south of Coldwells). Another sixteenth-century link with France was provided by Father Edmund Hay, who was superior of the French Jesuits.

During the Civil War, the Hays were staunch royalists. Gilbert, 11th Earl of Erroll, was a colonel of horse in the army of Charles I and supported his son, even after the defeat at Worcester. Sir William Hay of Delgatie, Montrose's chief of staff, was beheaded by the Covenanters at Edinburgh in 1650. In the eighteenth century, Slains was a centre of Jacobite intrigue. Charles, 13th Earl of Erroll, was imprisoned after the abortive rising of 1708, which he helped to organize; his sister Mary, who succeeded him as Countess of Erroll in 1717, raised her clan for Prince Charlie during the 'Forty-five. John Hay, of the house of Kinnoull, was Secretary of State to the Old Chevalier, who created him Jacobite Duke of Inverness in 1727. Another branch, the Hays of Kingask, were for a time Earls of Carlisle and hereditary proprietors of Barbados.

Today the Earl of Erroll retains his office of Lord High Constable of Scotland, as well as being clan chief. The sept names are, firstly, variants of Hay, such as Hayburn, Hayes, Hayfield, Haynes, Haystoun and De La Haye; other septs are Alderston, Ayer, Beagrie, Dalgety, Erroll, Gifford, Kinnoull, Laxfrith, Leask, Leith, Lockerwort, MacGaradh, Slains, Turriff and Yester. The chief is styled MacGaraidh Mór and the clan's badge is mistletoe; its slogan is 'A Hay, A Hay, A Hay!' and its Gaelic name Clann Chuidh.

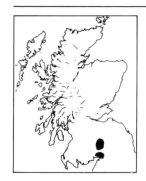

CLAN
JOHNSTONE

THE JOHNSTONES HAVE THE DISTINCTION OF having been involved in the bloodiest of all clan feuds; their struggle with the Maxwells was outstanding even among the feuds of Border clans for its bitterness and tenacity. There were, of course, other claims to fame which the Johnstones could advance: their chiefs rose in the peerage to the rank of a marquessate, they contributed one of the greatest poets and dramatists to English literature, and one of the clan left memoirs of vital interest to historians of the Jacobite movement. Their pedigree, too, goes further back than is the case with most Scottish Border clans.

As the name suggests, the progenitor of the clan was a man named John, who received a grant of land in Dumfriesshire from the Bruce lords of Annandale late in the twelfth century. This estate became known as 'Jonestun' or Johnstone, so that John's son, who lived between 1194 and 1240, was called Sir Gilbert de Johnstoun, the first to bear the surname. His son, also Gilbert, seems to have been a man of less importance than his father and did not attain the honour of knighthood. The 4th chief, however, Sir John Johnstone, married Mary, daughter of the Earl of Strathearn; both he and his son, Sir Gilbert, signed the Ragman's Roll in 1296, swearing fealty to Edward I of England. Yet their patriotism was not in doubt when war broke out. After Sir William Wallace took Lochmaben Castle, he appointed Johnstone, 'a man of good degree who had married the second daughter of Halliday, Wallace's dear nephew', to be its captain. In the late fourteenth century, the 6th chief, Sir John, was a warden of the West Marches and won a striking victory over the English in 1378:

> 'When at the wattyr of Sulway,
> Schyr Jhon of Jhonystown on a day
> Of Inglis men wencust a gret dele.'

His son, Adam Johnstone, 7th of Johnstone, who was laird by 1413, has often been claimed as the common ancestor of the houses of Annandale and Westerhall, though the evidence is inconclusive. Adam was involved in a large-scale battle against English invaders in 1448 and died about 1454. During the chiefship of his son John, the

war between James II and the Douglases reached its climax. The Johnstones fought in the king's army at the Battle of Arkinholm (now Langholm) on 1st May 1455. They then assisted King James at the siege of Threave Castle, the Douglas stronghold in Galloway, receiving the lands of Buittle and Sannoch, near Threave, as a reward. Finally, the Johnstones were in at the kill when the Douglas insurrection was crushed at the Battle of Lochmaben (1484), again receiving grants of land.

John, 8th of Johnstone, was succeeded by his elder grandson within his lifetime, having grown too old to lead the clan himself. Yet even this grandson predeceased him in 1488, so that by the time the old chief died, around 1493, his younger grandson Adam was reigning as 10th Laird of Johnstone. In 1498 Adam was one of a band of 60 men who raided the house of the Laird of Glendinning, Sheriff of Eskdale; they carried off four horses, 14 cows and oxen, with cutlery and furniture to the value of 100 merks. This crime seems to have done Johnstone little harm with the authorities, for he was knighted shortly afterwards. At his death in 1509 his son James became Laird of Johnstone; he married Mary, daughter of John, 4th Lord Maxwell. Despite this marriage, indicating an amicable relationship between the Johnstones and Maxwells at the beginning of the sixteenth century, the two clans were set on a collision course made inevitable by their geographical position. It is even possible that the marriage aggravated the situation: the eldest offspring, John, who succeeded as 12th Laird of Johnstone in 1524, was regarded jealously by his uncle, the 5th Lord Maxwell. From this minor friction a terrible clan feud developed which claimed hundreds of lives. Whatever the immediate provocations, the underlying cause was the proximity of two such strong clans — the Johnstones' power increasing, the Maxwells' receding throughout the sixteenth century — in the warlike arena of Annandale in the Scottish West March.

The Johnstone country was divided into two unequal parts, of which the northern section was by far the larger. It was bounded on the north by a line running roughly from the eastern slopes of the Lowther Hills, skirting

Wamphray Glen, over which looked Wamphray Castle, an impregnable Johnstone fortress.

Johnstone

MOTTO: *Numquam non paratus* (Never unprepared)
ORIGIN OF NAME: John's tun (farm)
WARCRY: *Light thieves all!*
PLANT BADGE: Red hawthorn

Hart Fell (2,651 ft), to Andrewhinney Hill (2,221 ft); below that line, the Johnstone territory lay on both banks of the River Annan to as far south as Newton, except for an enclave of land belonging to the Carlyle family on the west bank. South of Newton, there was a similar enclave of Jardine land on both banks of the Annan, around Applegarth; the Johnstone lands rejoined the river south of Applegarth, though only on the east bank, and stretched further eastwards until the River Esk became their new boundary. This whole area was approximately 30 miles long, with an average breadth of about 14 miles. Further south there was another Johnstone settlement on the northern shore of the Solway Firth, from Cummer-trees to Gretna. This southern sphere of Johnstone influence was separated from the main clan territory in Annandale by the Maxwell country lying between the Annan and the Esk; the larger Maxwell land-holding, however, lay beyond Dumfries, on the western side of the River Nith.

As regards strongholds, the Johnstones were at various times keepers of the great castle of Lochmaben, a post which brought them increased power, an annual salary of £300 Scots and the right to fish the lochs beside the castle; it is now a ruin, 1 mile south of the town of the same name (on the B7020). The Johnstones' own chief seat, however, was Lochwood Tower, 6 miles south of Moffat (on the east side of the A701). Dating back at least to the fourteenth century, it was burned by the Maxwells in 1585, rebuilt, and again destroyed by fire — accidentally this time — in 1710. Other Johnstone strongholds were Newbie Tower, on the shore of the Solway Firth, and Wamphray Castle, long since ruined, an impregnable fortress on a hill overlooking Wamphray Glen, north-east of Newton. John Johnstone of Wamphray joined in the Jacobite rebellion of 1745 and was imprisoned in his own castle, under sentence of death; his kinsman, Johnstone of Kirkhill, changed places with him and the guards only discovered the substitution when they came to execute the sentence, by which time the Laird of Wamphray was beyond their reach.

It was in the sixteenth century, however, that the

The Lowther Hills mark the northern edge of Johnstone territory.

Johnstones were at the peak of their power and most heavily involved in the murderous clan politics of the Borders. Although John, 12th Laird of Johnstone, ruled the clan from 1524 to 1567, an exceptionally long period, he spent much of his life either as an outlaw or actually in prison. He antagonized the Armstrongs by the killing of Meikle Sym Armstrong, which provoked a blood feud. The Maxwells, while keeping in the background, discreetly fanned the flames by encouraging the Armstrongs against the Johnstones. In 1530 Johnstone served the first of many terms of imprisonment, being released on giving a bond of fidelity on behalf of his clan. About this time the English Warden, Lord Dacre, wrote to Cardinal Wolsey: 'The Debateable Land is now clear waste owing to the Johnstoun and Maxwell feuds'. The Maxwells were allied with the English, but the Johnstones remained patriots, if only because their enemies were in the other camp. In 1543 Johnstone obtained a charter erecting his lands into the feudal barony of

Johnstone and two years later he sat in the Parliament at Stirling which bound Scotland in alliance with France. Soon after, however, in April 1547, he was captured by the English and spent three years as a prisoner in a succession of castles: Carlisle, Lowther, Pontefract, Whartonhall and Hartlie. Although liberated in 1550, the Laird spent further periods in Scottish prisons before his death in 1567, when his effects included not only a large amount of grain, wool and linen, but a hoard of gold and silver worth £200.

His grandson, Sir John Johnstone, 13th Laird, inherited the quarrel with the Maxwells. Despite this, both clans supported Mary Queen of Scots and fought for her at the Battle of Langside (1568). However, as Mary's imprisonment in England made her increasingly remote from Scottish affairs, the old feuds broke out again among her supporters. One of the chief bones of contention was the office of Warden of the West March. In 1579 this post was given to Johnstone, but with the fall of the Regent

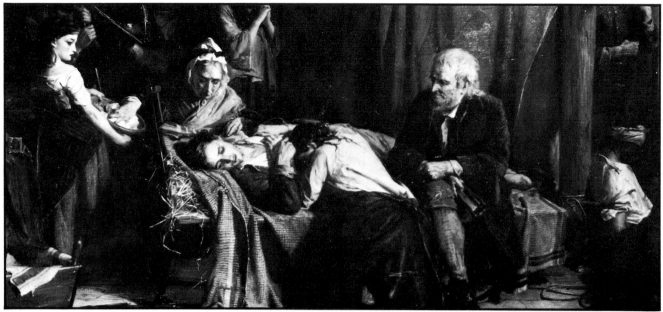

'After the Battle: A Scene in Covenanting Times', by R. Herdman. Among the Johnstones who supported the Covenant was the fanatical Lord Warriston.

Morton, Lord Maxwell replaced him in 1581. The following year, the positions were reversed and Johnstone found himself Warden again and high in the king's favour, partly due to the influence of his wife, who was an accomplished courtier. Maxwell also played into his hands by flagrantly breaking the law again and again; in 1585, as already mentioned, he burned Johnstone's tower of Lochwood. The Johnstones' weakness was numerical. They could only muster 400 fighting men from their own clan, while Maxwell's forces, swollen by many outlaws, sometimes numbered nearly 2,000. The royal authority was invoked to redress the balance, but in vain. Maxwell devastated the entire West March, took every Johnstone stronghold, captured the Laird himself and secured the submission of Clan Johnstone.

Yet, a month later, the Johnstones and Maxwells came together as allies in another cause which alarmed James VI more than any Border feuding. The two clans met at Lincluden to hear Mass celebrated, in defiance of the law, by a priest under Maxwell's protection; the English Lord Warden Scrope reported that 'this infection spreadeth itself into divers other places'. The Johnstones were reluctant to accept the Reformation and up until 1603 there were various outlawries passed against Johnstone chiefs and their dependents for hearing Mass and having their children 'baptized and taught by Roman priests, and entertaining the same'. This fidelity of the Johnstones and Maxwells was unusual on the Border, where all religion was largely discounted; yet their status as co-religionists was not sufficient to heal their clan feud. The warfare reached a climax on 6th December 1593, when Sir James Johnstone, 14th Laird, with 400 men, routed a Maxwell army five times as large at Dryfe Sands, near Lockerbie. After years of fluctuating fortunes, the chiefs of the two warring clans met on 4th April 1608 to settle a lasting peace. During the meeting, a quarrel arose and Lord Maxwell shot the Laird of Johnstone, who fell from his horse, exclaiming, 'Lord have mercy on me! Christ have mercy on me! I am deceived!' and promptly expired. Maxwell fled abroad, but, returning five years later, was arrested and beheaded for the murder. The

terrible feud between the Johnstones and Maxwells was finally ended in 1623 when the chiefs and chieftains of both clans met in the presence of the Privy Council and 'choppit hands'.

By the seventeenth century, the clan system had virtually disappeared from the Borders. James Johnstone, 15th Laird, was created Lord Johnston in 1633 and Earl of Hartfell 10 years later. A moderate Covenanter, he later joined Montrose and was one of the royalists captured at Philiphaugh in 1645. His son was created Earl of Annandale and Hartfell after the Restoration and it was about this time that Moffat, in the Johnstone country, first became a fashionable spa. The 2nd Earl of Annandale was a supporter of William of Orange who raised him in the peerage as Marquess of Annandale in 1701; during the 'Fifteen rebellion he was active on the government side. The marquessate of Annandale became dormant on the death of the 3rd Marquess in 1792; it was later unsuccessfully claimed by the Johnstones of Westerhall.

The most distinguished member of the clan was Ben Jonson (1573-1637), the great English dramatist, whose grandfather came from Annandale. He was so proud of his ancestry that he travelled on foot to Scotland in 1618 and was made a burgess of Edinburgh. A less attractive figure was Archibald Johnstone, Lord Warriston (1611-63), a fanatical Covenanter who jeered at Montrose on his way to execution, only to be hanged himself in Edinburgh 13 years later. James, Chevalier de Johnstone (1719-1800), was aide-de-camp to both Lord George Murray and Bonnie Prince Charlie during the 'Forty-five, after which he escaped to Holland and entered the French service. His *Memoirs of the Rebellion of 1745-46* provide an important source for historians.

The principal cadet houses of Johnstone were Elphinstone, Westerhall, Newbie, Elsieshields and Graitney; the Johnstons of Caskieben are a separate race from the Border clan. Today the chiefly line is the family of Hope-Johnstone of Annandale. Clan Johnstone's plant badge is red hawthorn, and its warcry is 'Light thieves all!' There is a recognized Johnstone tartan.

CLAN
MACGREGOR

ALTHOUGH MOST HIGHLAND CLANS HAVE A HISTORY of bloodshed and struggle for survival, only the MacGregors have experienced a systematic effort to exterminate their race, as well as the outlawing of their very name. Since several generations were forbidden to call themselves MacGregor, many unrecognized descendants of the clan flourish today, dispersed at home and abroad under inherited pseudonyms. The other reason for the MacGregors' notoriety is, of course, the career of Rob Roy, the most famous Highland outlaw of all time.

Clan Gregor claims a royal descent from Alpin, whose son Kenneth united the monarchies of Dalriada and Caledonia to become first King of Scots in 844. The chief's motto records this tradition: ''S Rioghal mo dhream' ('My race is royal'). According to the legend, one of King Alpin's younger sons was ancestor to Hugh of Glenorchy, who lived about the middle of the twelfth century. From his son Giolla Fhaolain (the Devotee of St Fillan) descended two brothers, Iain of Glenorchy and Duncan. Iain did homage to Edward I of England in 1296; his line ended in an heiress who married into the house of Campbell of Lochawe, who thereafter claimed the superiority of Glenorchy. Duncan, the younger brother, had a son, Gregor of the Golden Bridles, who gave his name to the clan.

Gregor's son, Iain Càm (One-eyed), held the three glens of the rivers Orchy, Strae and Lochy, but was probably by then only a tenant of Campbell of Lochawe. The MacGregors, however, still asserted their ancient right to these lands, so that the seeds of a long feud with the Campbells were already sown when Iain Càm died in 1390. The three glens which were the cradle of the Gregarach (as the MacGregors were known) are situated in eastern Argyll, near the Perthshire border. The River Orchy, which flows for 16 miles in a south-westerly direction from Loch Tulla to Loch Awe, gives its name to Glenorchy (through which the B8074 road now passes, linking the A85 and A82). Its southern tributary, the Lochy, flows down the glen of the same name (through which runs the A85); its northern tributary, the Strae, has its course through the third and wildest glen, which has

limited road access only to its southern reaches (by the B8077, north-east of the village of Lochawe).

The third MacGregor chief, Iain Dubh (the Black), reigned for 25 years and died in 1415. It was during the chiefship of his son Malcolm that the clan finally lost its ancient patrimony of Glenorchy. In 1432 Sir Duncan Campbell of Lochawe gave Glenorchy to his third son, Colin. To maintain this overlordship, Colin Campbell built Kilchurn Castle, now a ruin, at the head of Loch Awe, about 2 miles west of Dalmally (A85 road). So Malcolm MacGregor, his son Patrick and grandson Iain Dubh II had to retire to Glenstrae where, from their tower at Stronmelochan (on the B8077 road), they ruled over a reduced and land-hungry clan.

When Iain Dubh II of Glenstrae died in 1519 he left no heir. Passing over the senior cadet houses of Brackly and Roro, the MacGregors' superiors, the Campbells of Glenorchy, enforced the succession of Iain, chieftain of the line known as Clan Dugall Ciar, as 7th Chief of MacGregor. This was because Iain was married to the daughter of Sir Colin Campbell of Glenorchy, who hoped to control the Gregarach through his son-in-law. The Campbells miscalculated, however, for the Clan Dugall Ciar, which included the notorious MacGregors of Glengyle, was the most unruly branch of the family. Iain was succeeded in 1528 by his son Alasdair, 8th of Glenstrae, who fought at the Battle of Pinkie in 1547 and died shortly afterwards.

As a result of their loss of land, the MacGregors began to spill out of their original territory, settling where they could and showing as little sensitivity to other men's rights as the Campbells had shown towards themselves. They moved eastward into Perthshire, first to Glenlyon where a cadet house, descended from a nephew of the first Iain Dubh, was already established at Roro, as tenants of Menzies. MacGregors also settled in Glendochart, where they had ancestral connections with the old abbey, and further east at Fortingall. A branch of the Gregarach had held a lease of the church lands of Fortingall since the early fifteenth century; one of them compiled the *Book of the Dean of Lismore*, which contains much of the clan's

Glenstrae and Glenlochy, two of the MacGregor glens in Argyll, with snow-capped Ben Lui in the distance.

history. Still further afield, MacGregors penetrated as far north as Rannoch and south-east to Balquhidder.

By the late sixteenth century, Clan Gregor had become a national problem. Though nominally settled as tenants of other chiefs, the scattered clansmen recognized only MacGregor and led a bandit existence, preying on their neighbours' cattle. The problem, of course, had been created by the government two hundred years earlier, by surrendering Glenorchy to Campbell greed, instead of recognizing the MacGregors' unwritten title to their land by ancient occupation. Throughout the 1560s, Gregor MacGregor, 10th Chief, waged war against Campbell of Glenorchy, who had now also purchased the superiority of Glenstrae from the Earl of Argyll and refused to recognize Gregor's succession. In 1570 he captured and beheaded MacGregor.

Worse was to come. In 1589 the branch of the clan known as the 'Children of the Mist' murdered John Drummond of Drummond-Ernoch, the King's Forester of Glenartney, who had hanged some Gregarach for poaching deer. The executed chief's son, Alasdair, 11th of Glenstrae, supported his clansmen. He mustered the whole clan at Balquhidder church, where each man laid his hand upon Drummond's severed head and took upon himself a share of the blood-guilt. For this, MacGregor was condemned by the Privy Council, but later reconciled to James VI through the mediation of friendly nobles. By now, however, the chief had lost control of his far-flung, landless and embittered clan, so that he was powerless to restrain the more lawless elements. Some of them attacked the Colquhouns of Luss in 1602, whereupon the victims' widows paraded their menfolk's bloodstained shirts before the king, who was enraged by the sight and granted Colquhoun a commission to punish the MacGregors. Without waiting to be attacked, Alasdair MacGregor ambushed the combined army of Colquhouns, Buchanans and Dumbarton townsmen at Glenfruin on the 7th February 1603. The site of the battle is about 3 miles south-east of Garelochhead, just beyond Strone (access by an unclassified road off the A814). Glenfruin was a sweeping victory for the MacGregors, but its

MacGregor

MOTTO: *'S rioghal mo dhream* (My race is royal)
GAELIC NAME: Clann Ghriogair
WARCRY: *Àrd Choille!* (The High Wood)
PLANT BADGE: Pine
PIPE MUSIC: *Ruaig Ghlinne Freoine* (Chase of Glenfruin)

Glenorchy, long disputed between the MacGregors and Campbells.

consequences were worse for them than if they had been defeated.

On 3rd April 1603, the same day that he said farewell to the citizens of Edinburgh, having inherited the throne of England, James VI held a council meeting 'whereby it wes ordainit that the name of McGregoure sulde be altogidder abolisched, and that the haill persounes of that Clan suld renunce thair name and tak thame sum uther name, and that they nor nane of thair posteritie suld call thame selffis Gregour or McGregoure thair efter, under the payne of deade.' This was the last governmental act of the old Scots monarchy. MacGregor eventually gave himself up and was hanged, with 11 of his chieftains, at the Mercat Cross in Edinburgh on 20th January 1604. For the next half-century, the MacGregors lived mostly as outlaws or relied on the protection of friendly chiefs, notably the Laird of Grant. The men were hunted down and slaughtered, the women had their faces branded.

During the Wars of the Covenant, despite their cruel treatment at the hands of the Stuart kings, the MacGregors took the royalist side. In reward for this, the laws against them were repealed by Charles II in 1661. At the Revolution, therefore, the clan rallied to James VII, but this loyalty rebounded against them in 1693 when the victorious William of Orange reintroduced the legislation

suppressing Clan Gregor. Then, early in the eighteenth century, Archibald, 16th Chief of MacGregor, died and the house of Glenstrae became extinct. In this emergency, a dozen gentlemen of the clan held a meeting in July 1714, and recognized Alexander MacGregor, alias Drummond, of Balhaldie as chief of the name. This arbitrary decision, however, ignored the superior claim of John MacGregor, alias Murray, of Glencarnoch, Chieftain of the 'Children of the Mist'.

Both the *de facto* and *de jure* chiefly lines were Jacobite. Alexander of Balhaldie was 'out' in the 'Fifteen and was created a baronet by the exiled James VIII in 1740. Glencarnoch's successor, Robert MacGregor, commanded a force of Gregarach in Prince Charlie's army and was subsequently imprisoned for three years; a MacGregor was one of the Seven Men of Glen Moriston who guarded the fugitive prince, and Clan Gregor was specifically excluded from the Act of Grace of 1752. Yet one member of the clan eclipsed all others in fame during the first half of the eighteenth century: Robert MacGregor, alias Campbell, better known as Rob Roy.

He was born in 1671, the younger son of Lieutenant-Colonel Donald MacGregor of Glengyle and his wife, a Campbell of Glenfalloch. In 1691 he took part in a raid on the village of Kippen, but after the re-imposition of the

Rob Roy, here seen separating the duellists Rashleigh and Osbaldistone, an incident from Sir Walter Scott's novel about the famous MacGregor outlaw.

anti-MacGregor laws in 1693, he assumed his mother's name of Campbell and became a cattle dealer. At first he enjoyed the patronage of the Duke of Montrose, but after Rob Roy had absconded with certain funds, the relationship turned sour. When Montrose's kinsman and factor, Graham of Killearn, humiliated MacGregor's wife and evicted her in mid-winter, Rob Roy embarked on a long feud. For years he preyed upon Montrose's cattle and lands, even seizing the government-built fort at Inversnaid. During the 'Fifteen Rebellion, he attached himself loosely to the Jacobite army, but his alliance with his Campbell kinsmen held him back from committing himself totally. Even so, his exploits included the proclamation of James VIII at Drymen and the occupation of Falkland Palace in 1716.

Later that year, his enemies having destroyed his home at Craigroyston, he boldly kidnapped Graham of Killearn from the inn at Menteith and appropriated Montrose's rents. In 1717 he was captured at Blair Atholl, but escaped after three days to resume his war against Montrose. Since he no longer had anything to lose by declaring his true loyalties, he joined in the Jacobite Rebellion of 1719 and fought at the Battle of Glenshiel. Three years later, with the help of the Duke of Argyll, he was reconciled with Montrose. The government, however, was not so easily placated and, in 1727, Rob Roy boarded a convict ship at Gravesend, bound for slavery in Barbados. Luckily he was pardoned before the ship weighed anchor. He lived at Balquhidder in Perthshire for the rest of his days, fighting a duel with Stewart of Invernahyle shortly before his death in 1734. Rob Roy is buried in Balquhidder churchyard (access by an unclassified road running west from Kingshouse, about 3 miles

south of Lochearnhead, on the A84), between his wife and two of his sons, one of whom was hanged in 1754 for abducting and forcibly marrying a widow from Balfron. It is a measure of Rob Roy's celebrity that he was the subject of a biography by Daniel Defoe, a novel by Sir Walter Scott and a poem by Wordsworth.

The laws against Clan Gregor were repealed in 1774 and a few years later a gathering of more than 800 clansmen declared John MacGregor, alias Murray, of Lanrick to be 18th Chief of MacGregor. In 1795 he was created a baronet and the chiefship has since then continued in his line. MacGregor's seat is Edinchip, near Lochearnhead, in Perthshire. Because of the statutes prohibiting the clan name, many Scots have inherited assumed surnames which conceal Clan Gregor origins, for example Field-Marshal Sir Colin Campbell, Lord Clyde, who commanded the 'Thin Red Line' at Balaclava and whose father's name was MacLiver, a MacGregor alias. This widespread adoption of pseudonyms has resulted in Clan MacGregor having a disproportionate number of sept names. Principal among them are the obvious derivatives from the clan name, such as Gregor, Gregorson, Gregory, Gregson, Greig, Grigor and Macgruder; other identifiable septs are Comrie, Crowther, Fletcher, Grier, Grierson, King, Leckie, MacAdam, MacAra, Macaree, MacChoiter, MacLiver, MacNee, MacNeish, MacPeter, Malloch, Peter and Petrie.

In commemoration of their alleged descent from King Alpin, the MacGregors are also known as Clan Alpin and their chief as An t-Ailpeineach. Their badge is the pine, their warcry '*Àrd Choille!*' ('The High Wood!') and their Gaelic name Clann Ghriogair.

CLAN
MACKAY

'THE REAL MACKAY' HAS BECOME AN EVERYDAY expression to describe something genuine and reliable; it is a fair tribute to a clan which has always stood by its principles, even when such loyalty was bound to bring misfortune. In fact, the origin of the phrase was simply an attempt to distinguish between the overall chief of the name (the real Mackay) and the chieftain of an unruly junior branch which often gave trouble to the rest of the clan. Many unusual features distinguish the Mackays. The chiefly family became Dutch for several generations and produced a prime minister of the Netherlands; the 'White Banner' of Mackay, still preserved, is one of the mysterious old flags of legendary origin which have been handed down in several Scots clans; and the Mackays also have the distinction of having founded the first clan society in Scotland.

Originally the Mackays belonged to the old ruling house of Moray. Malcolm MacEth, Earl of Ross, was displaced from the province of Moray by King Malcolm IV in 1160. His grandson Kenneth joined in a rebellion against William the Lion and was killed about 1215. Kenneth's son, called Iye, was the progenitor of the Mackays; he became chamberlain to Walter de Baltrode, Bishop of Caithness, and his son, Iye Mór, married the bishop's daughter, thus acquiring lands in Durness, in the north-western corner of Sutherland. Iye Mór (the Great) was in turn succeeded by his son Donald, born in 1265, who married a daughter of Iye Macneill of Gigha. Their son, another Iye, became chief in about 1330. It was during his chiefship that the bitter feud between Clan Mackay and the Sutherlands first flared up. David II granted the earldom of Sutherland 'in regality' to William, Chief of Sutherland, in 1345, giving him almost royal power in the most northerly part of Scotland. He immediately claimed feudal superiority over the Mackays, provoking fierce resistance on their part. Eventually the question was put to arbitration, with a strong likelihood of a verdict in favour of the Mackays' independence. The Sutherlands, however, struck first. In 1372, Iye Mackay and his heir, Donald, were murdered in Dingwall Castle by Nicolas Sutherland of Duffus.

Donald's son, Angus, then became 5th Chief of Mackay. He married a daughter of Torquil MacLeod of the Lewes and died in 1403, when his son Angus Dubh (the Black) inherited the chiefship.

Under Angus Dubh the Mackays began to make their presence felt throughout Sutherland and other parts of the Highlands. Yet Angus's reign did not start auspiciously. His uncle, Huisdean Dubh, acted as 'tutor' or regent of the clan during his minority, but quarrelled with the young chief's widowed mother who thereupon summoned her MacLeod kinsmen to her aid. So they invaded the Mackay country of Strathnaver in 1408. After laying waste the area, they withdrew, but were overtaken by the pursuing Mackays in Strathoykel, far to the south, at a place 3 miles east of Oykel Bridge (on the north side of the A837 road), where a fierce battle took place. This fight was known as *Latha Tuiteam Tarbhach* (the Day of Great Slaughter); it was a victory for the Mackays and it is said that only one MacLeod escaped alive. Soon afterwards the young chief, Angus Dubh, took the field himself, commanding a joint force of Mackays, Sutherlands, Munros and Rosses which marched in 1411 against Donald, Lord of the Isles, who was in rebellion against the Regent Albany. When Angus tried to prevent Donald taking Dingwall, he was defeated and taken prisoner. Donald of the Isles was beaten in his turn at Harlaw, so he released Mackay and tried to patch up an alliance with him, giving him his sister Elizabeth in marriage.

The remainder of Angus Dubh's chiefship saw a further strengthening of Mackay power. In 1425 Angus 'tuk an gret prey of gudis out of Moray' and the following year he invaded Caithness 'with all hostility and spoilt the same'. When he attended the parliament held at Inverness in 1427 he was described as 'a leader of 4,000 men'. Shortly after this, Angus suffered a setback. His first cousin, Thomas Neilson Mackay of Creich, committed sacrilege by burning the chapel of St Duthac at Tain and was outlawed. Thomas's lands were held from Angus Dubh who had been granted them in a charter by the Lord of the Isles. James I, however, ignored this fact and apportioned the land between Thomas's brothers and

Ben Stack *rises proudly above the Mackay lands in northern Sutherland.*

Mackay

MOTTO: *Manu forti* (With a strong hand)
GAELIC NAME: Clann Mhich Mhorgain, Clann Aoidh
WARCRY: *Bratach bàn Mhic Aoidh*!
(The White Banner of Mackay)
PLANT BADGE: Great bulrush, reed grass
PIPE MUSIC: Mackay's March

Eddrachillis Bay *with its many islands lies on the southern frontier of Mackay power.*

their father-in-law, all dependents of the Sutherlands. Then, in 1433, they and the Sutherlands marched on Tongue, determined to destroy the Mackays once and for all. Angus Dubh's predicament was grave: he himself was ill and had to be carried in a litter, while Neil, his heir, was being held hostage on the Bass Rock by James I. In this crisis, the clan was led by Angus's teenage younger son, Iain Abrach. The Mackays met the invaders at Druim nan Ceap, near Tongue. Both armies were evenly matched — about 1,500 men each — but the Sutherlands taunted the Mackays with the youth of their leader: 'We will put a hobble on yonder calf!' they jeered. Their laughter was short-lived. In the ensuing battle the Mackays routed their enemies and hunted them from the slopes of Ben Loyal to the loch of the same name, where a stone marks the grave of the last Sutherlands slain in flight. Only the death of Angus Dubh, killed by an arrow in the moment of victory, detracted from this triumph of the Mackays.

In 1437 the Mackays retaliated against the Sutherlands by invading Caithness where they again defeated their enemies at the battle known as Sandside Chase. Neil of the Bass (so called because of his imprisonment there) was overshadowed during his chiefship by his younger brother, Iain Abrach, who was ancestor of the clan's principal cadet family, the Aberach Mackays. It was Neil's son, Angus Roy, however, who carried on the main

Ben Loyal, on whose slopes the Sutherlands were hunted down after their defeat by the Mackays in 1433.

line and became 8th Chief of Mackay. In the time of Angus Roy the Mackays settled their feud with the Sutherlands by the marriage of one of the chief's daughters to Sutherland of Dirled. Yet they became involved almost immediately in another feud with the Rosses of Balnagown who, in 1486, burned Angus Roy to death in the church at Tarbet where he had sought sanctuary. The Mackays' vengeance was swift. They invaded Strathcarron of Ross and routed the Rosses and their allies at Aldicharrish on 11th July 1487. Iye Roy Mackay, son of the murdered Angus Roy, was now chief and it was during his reign that the clan finally obtained royal charters for their lands, after helping the king to crush the Lordship of the Isles and the MacLeods in Lewis.

The cradle of the Mackays was Strathnaver, bounded on the west by the Minch, on the north by the Atlantic; its eastern boundary ran down Strath Halladale (through which passes the A897 road from Golval to Kinbrace); the southern frontier stretched from Eddrachillis Bay to just south of Forsinard (on the A897). This territory was known as Duthaich 'Ic Aoidh (the Land of the Mackays).

The chief's seat was the House of Tongue, just north of the village of that name, on the eastern shore of the Kyle of Tongue (A836). Older Mackay strongholds were Castle Varrich, on the southern outskirts of Tongue, and Castle Borve, near Farr Point (access by an unclassified road off the A836 between Bettyhill and Strathy); both are now meagre ruins. Altogether the Mackay country was about 50 miles long by 25 miles broad. It was well-populated and watered by many rivers with fertile valleys — Strath Dionard, Strath More, Strathnaver, Strath Halladale — and by Lochs More, Hope, Loyal and Naver. The Laxford is still a famous salmon river and the Mackays also supplemented their diet with sea-fishing. There was arable land on the coast as well as in the river valleys and sheep and black cattle were kept in the inland areas; small horses were also bred. Reay Forest was renowned for its venison. Old accounts of life in Strathnaver make it clear that the Mackays were a very prosperous clan who wanted for nothing.

Iye Roy Mackay consolidated the clan's legal position, as has been said, by getting confirmation of his lands in 1499, 1504 and 1511. In 1493 he again harried the Rosses

A ruined croft on Loch Eriboll stands as a sad reminder of clansmen long gone from their homeland.

and in 1513 he fought at Flodden and was among the survivors, though his brother, John Riabhach (the Freckled) was killed. Iye Roy's son, John of Strathnaver, chief from 1517 to 1529, left no male issue, so was succeeded by his brother Donald. Donald Mackay supported the Forbes clan, with whom he claimed kinship, in their feud against the Seatons. Probably his real motive was to make common cause against the Gordons, who had by now inherited the earldom of Sutherland and who were also enemies of the Forbeses in Aberdeenshire. The Mackays fought under James V at Solway Moss in 1542 and were rewarded with some grants of land shortly before the king's death. Iye Dubh (the Black), 12th Chief of Mackay, led the clan from 1550 to 1572, the period of the Reformation. He sided with the Protestant party and became the enemy of the Queen Mother, Mary of Guise. In 1554, the Sutherlands were empowered to arrest Mackay, so they invaded his country, destroyed Castle Borve and took Iye Dubh prisoner, all with royal approval. Then, in 1565, when Mary Queen of Scots married Darnley, she granted him the Mackay patrimony of Strathnaver; after Darnley's death, Strathnaver was given to Lord Huntly, who promptly transferred it to the Earl of Sutherland, the Mackays' old enemy. Iye Dubh, however, was free by this time and he asserted his rights violently, burning Dornoch in 1566 and 1571. A question had already been asked in Parliament 'be quhat means may all Scotland be brocht to universal obedience, and how may McKy be dantonit'. Eventually Strathnaver was restored to the Mackays, but under the feudal superiority of the Earl of Sutherland.

During the chiefship of Iye Dubh's son, Huisdean Dubh, the Aberach Mackays (descended from Iain Abrach, the victor of Druim nan Ceap) rebelled against their chief (the real Mackay) and joined with Sutherland. This was a serious blow to the clan. Huisdean Dubh's son, Sir Donald Mackay, 14th of Strathnaver, raised 3,600 men to fight for Gustavus Adolphus and the Protestant cause in the Thirty Years War. In 1627, Mackay's Regiment earned fame by its heroic defence of the Pass of

Oldenburg and the following year Sir Donald was created Lord Reay. He fought for Charles I in the Civil War and died in exile in 1649. By now the Mackay chiefs' finances were too embarrassed to allow them to play a prominent part in affairs. Members of the clan, however, served in the Scots Brigade in Holland and in 1688 its commander was General Hugh Mackay of Scourie, who led the Williamite army defeated by Dundee at Killiecrankie, a fact commemorated in the song:

> 'O fie, Mackay, what gart ye lie
> I' the bush ayont the brankie-o?
> Ye'd better kissed King Willie's loof
> Than come tae Killiecrankie-o!'

In both the 'Fifteen and the 'Forty-five Rebellions, the Mackays took the Hanoverian side and helped secure the far north for the government. Their way of life was breaking down, however, and they suffered badly in the Strathnaver clearances between 1815 and 1818; finally, in 1829, the Reay estate was sold to the Sutherland family. Some of Lord Reay's kinsmen had emigrated to Holland and in 1875 the chiefship passed to the Dutch Baron Aeneas Mackay d'Ophemert, who became 10th Lord Reay; his nephew, father of the 12th Lord Reay, was Prime Minister of the Netherlands. Since 1929 the earldom of Inchcape has also been held by a Mackay.

The emblem of Clan Mackay is the *Bratach Bàn* (the White Banner) preserved in the Scottish National Museum of Antiquities; it is owned by the Clan Mackay Society, founded in 1806, the oldest clan society in Scotland. Principal cadets were the Aberach Mackays and the houses of Scourie, Bighouse, Strathy, Melness and Sandwood. Lord Reay, as Chief of Mackay, is styled MacAoidh and the clan badges are the great bulrush or reed grass. Sept names are Bain, Bayne, MacBain, MacCay, MacCrie, MacKee, Mackie, MacPhail (where there is a Sutherland connection), MacQuey, MacQuoid, Neilson, Polson, Reay, Scobie and Williamson. The Clan Mackay warcry is 'Bratach bàn Mhic Aoidh!' ('The White Banner of Mackay') and its Gaelic name is Clann Mhich Mhorgain (the more ancient style) or Clann Aoidh.

CLAN
MACKENZIE

IT IS NOT DIFFICULT TO PINPOINT THE OUTSTANDING feature of Clan Mackenzie: if the extent of a clan's lands were the sole criterion of its importance, then the Mackenzies would be historically the principal family of Scotland. They were the only clan whose unbroken territory straddled the country from coast to coast, making it possible to travel from Applecross to the Moray Firth without leaving Mackenzie land. In fact this huge land-holding, covering the greater part of Ross and Cromarty, did not give the Mackenzies ascendancy over the other Highland clans. Much of it was barren, while the more scattered property of the Campbells, as well as being richer and closer to the seat of political power in the Lowlands, probably amounted to an even greater area. Nevertheless, this great belt of Mackenzie country, cutting the Highlands in two, obviously gave the clan considerable influence.

There has been some debate over the origin of the Mackenzies. One tradition identified them with the great Irish family of FitzGerald; a cadet of that house was said to have fought in the Scots army against the Norsemen at the Battle of Largs in 1262 and to have received a grant of land from Alexander III. This theory is now discredited and it is generally accepted that they derive from a younger son of Gilleoin of the Aird (from whose elder son descended Farquhar Mac an t-Sagairt, ancestor of the Rosses). The forefathers of Clan Mackenzie, therefore, were originally junior kinsmen and vassals of the ancient O'Beolain Earls of Ross. Their earliest territory was Kintail, the district to the north-east of Loch Duich, the inland continuation of Loch Alsh, in south-west Ross-shire. In the late thirteenth century their chief was one Kenneth, twelfth in descent from Gilleoin of the Aird, according to the old genealogies.

Kenneth was governor of Eilean Donan Castle, on Loch Duich, under the Earl of Ross. Eilean Donan, built on a tidal islet commanding Loch Long and Loch Duich, remained the Mackenzies' western stronghold throughout the centuries and is still standing today, its site making it one of the most spectacular castles in Scotland, at Dornie (on the A87 road, between Kyle of Lochalsh and Shiel Bridge). Kenneth rebelled against his superior, Earl William of Ross, and successfully held Eilean Donan against him, thus establishing himself as an independent chief. He married Morna, daughter of Alexander Macdougall of Lorn, and died in 1304. From him the clan took its name Mac Coinnich (Mac Kenneth), Anglicized as Mackenzie.

Kenneth's son John sheltered Robert the Bruce at Eilean Donan in 1306 and led 500 of his men at Bannockburn. John's son, Kenneth, and grandson, Murdoch, were engaged in a constant feud with the Earls of Ross, against whom they managed to preserve their independence. It is from the time of Murdoch's grandson, Alexander Ionraic (the Upright), 6th Chief of Kintail, that Clan Mackenzie's history can be traced from records, rather than legends and traditions. Alexander was one of the Highland chiefs seized at Inverness by James I in 1427. The king was determined to establish order in the Highlands, having sworn 'there shall not be a spot in my dominions where the key shall not keep the castle, and the furze bush the cow.' Alexander Mackenzie, being a mere youth, was not imprisoned by the king, but ordered to attend the High School at Perth. By now the Mackenzies' overlords were the Macdonald Lords of the Isles who had acquired the earldom of Ross by marriage. When the Lord of the Isles raised a rebellion, however, in 1429, Alexander Mackenzie fought in the king's army.

Alexander's 'uprightness' proved profitable. In 1476 he received a royal charter of many of the lands forfeited from the rebel Macdonald, including Strathconon and Strathgarve, in the area west of Dingwall. This brought the Mackenzies' extensive territory in the east, now held directly from the Crown, almost to the shores of the Cromarty Firth. Alexander the Upright died in 1488 and was succeeded by his son Kenneth a'Bhlàir (Kenneth of the Battle). Kenneth earned this name by his victory over the Macdonalds at Blàr-na-Pàirc' in 1491, near Kinellan in Strathpeffer. He died shortly afterwards and was buried at Beauly Priory. The eldest of his sons, Kenneth Òg, held the chiefship very briefly until he was murdered by the Laird of Buchanan in 1497; his half-brother, John

The Five Sisters of Kintail. Kintail was the earliest territory held by the Mackenzies.

Mackenzie

MOTTO: *Luceo non uro* (I shine, not burn)
GAELIC NAME: Clann Choinnich
WARCRY: *Tulach Àrd!* (The High Hill)
PLANT BADGE: Deer's grass, holly
PIPE MUSIC: *Caberféidh*

of Killin, became 9th Chief of Kintail.

John was a man of exceptional cunning who, recognizing the power of the Scots Crown in the north, built his clan's fortunes on the law, rather than the sword. In 1509 he obtained a charter of Kintail, Eilean Donan and other lands erected into a barony; he received seven further charters of land in the course of his long reign, as well as the revenue from gathering the customs of Inverness and the keepership of Sleat Castle. He was taken prisoner at Flodden in 1513, but rescued by a woman in whose house his English escort stopped for the night: by an amazing coincidence she had once been shipwrecked and sheltered in the Mackenzie country. Soon after his return to Scotland he was appointed Lieutenant of Wester Ross. In 1547, at the age of about 65, he fought at the Battle of Pinkie where he was wounded. His resourcefulness did not desert him in old age. When the young Mary Queen of Scots sent her chamberlain north to assess the wealth of the Highland chiefs, Mackenzie filled his house at Killin with dogs and cattle, his servants creating such squalor with discarded offal and straw palliasses that the disgusted courtiers left at dawn. They reported to the Queen that the Highland chiefs lived like princes, except for Mackenzie. 'It were a pity of his poverty', observed the Queen sympathetically and she assessed his feu at much less than the others, though he had by now created a small empire in the Highlands.

John of Killin died in 1561 and his son and grandson both continued the expansion of Mackenzie power. During the chiefship of the latter, Colin Mackenzie, a feud started with the Macdonells of Glengarry which continued into the time of Colin's son, Kenneth, 12th of Kintail, who succeeded in 1594. By 1607 the Macdonells were defeated and their lands of Lochalsh and Lochcarron ceded to the Mackenzies by royal charter. Two years later, after the failure of the Fife Adventurers' efforts to colonize Lewis in the name of James VI, Mackenzie managed to buy their rights from the king and establish himself as overlord of the MacLeod lands on Lewis and the mainland. At the same time he was raised to the

Glen Shiel, where in 1719 a Jacobite army of Mackenzies, MacGregors and Spaniards was defeated by superior Hanoverian forces.

peerage as Lord Mackenzie of Kintail and his son, Colin, who succeeded as a minor in 1611, was created Earl of Seaforth in 1623. This marked the zenith of the Mackenzie fortunes.

The lands over which the new Earl of Seaforth was master amounted to a miniature kingdom. From their early home in Kintail the clan had spread west, north and east. Their great castle of Eilean Donan was held for them by its hereditary governors the Macraes, nicknamed 'Mackenzie's Shirt of Mail'. Northwards up the west coast, Mackenzie's lands reached, almost unbroken, as far as Enard Bay. Of the three alien enclaves that had formerly disrupted this coastline, the Macdonells had been deprived of Lochalsh, the MacLeods of the Gairloch and the Macdonells around Loch Broom outflanked by the Mackenzie overlordship of Coigach. To the west, they also settled on the island of Lewis. To the east, the clan held territory all the way to the coast, including most of the Black Isle.

The northern frontier extended roughly from Enard Bay eastwards, bounded on the north by the MacLeod lands of Assynt, then running southwards along the boundary with Clans Ross and Munro, from Glen Oykel to Dingwall. The southern boundary ran north-eastwards from Kintail, skirting the Fraser and Chisholm country which lay to the south, and ending at the Beauly Firth. The Mackenzies' lands on the east coast, though less extensive, were far the richest and their cultivation produced the bulk of their income. It would be unrealistic to attempt to detail so large an area, but the principal places of interest in Mackenzie history (apart from Eilean Donan, described above) may briefly be mentioned. Strathpeffer, 4 miles west of Dingwall (A834 road), adjoins Kinellan, where the fifteenth-century Mackenzie

chiefs lived; nearby are the sites of their victories over the Macdonalds in 1478 and 1491, as well as of Brahan Castle, their seventeenth-century home. At Beauly Priory, about 10 miles south of Dingwall (on the A9) are the tombs of many Mackenzie chiefs. The distance separating these east coast sites from Eilean Donan is an inconvenience to the visitor, but also a testimony to the former greatness of the Mackenzies.

During the minority of the 1st Earl of Seaforth, his much feared uncle, Sir Roderick Mackenzie of Coigach, Tutor of Kintail, consolidated the clan's hold on its possessions; he was ancestor of the Earls of Cromartie. George, 2nd Earl of Seaforth, who inherited in 1633, was at first an opponent of Montrose, against whom he fought at Auldearn, but he became disillusioned with his Covenanting allies and joined the royalists in 1646. From then onwards, the Mackenzies adhered staunchly to the House of Stuart and this was their eventual undoing. Seaforth followed Charles II into exile, where he held the empty title of Secretary of State for Scotland until his death in Holland in 1651. His son Kenneth, 3rd Earl, fought in the royal army at Worcester and led an unsuccessful Highland rebellion against Cromwell in 1654.

The Restoration brought a return to prosperity for the Mackenzies, but at the Revolution the 4th Earl of Seaforth, who was one of the eight original Knights of the Thistle, went overseas with James VII. He returned to Scotland and raised his clan for the Stuart cause, but was forced to surrender to General Mackay and remained in prison until 1697. The exiled James VII created him Marquess of Seaforth. William, 5th Earl (and titular Marquess) of Seaforth, brought 3,000 men to the Jacobite army during the 'Fifteen Rebellion and fought at

Eilean Donan Castle, built on a tidal islet commanding Loch Duich and Loch Long, was the Mackenzies' great western stronghold.

'Rent-day in the Wilderness'. Landseer's painting depicts the scene as the rents are collected on behalf of the Mackenzie chief, exiled after the 'Fifteen.

Sheriffmuir. After the collapse of the rising, he fled to France and his estates and peerage were forfeited. Four years later, however, Seaforth was the prime mover in the smallest of the Jacobite rebellions, 'the 'Nineteen'.

In May 1719, Seaforth, the Earl Marischal and the Marquess of Tullibardine landed in Kintail with 300 Spanish troops. They were joined by 500 Mackenzies and by Rob Roy with his wild MacGregors, but defeated at Glenshiel on 11th June by superior Hanoverian forces under General Wightman; Seaforth himself was wounded and carried off the field by his clansmen. The site of the battle is about 6 miles south-east of Shiel Bridge (just north of the point where the A87 road crosses from the south to the north bank of the River Shiel). Eilean Donan was blown up by English sailors, but Seaforth escaped to France, was pardoned in 1726 and died in Lewis in 1740. During the 'Forty-five, his impoverished heir, Kenneth, was understandably reluctant to join the rising and even sent a token number of Mackenzies to officer one of the government's Independent Companies of Highlanders. However, about 500 Mackenzies under the Earl of Cromartie did fight for Prince Charlie.

In 1771 the Mackenzie chief was again created Earl of Seaforth and in 1778 he raised the 1st Battalion, The Seaforth Highlanders, a regiment which still wears the Mackenzie tartan. The last Lord Seaforth died in 1815, a deaf mute, thus fulfilling the curse put on his house by Coinneach Odhar, the sixteenth-century 'Brahan Seer': 'I see a chief, the last of his house, both deaf and dumb.' There were more than 40 cadet houses of this great clan, of which the principal survivors are the Earls of Cromartie and the Mackenzies of Scatwell. In 1979 the Earl of Cromartie was recognized by the Lord Lyon as the Chief of Clan Mackenzie. Though clans in their own right, the Mathesons, Maclennans and Macraes have an historic attachment to the Mackenzies. The septs of Clan Mackenzie are: Charleson, Kenneth, Kennethson, MacBeolain, MacConnach, MacIver or MacIvor (where there is a connection with Ullapool and district), MacKerlich, MacMurchie, MacVanish, MacVinish, Murchie and Murchison. The chief's title is MacCoinnich (son of Kenneth) or Caberféidh (Deer's Antlers, which appear on his coat of arms). The clan's badges are deer's grass or holly, its slogan '*Tulach Àrd!*' ('The High Hill!' — a rallying-point in Kintail) and its Gaelic name Clann Choinnich.

CLAN
MACLEAN

ALTHOUGH THEY HELD SOME TERRITORY ON the mainland, the Macleans were first and foremost islanders. Their many and varied homes in the Western Isles provided a romantic and picturesque setting for their equally romantic history. They were a populous and thriving clan, notable for the colourful legends surrounding them. Those who look for romance in the story of the Highland clans will find much to enthral them in the chronicle of the Macleans.

Their earliest known ancestor was called Old Dugald of Scone, whose name would seem to indicate a Perthshire origin; he is thought to have lived about 1100. There is also a tradition that the Macleans were one of the clans transplanted from the Province of Moray by Malcolm IV in the second half of the twelfth century. Clan Maclean takes its name from Gilleathain na Tuaighe (Gillean of the Battle-axe), seven generations after Old Dugald of Scone; in commemoration of their first chief, the Macleans are also known as Clan Gillean. In 1263 Gillean fought in the army of Alexander III against the Norsemen at the Battle of Largs; his nickname was given to him because of his skill in wielding a battle-axe. Gillean's grandson, Malcolm, similarly fought for Bruce and Scotland at Bannockburn. He married a daughter of the Lord of Carrick and had three sons, including his heir, Iain Dubh (the Black).

It was in the time of Iain Dubh that the Macleans first acquired the lands of Duart, in eastern Mull, from which they were destined to expand into a great power in the Western Isles. Iain Dubh had two sons: Lachlan Lùbanach (the Crafty), who succeeded him in Duart, and Hector Reaganach (the Stubborn), ancestor of the house of Lochbuie and of the Macleans of Urquhart, on the mainland. The brothers, who had formerly been vassals of Macdougall of Lorn, renounced this allegiance and attached themselves to the Macdonald Lord of the Isles. Lachlan Lùbanach got charters confirming his lands in Mull from the Lord of the Isles in 1390 and became Steward of the Household to Macdonald. The Mackinnons, the previous lords of Mull, were driven out by the Macleans and took refuge in Skye.

It is important at the outset to understand the structure of Clan Maclean and the geographical situation of its various territories. Broadly, the Macleans were divided into four main branches: Duart, Lochbuie, Ardgour and Coll. The houses of Ardgour and Coll descended from the grandson of Lachlan Lùbanach. The Maclean lands, though separated by water, formed a single geographic concentration, with the exception of the Northern Macleans' lands in Glen Urquhart. This isolated cadet house, known as Clann Thearlaich (because of its descent from Charles, son of Hector Reaganach, who became constable of Urquhart Castle in 1394), acquired rich land in Glen Urquhart, on the northern shore of Loch Ness, between Corrimony and Drumnadrochit (now traversed by the A831 road). These lands were lost in 1482, but the junior branch of Dochgarroch managed to retain some land-holdings in Inverness-shire.

Otherwise, the Macleans' territory was situated on the west coast and its adjoining islands. On the mainland they held Morvern and Ardgour, whose south-eastern boundary was the entire 30 mile expanse of Loch Linnhe, from the Sound of Mull to Loch Eil. The northern boundary reached from Glenfinnan eastwards to the mouth of Loch Eil, and on the west the borders ran from Glenfinnan down to Glen Tarbert; further south, the entire Morvern and Kingairloch peninsula was held by the Macleans. This was wild, infertile land, mostly rough pasture or waste; the small quantity of arable land lay along the coast on the Sound of Mull, but the one abundant harvest was fish, both from the sea and from fresh-water lochs.

Offshore, the Macleans held the islands of Mull, Coll, Tiree, Luing, Scarba, the northern half of Jura and part of Islay. Of this island empire, Mull was the most important territory. It is the third largest Hebridean island, after Skye and Lewis, with an area of about 350 square miles (including its satellite islets, of which there are more than 400). The climate is wet, but mild, and the soil is fertile and provides good pasture; the island was always rich in cattle. Ben More, in the west of the island, rises to 3,169ft. Crofting and fishing provided the islanders' livelihood and there is still a salmon fishing station today at Caliach

Duart Castle, the ancient stronghold of the Maclean chiefs, is situated on the most easterly point of Mull.

Maclean of Duart

MOTTO: Virtue mine honour
GAELIC NAME: Clann Ghilleathain
WARCRY: *Beatha no Bàs!* (Life or death), *Fear eil airson Eachainn!* (Another for Hector)
PLANT BADGE: Crowberry
PIPE MUSIC: The Maclean's March

Point, in the north-western extremity of Mull (on a minor road beyond Calgary). The capital is Tobermory (Tobar Mhoire, meaning the Well of Mary), but the ancient stronghold of the chief is Duart Castle on the most easterly point of the island (off the A849 road). Moy Castle, now a ruin, beside the village of Lochbuie, was the stronghold of the chieftains of that branch.

Mull contains many other relics of Maclean power. On the north-east shore of Loch Spelve are the remains of the slipways for Maclean of Duart's fleet of war-galleys and on the road between Salen and Gribun (B8035), 6 miles from Salen, is the lucky stone on which the Macleans sharpened their swords before battle, the groove worn by the blades having by now become a deep cleft. Most important of all, off the south-western peninsula called the Ross of Mull (featured in R. L. Stevenson's *Kidnapped*), is the sacred monastic island of Iona. The island of Ulva, off the west coast of Mull, was something of a curiosity in the midst of this Maclean archipelago, being held in semi-independence by the Macquarries, though they naturally followed the Macleans in war. North-west of Mull are the Maclean islands of Coll and Tiree. These are flat and fertile by Hebridean standards. Breachacha Castle, a ruin on the shore of the sea-loch of the same name, on the south coast of Coll, was the stronghold of Maclean of Coll, who received Dr Johnson and Boswell there in 1773. The Maclean country in Jura comprised the area to the north of the narrow isthmus between Loch Tarbert and the Sound of Jura; in Islay the Macleans were restricted to the small western peninsula known as the Rhinns of Islay. Altogether, this was a large and populous territory occupied by thousands of clansmen.

The Macleans of Duart were the senior line. Lachlan Lùbanach was succeeded about 1405 by his son Eachan Ruadh nan Cath (Red Hector of the Battles) who was killed at the Battle of Harlaw in 1411, during a deadly man-to-man duel with Irvine of Drum who was also slain by Maclean's dying stroke. Red Hector's son, Lachlan Bronnach (the Big-bellied), had several sons, among them the progenitors of the branches of Ardgour and

Moy Castle, in the south of Mull, was the seat of the Maclaines of Lochbuie.

Tobermory Bay, where a treasure-laden galleon from the Spanish Armada sank in 1588, apparently blown up by a Maclean.

Ben More, Mull. Whenever a Maclaine of Lochbuie is about to die, it is said that a headless ghost of one of their ancestors rides through Glen More.

Maclaine of Lochbuie

CREST BADGE: A battleaxe in pale with two branches in saltire, dexter a laurel, sinister a cypress, all proper
MOTTO: *Vincere vel mori* (To conquer or die)
PLANT BADGE: Blaeberry
PIPE MUSIC: Lament for Maclaine of Lochbuie

Coll; his grandson, Hector Odhar (Sallow Hector), 10th of Duart, was killed at Flodden (1513). This chief's natural son, Lachlan Cattanach (so called because he had been brought up among the Clan Chattan), married a daughter of the Earl of Argyll, with disastrous consequences. According to tradition, he eventually marooned his wife, whom he hated, on the Lady's Rock, at the northern end of the Firth of Lorn, between Duart Point and the southernmost tip of Lismore Island. In revenge, her brother, Sir John Campbell of Calder, murdered Maclean in Edinburgh in 1523.

By the sixteenth century, the Macleans were profiting hugely from the collapse of the Macdonald Lordship of the Isles; apart from the independence they now enjoyed, they felt strong enough to attack the Macdonalds' trade-routes in Jura and Islay. Sir Lachlan Mór Maclean (Lachlan the Great), 14th Chief of Duart, fought in the royal army against the Catholic lords at Glenlivet in 1594, but survived this defeat, only to be killed four years later in battle against the Macdonalds at Tràigh Ghruineard in Islay. Legend has it he was killed by a native of Jura called Dubhsìth, a dwarf whose services Maclean had contemptuously rejected; the dwarf was a fine archer who vengefully joined the Macdonalds and, from his perch in a tree, shot an arrow which slew Lachlan Mór.

It was during the chiefship of Lachlan Mór, in 1588, that the *Florencia*, a galleon belonging to the scattered Spanish Armada, was sunk off Tobermory. Apparently it was blown up by a Maclean who had gone on board to demand payment for the stores with which Lachlan Mór had supplied the Spaniards; the messenger was clapped in irons, but escaped and crippled the ship before it could sail. Some accounts estimate the *Florencia's* treasure at

The Abbey of Iona, the sacred monastic island beyond the Ross of Mull.

30 million ducats. Today it lies embedded in mud, maddeningly inaccessible, just 80 yards off Tobermory pier.

Lachlan Mór's grandson and namesake was created a baronet in 1631. He was a royalist who fought under Montrose, so that Argyll and his Covenanters laid waste the Maclean lands. In revenge, Sir Lachlan Maclean razed Castle Campbell (near Dollar) to the ground. His heir, Sir Hector, was killed fighting in the royal army at the Battle of Inverkeithing in 1651. This episode was the origin of the Maclean warcry. The chief, who was his enemies' constant target, was protected by eight successive gentlemen of his clan who were cut down in turn as they shielded him. When one fell, the next stepped forward, crying 'Another for Hector!' Sir Hector's grandson, Sir John, 4th baronet, fought at the head of his clan for the Stuarts at Killiecrankie and Sheriffmuir. A combination of debt and Jacobitism deprived Maclean of his lands, which were taken over by his enemy, the 1st Duke of Argyll. His son, Hector, was created Lord Maclean by the exiled Pretender, but was arrested before he could join Prince Charlie in 1745. The clan, however, fought at Culloden under Maclean of Drimnin. Duart Castle was occupied by the Hanoverian army and fell into ruin until it was repurchased and restored by Maclean of Duart in 1912. The principal cadet houses of Duart were Lehire, Brolas (now the chiefly line), Pennycross, Drimnin, Torloisk, and the Macleans of the Ross of Mull. The Barons Maclean of Sweden descended from a younger son of Sir Lachlan Mór of Duart.

The Maclaines of Lochbuie, also on Mull, whose distinctive spelling of the name dates from the late sixteenth century, were the most important branch after Duart. They have often disputed the seniority of the house of Duart, claiming that their ancestor, Hector Reaganach, was the elder brother, rather than Lachlan Lùbanach, the progenitor of Duart. They are still haunted by the ghost of their 5th Chieftain's son, Eòghann a' Chinn Bhig (Ewen of the Little Head), who was decapitated in battle in 1538. Whenever a Maclaine of Lochbuie is about to die, the headless ghost of Ewen on horseback is said to appear, riding through Glen More (now the route of the A849 road from Strathcoil to Pennyghael) as a warning to his kin. The house of Scallasdale was the most notable junior branch of Lochbuie.

The Macleans of Ardgour are descended from Lachlan Bronnach, 8th of Duart. They have been more fortunate in retaining their lands than other branches of the clan and their chieftain is still seated at Ardgour. In 1760, Hugh Maclean, 12th of Ardgour, was a Knight Companion of the Beggar's Benison, an ancient royal charity which had turned into the Scots version of the Hellfire Club. Cadet houses of Ardgour were the Macleans of Borreray, Treshnish, Inverscaddel and Blaich. Also descended from Lachlan Bronnach were the Macleans of Coll, whose cadet houses were Arnabost, Achnasaul, Muck, Drimnacross, Totaranald, Grishipol and Crossapol. Lachlan Maclean of Arnabost (1798-1848) was a distinguished Gaelic writer. Archibald Maclean, premier lieutenant of the Prussian Life Guards, who won the Iron Cross in the Franco-Prussian War, was descended from the family of Grishipol. The house of Achnasaul is the senior surviving cadet of Coll. The houses of Kingairloch and Dochgarroch descend from the Northern Macleans.

Today, the Chief of Clan Maclean is once more resident in Duart Castle; his Gaelic title is Mac'ill-Eathain. Of the lesser chieftains, Maclaine of Lochbuie is styled Mac'ill-Eathain Lochabhuidhe; Maclean of Ardgour, Mac-'ic-Eoghain; and Maclean of Coll, Mac-Iain-Abraich. The septs of Maclean of Duart are Clanachan, Garvie, Gillan, Gilzean, Lean, Macilduy, MacLergain, MacVeagh, MacVey and Rankin; Maclaine of Lochbuie sept names are MacCormick, MacFadyen, MacFadzean, MacGilvra (where there is a Mull connection), MacIlvora, MacPhadden and Patten. The clan badges are crowberry for Duart, blaeberry for Lochbuie and holly for Ardgour and Coll. The Clan Maclean warcries are *'Beatha no Bàs!'* ('Life or death!') and *'Fear eil' airson Eachainn!'* ('Another for Hector!'). Its Gaelic name is Clann Ghilleathain.

CLAN
MACLEOD

TECHNICALLY, THE MACLEODS ARE TWO SEPAR-
ate clans. Since, however, they descend from two
brothers, share the same patronymic and have historically occupied neighbouring territories, it is both reasonable
and practical to treat them as one family. Like Clan
Donald they are notable for having one foot on the
mainland and the other in the Hebrides. They have
further claims to fame in the rich legends and traditions
associated with their history — for example, the Fairy
Flag — and in the particularly close bond which united
them with their chiefs, even during the nineteenth-
century famines and clearances, when such loyalties had
been abandoned in many other clans.

The MacLeods are of Norse origin, descended from
Olav the Black, King of Man and the Isles from 1225 to
1237. One of Olav's sons by his third wife was called Leod.
As a youth, Leod was fostered in the household of Paal
Baalkeson, Sheriff of Skye under the Kings of Man.
When Baalkeson died in 1231, Leod inherited the lands of
Sleat, Trotternish, Waternish and Snizort in Skye, as well
as Harris and North Uist. From King Olav, his natural
father, Leod obtained Glenelg, on the mainland
adjoining Skye, and a portion of Lewis. He married the
heiress of MacArailt, the Norse governor of Dunvegan,
and so acquired the famous castle of that name in western
Skye. Leod, from whom the clan took its name, had four
sons, of whom the eldest were Tormod and Torquil.
Tormod was ancestor of the senior line, MacLeod of
MacLeod, the house of Harris and Dunvegan, known as
the Siol Thormoid (Descendants of Tormod); Torquil
was ancestor of the MacLeods of the Lewes, the house of
Lewis and Raasay, known as the Siol Thorcuil.

To deal first with the former, when Leod died around
1280, his heir Tormod had predeceased him, so that his
successor was his grandson, also called Tormod. His
patrimony was Leod's possessions in Skye, Harris and
two-thirds of Glenelg. He married Christina, sister of Sir
Alexander Fraser of Touch, Great Chamberlain of
Scotland, and was succeeded by his son Malcolm. David
II gave Malcolm MacLeod a charter of his lands in
Glenelg about 1342; his other lands were held from the

Lord of the Isles. The remaining one-third of Glenelg was
owned by the Frasers and there is a tradition that Malcolm
MacLeod was the lover of Fraser of Glenelg's wife.
Returning from a secret meeting with her, he is said to
have met and killed a savage bull, breaking off one of its
horns in the struggle. The horn is preserved at Dunvegan
and each MacLeod chief, on his succession, is supposed to
drain it of liquor in one draught — its capacity is half a
gallon!

In the time of Malcolm's grandson, William Cleireach
(the Clerk), the feud with the Frasers revived, while a
more serious attack by the Macdonalds endangered the
Siol Tormod's possessions in Harris and Skye. About
1391 the Macdonalds invaded Skye, only to be routed in a
pitched battle at the head of Loch Sligachan, on the
eastern shore, opposite Raasay. William's son, Ian Borb
(the Fierce), 6th Chief of the Siol Tormod, fought for the
Lord of the Isles at Harlaw in 1411, married a
granddaughter of the Earl of Douglas and reigned till
about 1442 when his son, William Dubh (the Black),
succeeded. William was drawn into the war between the
last Lord of the Isles and his bastard son Angus Òg, with
disastrous consequences. At the Battle of Bloody Bay, a
sea engagement fought in 1480 off the north coast of Mull
(between Ardmore Point and Tobermory), William
Dubh and many of his clansmen, as well as the heir of the
Siol Torquil, were slaughtered.

The lands which the Siol Tormod were defending were
far-flung and disconnected. They consisted, firstly, of
Harris — the peninsula to the south of Lewis — whose
northern frontier reached from Loch Resort to Ardvour-
lie on Loch Seaforth; the MacLeod territory included
Berneray and other islands in the Sound of Harris. In
Skye, the Siol Tormod held the western part of the island,
consisting of the districts of Dunvegan, Duirinish,
Bracadale and Minginish, i.e. south-west of a boundary
running eastward from Loch Bay to Mugeary, then south
to Loch Scavaig. This area included the 'far Cuillins' and
the island of Soay. On the mainland, MacLeod of
MacLeod continued to hold his ancient patrimony of
Glenelg, the peninsula between Loch Duich and Loch

Dunvegan Castle, the seat of the MacLeod of MacLeod.

The Black Cuillin rear jaggedly above the MacLeod lands in south-west Skye.

Macleod of Harris
MOTTO: Hold fast
GAELIC NAME: Clann Thormoid
PLANT BADGE: Juniper
PIPE MUSIC: Macleod's Praise

Hourn; the most northern part of it, however, on the shore of Loch Duich, was the property successively of Bissets, Frasers, Mackenzies and Macraes. As will be seen later, these lands of the Siol Tormod, though belonging to the senior line of MacLeod, were not so extensive as the territories of the more junior Siol Torquil. This was because of the reverses suffered by the Siol Tormod during the fifteenth century: Ian Borb had lost his part of North Uist in 1406, Sleat was lost in 1435 and Trotternish (in the north of Skye) in 1482.

About 1490 the Macdonalds laid waste Skye until checked by Alasdair Cròiteach (the Hump-backed), 8th Chief of MacLeod, at the Battle of Glendale. This costly victory, the greatest battle in MacLeod history, was attributed to the chief's mother having ordered the Fairy Flag to be unfurled. The flag, still preserved at Dunvegan, is of oriental origin. According to clan tradition, it may be flown on three occasions to save the MacLeods from disaster; so far it has been used twice. Alasdair Cròiteach also built the Fairy Tower at Dunvegan Castle and St Clement's Church at Rodel, on the southernmost tip of Harris (at the termination of the A859 road). He earned lasting fame by establishing the MacCrimmons, the greatest family of Scots pipers, at Boreraig on Loch Dunvegan, where a college of piping was founded.

In the sixteenth century, Tormod, 12th Chief of MacLeod, was a supporter of Mary Queen of Scots. His immediate enemies, however, were still the Macdonalds who, in 1580, raided Skye yet again and massacred the entire congregation in the church at Trumpan, whose ruin still stands near Ardmore Point (on the minor road, continuation of the B886, beyond Halistra). Tormod MacLeod at once counter-attacked and slaughtered the invaders at Trumpan Bay, where their galleys had become grounded at low tide, cutting off escape. His son Rory Mór (the Great), 15th Chief, failed to produce charters for his lands, as demanded by the Act of Parliament of 1597, so suffered forfeiture. He managed to retrieve the situation, however, though only by placing himself heavily in the debt of the Earl of Argyll. He gave

Slioch seen from across Loch Maree. The south side of the loch was settled by the MacLeods of Lewis.

The distant hills of Harris. The MacLeods of Harris descend from Tormod, son of Leod, son of Olav the Black, King of Man and the Isles.

such help as he could to his beleaguered kinsmen the Siol Torquil, who were being dispossessed in Lewis at this period, but he submitted to the statutes of Icolmkil, 1609, which brought the Isles firmly under the jurisdiction of James VI.

In 1626 Ian Mór (called 'Great' because of his size, not for any achievements) became chief. Though not ill-disposed towards Charles I, he refused to join Montrose, possibly because of his own Campbell connections. After his death in 1649, however, the MacLeods more than compensated for any previous backwardness in the Stuart cause. At the Battle of Worcester in 1651, the Siol Tormod was nearly wiped out, the whole MacLeod clan losing 700 men and being excused further military service by common consent of the other chiefs. Patrick Mór MacCrimmon, the great piper, who was presented to Charles II during the Worcester campaign, composed his famous pibroch 'I got a kiss of the king's hand' in commemoration of the occasion. After the Restoration, the MacLeods felt slighted by the king, who gave no tangible sign of gratitude, so that they refused to rise for James VII in 1689. MacLeod of Contullich, a Jacobite, was Tutor of Dunvegan, the title meaning regent of the clan, during the 'Fifteen, but kept his kinsmen out of the rising. The boy chief, Norman, 22nd of MacLeod, was created Baron MacLeod by the Old Chevalier in 1716, but during the 'Forty-five he took the Hanoverian side, being much under the influence of Forbes of Culloden.

Macleod of Lewis and Raasay

CREST BADGE AND MOTTO: same as Macleod of Harris
GAELIC NAME: Clann Thorcuil
PLANT BADGE: Red whortleberry

Ardvreck Castle, the MacLeod's stronghold in Assynt. Here Montrose was betrayed to the Covenanters after his defeat at Carbisdale in 1650.

Curiously, it was in the nineteenth century that the chiefs of the Siol Tormod possibly earned themselves greatest glory. The terrible times of the potato famine and the Clearances are a period that many clans would prefer to forget. For some, it marked the betrayal of thousand-year-old loyalties by their chiefs. It was not so with the MacLeods. In 1847, Norman, 25th Chief of MacLeod, fed nearly 7,000 people who were starving as a result of the potato famine. There was not a single death from starvation on his property, but he so impoverished himself that he had to let Dunvegan Castle and take a salaried post in London. Today, however, MacLeod of MacLeod is re-established at Dunvegan, where clan parliaments are held at regular intervals. The great castle stands at the head of the loch of the same name in western Skye (off the A864 road) and is a treasure-house of clan history.

The fortunes of the Siol Thorcuil, the MacLeods of Lewis, descended from Tormod's younger brother, were less happy. Torquil, from whom his house took its name, died during the reign of Robert the Bruce. His grandson, also Torquil, acquired the lands of Assynt in Sutherland by marriage with the MacNicol heiress in the time of David II. His son Roderick married the daughter of the Lord of the Isles and left two sons: Torquil, 6th of the Lewes, and Tormod, ancestor of the MacLeods of Assynt, Geanies and Cadboll. At the height of their power, the Siol Torquil held extensive territory. It consisted, firstly, of the whole of Lewis, though the most northerly part was occupied by Morrisons and the most westerly by Macaulays, under MacLeod superiority. Then there was the island of Raasay, between Skye and the mainland, where the chieftain lived at Brochel Castle, now a ruin, on the eastern shore. In Skye they held the district of Waternish, a narrow enclave between their Siol Tormod kinsmen and the Clan Donald country of Trotternish, with which Loch Snizort provided a natural boundary. On the mainland, they were settled in Assynt, where their stronghold was Ardvreck Castle, whose ruin still stands, 1½ miles from the head of Loch Assynt (A837 road). It was here that the great Montrose was betrayed into the hands of his enemies. A little to the south, they also held the Coigach peninsula. Their third and most southerly holding on the mainland was the Gairloch, bounded to the north-east by Loch Maree and on the south by a line running approximately from Diabaig on Loch Torridon to Kinlochewe.

Yet these broad lands were not destined to remain the patrimony of the Siol Torquil. In 1506, Torquil MacLeod, 8th of the Lewes, forfeited his estates which, however, were restored to his brother Malcolm in 1511. Malcolm's son, Roderick, 10th Chief, convinced of his wife's unfaithfulness, disinherited their son, Torquil Cononach, in favour of his son by a later marriage, Torquil Dubh. In the strife which followed, this Torquil was killed by his disinherited namesake. The tragic outcome of this internal dissension was the weakening and eventual dispossession of the MacLeods of Lewis. Torquil Cononach's daughter married Mackenzie, Tutor of Kintail, who first helped the MacLeods against the Fife Adventurers (a band of bloodthirsty colonists whom James VI had callously authorized to conquer Lewis), then seized the MacLeod inheritance for himself in 1610. The senior surviving male lines of the Siol Torquil since then have been MacLeod of Raasay, whose estate was sold in 1846 when the chieftain emigrated to Australia, and MacLeod of Cadboll.

The sept names of MacLeod of MacLeod and Harris (the Siol Thormoid) are MacCaig, MacClure, MacCrimmon, MacCuaig, MacHarold, Macraild and Norman; those of MacLeod of the Lewes (the Siol Thorcuil) are Callum (where there is a Raasay connection), Lewis, MacAskill, MacAulay (where there is a Lewis connection), MacNicol, Nicolson and Tolmie. The two branches of Clan MacLeod wear different tartans and have separate plant badges — juniper for MacLeod of MacLeod, red whortleberry for MacLeod of Lewis. MacLeod of MacLeod is styled in Gaelic by the simple patronymic MacLeòid, MacLeod of Raasay is known as Mac-'ille-Chaluim; for reasons already explained, the MacLeods of Harris are named Clann Thormoid, the MacLeods of Lewis are Clann Thorcuil.

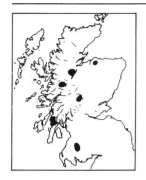

CLAN
MACMILLAN

THE MOST EXTRAORDINARY ASPECT OF THE MacMillans' history was their nomadic existence; few Scots families can have occupied such varied and widely distanced regions of the country. It has been suggested that they came originally from Ireland, though another theory traces their descent from the Siol O'Cain, an ancient Pictish tribe of Moray. The Buchanans and Munros have sometimes claimed them as a sept, but this notion is largely discredited and, if there is a connection, the MacMillans would appear to be the senior clan.

MacMillan, in Gaelic Mac Gille-Mhaoil, means 'Son of the Tonsured Servant' and commemorates descent from an old family of Celtic abbots. An Gillemaol, the Tonsured Servant, was living in 1132, when his name was listed as a witness in the Book of Deer, the oldest Scots religious record. At that time he was connected with a monastic community at Old Spynie, near Elgin. Shortly afterwards, David I overthrew the mormaership of Moray — the old-established Celtic jurisdiction — and settled the area with Norman feudal families. So the Tonsured Servant and his kin had to leave Old Spynie for Loch Arkaig in Lochaber, where they became known as Clann 'Illemhaoil Abrach (Clan MacMillan of Locha-ber). The Tonsured Servant had a son, Malcolm, who was mentioned in a document of 1150.

Ten years later, the MacMillans set out on their travels again when King Malcolm IV transplanted them from Loch Arkaig to Crown lands on Loch Tay in Perthshire. Here they settled at Lawers (now on the A827 road), mid-way along the north bank of Loch Tay, where they remained for two centuries. In 1306 Maolmuire MacMillan, great-grandson of Malcolm, sheltered the fugitive Bruce at Lawers. About 1360, however, the clan was moved on once more: Maolmuire's son, Malcolm Mór, was driven from Lawers by 'letters of fire and sword', on the orders of David II.

In this crisis the Clan MacMillan split up. Malcolm Mór and the chiefly line moved to Knapdale and became vassals of the Lord of the Isles. Knapdale is that strip of land immediately north of Kintyre, bounded on the north (in modern times) by the Crinan Canal and on the south

by the Tarbert isthmus. MacMillan's charter was engraved on a boulder standing at the Point of Knap which read:

'MacMillan's right to Knap shall be
As long as this rock withstands the sea.'

The rock was destroyed by Campbell of Calder in 1615. Malcolm Mór's grandson, Lachlan, was killed fighting for the Lord of the Isles at Harlaw in 1411; his son, Lachlan Òg, took part in the unsuccessful Douglas rebellion of 1455, but recouped his losses by marrying his son Alexander to a Macneill heiress who brought him Castle Sween (now a ruin, accessible by the unclassified road down the eastern shore of Loch Sween).

Alexander lost Castle Sween in 1481 when James IV conferred it, along with most of Knapdale, on the Earl of Argyll, drastically reducing the MacMillan lands. Yet Alexander left a striking memorial to his departed glory in MacMillan's Cross, a magnificent monument over 12 ft high, which stands beside the ruined chapel at Kilmory-Knap (between Castle Sween and Knap Point), bearing the inscription *Haec est crux Alexandri Mac Mulen* ('This is the cross of Alexander MacMillan'). His descendants retained only a small portion of land at Tiretigan (just south of Kilberry on the B8024 road). Even so, they were still harassed by the Campbells who had supplanted them.

Alexander's great-great-grandson, Malcolm MacMillan, supported the Macdonalds of Kintyre in their struggle against Campbell domination, with fatal consequences. In September 1615, Argyll ordered Sir John Campbell of Calder to annihilate the chiefly family. Only one of Malcolm's sons, Murachie, escaped the slaughter and passed on Tiretigan to his own son, known as MacMurachie. After killing a man who had tried to seduce his wife, MacMurachie fled overseas in 1665 and his hereditary enemies became the beneficiaries, Camp-bell of Lagg obtaining a charter of his lands. There is an unsubstantiated tradition that MacMurachie's descen-dants became connected by marriage with the French royal family. At home, the chiefship went to his cousin, Archibald MacMillan of Dunmore, who died in 1676. His

MacMillan, Dress

MOTTO: *Miseris succerrere disco* (I learn to succour the distressed)

ORIGIN OF NAME: Gaelic Mac Gille-Mhaoil, Son of the Tonsured Servant

GAELIC NAME: Clann Mhic 'Ille-Mhaoil

PLANT BADGE: Holly

MacMillan's Cross at Kilmory-Knap, a striking memorial to the MacMillans' lost power in Knapdale. It dates from the fifteenth century.

Ben Lawers on Loch Tay. The MacMillans were transplanted from Loch Arkaig to Lawers by Malcolm IV in the twelfth century.

son Alexander was coerced into joining Argyll's rebellion against James VII in 1685 and died in prison. His grandson, also Alexander, was Deputy Keeper of the Signet in the mid-eighteenth century and strongly anti-Jacobite. After his death in 1770 the chiefship passed to the Lagalgarve branch whose descendant, Lieutenant-General Sir Gordon MacMillan of MacMillan, was recognized by the Lord Lyon in 1951.

At the time of the migration from Loch Tay in 1360, scattered MacMillans established many junior branches. Some returned to Lochaber where, after two hundred years' absence, they attached themselves to Cameron of Lochiel and founded cadet houses of Glenpean, Glen Moriston and Murlagan. They fought for the Stuarts at Killiecrankie, but held back during the 'Forty-five, from distrust of the Pretender's religion. The MacMillans of Glen Urquhart, however, were 'out' with Grant of Glenmoriston and fought at Culloden. Hugh MacMillan was one of the Seven Men of Glen Moriston who guarded Prince Charlie (MacMillan was in fact the *eighth* man, legend having got its sums wrong). The chiefs of the Lochaber line emigrated to Canada in the early nineteenth century.

Another branch fled to Galloway in 1360, but lost most of their lands there a century later by supporting the Douglas uprising, like their cousins in Knapdale. They spread through Ayrshire, Galloway and Dumfriesshire, establishing cadet houses at Brochloch, Holm, Lamloch, Dalshangan and Arndarroch, in an area between Dalmellington and St John's Town of Dalry (on the western side of the present-day A713 road). The Brochloch family were well-known Covenanters. In 1825, Robert MacMillan of Holm married Mary Goldie, a great-great-granddaughter of Bonnie Annie Laurie. In 1836, a Dumfriesshire blacksmith named Kirkpatrick MacMillan invented the bicycle.

This far-flung clan also had lesser branches in Kintyre, Islay, Jura, Colonsay, Mull, Arran, Skye and the Outer Isles. The Rt. Hon. Harold Macmillan, Prime Minister from 1957 to 1963, was descended from the Arran branch. MacBaxter or Baxter is the principal sept name, derived from a MacMillan who, when pursued by his enemies, fled into the kitchen of Inveraray Castle where he disguised himself as a baker and was known ever after as Bacasdair (the baker). Other MacMillan septs are Bell, Blue, Brown (if connected with Kintyre), MacElmail, MacMoil, MacNucator and Walker. The clan badge is holly and its Gaelic name Clann Mhic 'Ille-Mhaoil.

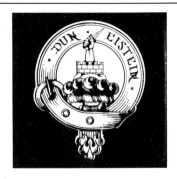

CLAN
MORRISON

TWO CHARACTERISTICS DISTINGUISH THE MORRISONS: their territory on the Isle of Lewis made them geographically the most remote Highland clan, and their hereditary office as Brehon judges gave them a peculiarly Celtic source of power which was not based on military strength. Due to their insular location they were never involved in national politics.

Originally, it appears that in the thirteenth century the heiress of Clan Gow — the hereditary armourers of Harris — married a man called Gillemhoire (Devotee of Mary), who was a natural son of Olav, the Norse King of Man and the Isles. There is a tradition that he was shipwrecked on Lewis, clinging to a piece of driftwood, which is the ancient clan badge. The early Morrison stronghold was a castle on the small island of Pabbay, 3½ miles north of Berneray in the Sound of Harris. The Dun of Pabbay eventually became a MacLeod fortress, but the Morrisons continued in their traditional craft as armourers in Harris.

Despite the antiquity of the Morrison line in Harris, it was the junior branch in Lewis which acquired most influence. At some time, probably late in the thirteenth century, their chief was granted the office of hereditary brieve of the island of Lewis. The brieve (*britheamh* in Gaelic) was a judge or arbiter to whom people appealed for adjudication in civil cases and who also had jurisdiction over minor criminal offences. When the Lordship of the Isles was abolished in 1493, the brieve's powers became correspondingly greater. From their tenure of the office the Morrisons of Lewis were also known as Clann Breitheamh. Their chief, the brieve, lived at Habost (on the main A857 road), towards the northernmost tip of the island — the Butt of Lewis.

Although the brieve was styled Morrison of Habost and Barvas, from his principal land-holdings, the clan's greatest stronghold was Dun Eistein, a sea-lashed castle north of Port of Ness (the nearest access road to its site is the B8014). This fortress testified to the importance of Clan Morrison, whose influence was increased by judicious marriages. In 1346 the Morrison heiress married Ceadhain Macdonald of Ardnamurchan and

Morrison
MOTTO: *Dùn Eistein* (Castle Eistein)
GAELIC NAME: Clann Mhic 'Ille-Mhoire
WARCRY: *Dùn Eistein!*
PLANT BADGE: Driftwood

The Butt of Lewis, *the most northerly point of the Morrisons' remote island home.*

insisted that he adopt her name. The chiefly line thus became related to the Lord of the Isles and, even after that jurisdiction was ended, maintained a friendship with the mighty Clan Donald, particularly with the Macdonells of Glengarry. Another profitable match gave the Morrisons a foothold on the Scottish mainland. In the fifteenth century, Hugh Morrison married the daughter of the Bishop of Caithness; as her dowry, she brought him the lands of Durness in Sutherland, where 60 Morrison families founded a new branch of the clan.

The Morrisons were one of the three clans who boasted themselves the original inhabitants of Lewis, the others being the MacLeods and Macaulays. Unfortunately, the Morrisons' relations with their two neighbouring clans deteriorated during the sixteenth century, beginning with a blood-feud with the Macaulays of Uig. Its origin was the killing of Donald Ban, brother of John Morrison of Habost, the brieve, by the Macaulays. When the brieve attacked the Macaulays in revenge, they were supported by the powerful MacLeods who defeated the Morrisons and overran Ness, the northern district of Lewis which was the brieve's territory. The succeeding brieve, Hucheon (Uisdean in Gaelic), also invaded North Harris, but was routed by the MacLeods on the island of Taransay; the brieve himself was the only Morrison survivor, saving his life by the remarkable feat of swimming, while wounded, 2 miles across the Sound of Taransay to the mainland of Harris.

Hucheon Morrison was not the kind of man to mend his ways and, not surprisingly, in 1551 he and Roderick MacLeod of Lewis were denounced by the government for sheltering rebels. The brieve, however, wrought the greatest mischief of his life as he lay on his death-bed, in August 1566: he confessed publicly that he was the real father of Roderick MacLeod's son, Torquil Cononach. The consequences were catastrophic. Roderick MacLeod disinherited Torquil Cononach, who sought help from his half-brother, the new brieve, Iain Dubh Morrison. Roderick was defeated and eventually, in 1577, forced by the Regent Morton to recognize his spurious son. Thereafter, MacLeod gradually recovered

the ground he had lost, so that when he died in 1595 he was able to bequeath a good part of his inheritance to his true son, Torquil Dubh, who declared war on the usurping Torquil Cononach. Iain Morrison, however, captured Torquil Dubh by treachery and handed him over to Torquil Cononach, who put him to death in 1597. Retribution came swiftly: the vengeful MacLeods and Macaulays drove the Morrisons from Lewis, to settle as refugees on the Scottish mainland.

There then followed a curious colonial episode. James VI granted a charter to a group of men called the Fife Adventurers, entitling them to pacify and colonize Lewis. The Morrisons joined with other Lewis clans in resisting the Adventurers, but Neil MacLeod, a natural son of the dead chief Roderick, went over to their enemies and turned the tide against them, so that the heads of a dozen leading Morrisons were soon decorating the walls of Edinburgh. Iain Dubh, the brieve, died at the hands of a MacLeod on the Scottish mainland in 1601. The Adventurers finally gave up their attempt to conquer Lewis and sold their rights to Roderick Mackenzie, Tutor of Kintail, who overthrew the MacLeods with the assistance of the Morrisons. The new brieve, Malcolm Mór Morrison, was killed in the struggle. Though restored to Lewis, the Morrisons were exhausted and powerless. In desperation, they allied themselves in 1616 with their old enemies, the MacLeods, in a rebellion against Mackenzie domination. Letters of fire and sword were granted to the Tutor of Kintail against Donald MacIndowie, the last brieve, and the ancient Morrison jurisdiction was extinguished.

The Morisons of Bognie and other east coast families have no connection with their Hebridean namesakes. There was a branch in Skye, however, one of whose members was John Morrison (1790-1852), a popular Gaelic poet. The senior surviving line is Morrison of Ruchdi, representing the Morrisons of the Dun of Pabbay. The clan's septs are Brieve, Gilmore, MacBrieve, Murison and any Smiths deriving from Harris; its slogan is '*Dùn Eistein!*', and its Gaelic name Clann Mhic 'Ille-Mhoire.

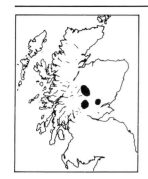

CLAN
MURRAY

AMONG THE UNUSUAL FEATURES OF THE MURRAYS' history are their former sovereignty of the Isle of Man, the exceptional number of peerages which they have acquired at various times and their privilege of maintaining one of the two legally permitted private armies in Britain. Blair Castle, the magnificent home of the Murray chief, the Duke of Atholl, is an imposing reminder of the clan's historic greatness.

From earliest times the Murrays boasted a royal origin. Their first known ancestor was the Flemish nobleman, Freskin, who was also progenitor of Clan Sutherland. He and his son were granted extensive lands in the province of Moray, newly conquered by the Scots kings, and probably intermarried with the old line of Celtic Mormaers of Moray. Freskin's grandson William assumed the name 'de Moravia' from these lands. William de Moravia's descendants became lords of Bothwell, their name changed to Moray or Murray by the end of the thirteenth century. To this line belonged Sir Andrew Murray, the great Scots patriot fatally wounded at the Battle of Stirling Bridge in 1297; after his death, Sir William Wallace assumed the leadership in the struggle for independence. Sir Andrew's posthumous son, also Sir Andrew Murray, married a sister of King Robert Bruce and was Regent of Scotland after his brother-in-law's death. The house of Murray of Bothwell became extinct about 1360.

The family of Moray of Abercairny claims descent from a younger son of Sir Andrew Murray the patriot, but this has never been definitely proved. Their estates are situated in Perthshire, near Crieff. The 1st Laird of Abercairny became Earl of Strathearn in 1344 by his marriage to Joanna, widow of the 7th Earl. His half-brother, Sir Alexander, succeeded him as 2nd Laird of Abercairny. During the Civil War this branch of Clan Murray was strongly royalist: William Moray, 10th of Abercairny, was a noted cavalier and his son, Robert, 11th Laird, was knighted by Charles II at the Restoration. The Murrays of Touchadam and Polmaise, in Stirlingshire, also claimed to belong to the senior line. They received a charter of Touchadam from David II in 1369 and became prominent in the county of Stirling. Sir William Murray, 6th of Touchadam, was killed at Flodden (1513); his grandson William acquired Polmaise by marriage to a Cunningham heiress in the sixteenth century. Three successive lairds represented Stirling in the Scots Parliament between 1609 and 1663.

The principal family, however, to which the chiefship of the Murrays unchallengeably belonged for most of the clan's history, was the house of Murray of Tullibardine. Sir Malcolm de Moravia, Sheriff of Perthshire, another descendant of Freskin, was succeeded before 1289 by his son William. This Sir William Murray obtained the lands of Tullibardine in Perthshire by marriage with Ada, daughter of Malise, Seneschal of Strathearn. His son Andrew sided with the Balliol faction in the War of Independence, helped defeat the Scots army at Dupplin in 1332, and was captured and executed for treason the following year. Andrew's grandson, Sir John Murray, added the lands of Pitcairlie in Fife to the estate of Tullibardine. In 1444, Sir David Murray, 6th of Tullibardine, had a charter erecting his lands into a feudal barony; he also established a church at Tullibardine, was an auditor of the Exchequer and Keeper of Methven Castle. Of his 10 sons, William succeeded as 7th Laird of Tullibardine, and Patrick, the fifth son, was ancestor of the Earls of Dysart and the Murray baronets of Ochtertyre. William, 7th of Tullibardine, was Sheriff of Perth and Keeper of Doune Castle, a responsibility for which he received £20 per annum from 1456 to 1458. His second son, Sir Andrew Murray, was ancestor of the Earls of Mansfield; his eldest son and heir, Sir William, became 8th Laird of Tullibardine. During his chiefship the Murrays suffered an outrage at the hands of the Drummonds, who burned the church of Monivaird where Tullibardine's followers had sought sanctuary.

In 1525, the 8th Laird was succeeded by his grandson, Sir William Murray, one of the Protestant Lords of the Congregation who demanded that the Queen Regent, Mary of Guise, should evacuate her French garrisons from Scotland; he also signed the instructions to the Commissioners for the Treaty of Berwick. His son,

The Atholl Highlanders at Blair Castle. Blair is the seat of the Murray chief, the Duke of Atholl, who still commands his own private army.

Murray of Atholl

MOTTO: *Tout prêt* (Quite ready)
GAELIC NAME: Siol Mhoireach
PLANT BADGE: Butcher's broom, juniper
PIPE MUSIC: Atholl Highlander

William, to whom he resigned his lands in 1560, was one of the leaders of the Reformation. He supported the marriage of Mary Queen of Scots to Darnley and became a Privy Councillor in 1565, but joined the faction opposed to Mary's second husband, Bothwell, and was one of the commanders of the rebel army at Carberry Hill (1567). Tullibardine approved of a proposal to execute Mary for Darnley's murder — a suggestion which was never carried out — and after the death of his brother-in-law, the Regent Mar, he became a joint-governor of the young James VI and Keeper of Stirling Castle. He died in 1583, the first Murray chief to play a prominent part in national politics.

The Murrays of Tullibardine, however, were firstly chiefs of a Highland clan; it was this important role which provided them with a power base. Their territory was Atholl in northern Perthshire, an area which comprehends every variety of Scots landscape — mountains, glens, lochs, forests and rivers. The most fertile and highly populated area is around Blair Atholl, about 7 miles north-west of Pitlochry (on the A9), which is watered by the River Garry. This country has always abounded in deer and game of all kinds, and in ancient times the Atholl Forest enjoyed special privileges and immunities. Blair Castle, seat of the Murray chiefs, stands less than a mile north-west of the village of Blair Atholl. This splendid fortress is one of the most striking in all Scotland and Cumming's Tower, the oldest part, dates back to 1269. Blair originally belonged to the Stewarts of Balvenie and came to the Murrays through marriage in the seventeenth century. The castle's history is especially rich in royal visitors: Edward III of England, Mary Queen of Scots, Bonnie Prince Charlie, and Queen Victoria and Prince Albert all stayed there. Larches, firs and beeches all around testify to the success of forestry in the district.

Although this area was the seat of the chief and the place where those of the Murray name lived as a Highland clan (with many Stewarts and Robertsons following the same banner), the Murray lands and cadet houses were scattered throughout Scotland. There were three Murray settlements around the River Tweed, including the

Doune Castle. In the fifteenth century, William Murray of Tullibardine was Keeper of this great fortress that guards the entrance to the Highlands.

The magnificent interior of Scone Palace, seat of the Earls of Mansfield, one of the senior cadets of Atholl.

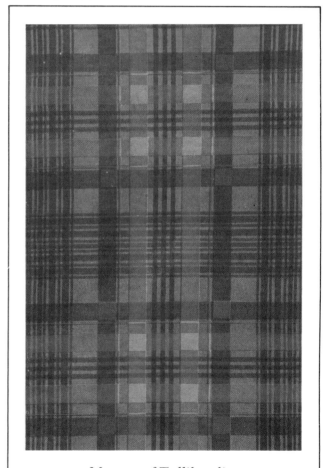

Murray of Tullibardine

CREST BADGE AND MOTTO: same as Murray of Atholl
GAELIC NAME: Siol Mhoireach

houses of Blackbarony and Elibank; in Dumfriesshire the Murrays of Cockpool became Earls of Annandale (extinct in 1658). It was in 1586 that the various branches first signed a bond recognizing Murray of Tullibardine as chief of Clan Murray. So, just three years after the death of his father (the Reformation leader), Sir John Murray, 11th of Tullibardine, found his authority augmented by this gesture of clan loyalty. In 1595, when the Highland chiefs were obliged to 'find caution' for the behaviour of their followers, Tullibardine had to raise £10,000, a testimony to his importance. He was created Lord Murray of Tullibardine in 1604 and Earl of Tullibardine in 1606.

William, 2nd Earl of Tullibardine, earned the favour of James VI by the part he had played as a young man in crushing the Gowrie Conspiracy in 1600, being rewarded with the hereditary office of Sheriff of Perthshire. He married Dorothea, heiress of the Earl of Atholl, and persuaded Charles I to revive the earldom of Atholl for his son John; the earldom of Tullibardine was relegated to his younger brother's line and became extinct in 1670. John, 1st Earl of Atholl, raised the Murrays for the king on the outbreak of the Civil War, but died in 1642 before he could perform any significant service. His son John, 2nd Earl of Atholl, took part in a rising on behalf of the exiled Charles II and resisted Cromwell's government until 1654. After the Restoration he was active against the Covenanters, and in 1676 he was created Marquess of Atholl. Two years later he joined 'the Highland Host' which harried the Whigs in western Scotland, and he

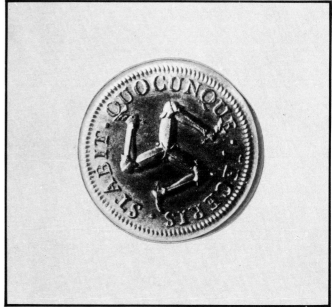

Murray coinage for the Isle of Man. From 1736 till 1765 the Dukes of Atholl held the sovereignty of the Isle of Man.

fought in the royal army at the Battle of Bothwell Brig (1679). The Marquess of Atholl also put down Argyll's rebellion in 1685 and was one of the founder Knights of the Thistle appointed by James VII. Since he was kept prisoner in 1689, he could not join Dundee, though his third son, James Murray of Dowally, led the Athollmen in the Jacobite army. Charles, his second son, was created Earl of Dunmore; his eldest son and heir, John, 2nd Marquess, was created Duke of Atholl a few weeks after succeeding to the chiefship.

The 1st Duke of Atholl was well-disposed towards William of Orange, but became disillusioned with Queen Anne's government over the Act of Union of 1707, which he opposed. His heir was killed at the Battle of Malplaquet (1709), whereupon the second son, William, Marquess of Tullibardine, should have been next in line for the dukedom. He was a fanatical Jacobite, however, and was attainted in 1715 for proclaiming James VIII and joining Mar's rising; the following year he escaped to France. In 1717 the Old Chevalier tried to compensate him for the loss of the dukedom of Atholl by creating him Duke of Rannoch in the Jacobite peerage. In 1719 Tullibardine returned to Scotland with a force of Spaniards, but was defeated at Glenshiel. A reward of £2,000 was offered for his capture, but he again escaped and lived abroad under the alias of Kateson. In 1745 the 56-year-old Marquess was given the honour of unfurling Prince Charlie's standard at Glenfinnan and, 12 days later, of receiving the prince at Blair Castle. After Culloden, it was third time unlucky for Tullibardine—he was captured and sent to the Tower of London where he died a prisoner in July 1746.

Tullibardine's younger brother, Lord George Murray, played a more important part in the 'Forty-five. He had been 'out' in the 'Fifteen and the 'Nineteen, but received a pardon in 1724. Having joined Prince Charlie in 1745, he served as Lieutenant-General of the Jacobite army throughout the campaign, though ill-feeling between himself and the prince contributed to the failure of the rebellion. The Chevalier Johnstone wrote that 'had Prince Charles slept during the whole of the expedition,

and allowed Lord George Murray to act for him according to his own judgment, he would have found the crown of Great Britain on his head when he awoke'. After Culloden, where he commanded the right wing, Lord George Murray was a fugitive for eight months, before escaping to Holland. The Atholl Highlanders, who fought at Culloden, have the distinction of being the only unit of the Jacobite army surviving today. They are regularly reviewed by the Duke of Atholl at Blair Castle, about the last Sunday in May (an event that draws many spectators), and they are one of only two forces exempted from the laws banning private armies in Britain. In 1845, a century after they last rose for the Stuarts, Queen Victoria presented them with colours, thus marking their reconciliation with the new dynasty. Besides having their own bodyguard, the Dukes of Atholl were also briefly distinguished by possessing a small kingdom. In 1736, the 2nd Duke inherited, through his grandmother, Lady Amelia Stanley, the sovereignty of the Isle of Man, with the privilege of striking his own coinage; the 3rd Duke surrendered it to the British government for £70,000 in 1765.

A less creditable part was played in the Jacobite cause by Sir John Murray of Broughton, the traitor who, having been secretary to Prince Charlie during the campaign, turned king's evidence against his fellow rebels. In later years he had cause to visit Sir Walter Scott's father on legal business, and during the visit he drank a dish of tea; after he had left, the elder Scott threw the china cup out of the window, remarking, 'Neither lip of me nor of mine comes after Murray of Broughton's'. In addition to the branches referred to above, mention should be made of the Earl of Mansfield, one of the senior cadets of Atholl. Lord Mansfield's seat is Scone Palace, at Old Scone, 2 miles north of Perth (on the A93), on the site where the ancient Kings of Scots were crowned.

As chief of the Murrays the Duke of Atholl is styled Am Moireach Mór. The sept names are MacMurray, Moray, Small, Spalding and Rattray. Clan Murray's plant badges are butcher's broom and juniper; its Gaelic name is the Siol Mhoireach.

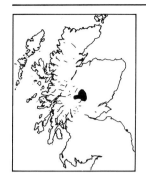

CLAN
ROBERTSON

THIS CLAN IS COMMONLY REFERRED TO, EVEN IN English, as Clan Donnachaidh, because the family of Duncan or Duncanson are also full members of it, their patronymic being more ancient than the surname Robertson. Of high lineage themselves, the Robertsons were distinguished down the centuries by their steadfast loyalty to the royal house of Stuart. All the elements which make the colourful histories of the Highland clans so fascinating are to be found in the annals of the Robertsons; their exceptional loyalty to the Crown, far back in the Middle Ages, is commemorated by a special supporter in their chief's coat of arms.

The ancestors of Clan Robertson were the ancient Celtic Earls of Atholl. Henry, 3rd Earl, left a son called Conan of Glenerochty whose descendants bore the designation 'de Atholia' until the time of his great-great-grandson, Duncan Reamhar (the Sturdy). This Duncan brought his clansmen to fight for Bruce at Bannockburn and there is an old tradition that, after the battle, the king told them: 'Hitherto ye have been called the sons of Duncan' (a reference to their remote ancestor, not their contemporary chief), 'but henceforth ye shall be called my children'. While this pleasing legend cannot be discounted, it is also possible that the modern surname derived from Robert, the 4th Chief. Duncan Reamhar is said to have been taken prisoner by the English at the Battle of Durham, or Nevill's Cross (1346), and he was described as Earl of Atholl in a charter of David II. He died about 1355, leaving two sons: Robert, from whom descended the chiefly line of Struan, and Patrick, ancestor of the house of Lude. Robert's grandson, also named Robert and distinguished by the nickname Riabhach (the Grizzled), gained royal favour in February 1437 by capturing Sir Robert Graham, the regicide. Graham had murdered James I in the Blackfriars at Perth and was tortured to death for this crime; years later, in 1451, when he came of age, James II rewarded Robert Riabhach by erecting his lands of Struan into a feudal barony and by granting him the privilege of an extra supporter beneath the shield bearing his arms — a naked man in chains, to commemorate the capture of Sir Robert

Graham. Robert Riabhach was killed in battle, around 1460, when his son Alexander became 5th Chief; a younger son, Robert, was ancestor of the Earls of Portmore. At this period the clan was involved in a feud with the Bishop of Dunkeld over their rights to the lands of Little Dunkeld. Yet, despite this threat to their territorial integrity, the Robertsons were also building up an impressive network of cadet houses.

From the house of Lude, mentioned above, there also descended the Robertsons or Reids of Straloch, known as the Barons Reid. Unlike the rest of the clan, the Barons Reid became Whigs; the last of the line was General John Reid, who composed the famous Black Watch march 'The Garb of Old Gaul'. Of the sons of Alexander, 5th Chief of Clan Donnachaidh, Andrew was ancestor of the houses of Killichangy, Ladykirk, Eastertyre and Edradynate; James was ancestor of the house of Auchleeks (now Dundas Robertson); and Alexander was ancestor of the lines of Faskally and Kindrochit. Since his heir had predeceased him, the 5th Chief was succeeded in 1506 by his grandson William. By now the Robertsons' feud was not with the Bishop of Dunkeld, but a much more formidable enemy, the Stewart Earls of Atholl. The cause of the quarrel was the eagerness of successive Earls to acquire as much as possible of the Robertsons' large land-holding in Atholl.

The Robertson lands were concentrated in three main areas. Firstly, there was an extensive strip of territory bounded on the west by Rannoch Moor and running eastwards for about 22 miles, confined on the north by the River Gaur and Loch Rannoch, on the south by Glen Lyon; skirting the western extremity of Loch Tummel, it then turned northwards for about 13 miles, as far as Dail-na-Mine Forest, the Pass of Drumochter and Loch Garry marking its western frontier, and with the Earl of Atholl's lands beyond the Bruar Water as its eastern boundary. The next largest parcel of Robertson land was in the area south-east of the River Tilt, approximately 8 miles in both length and breadth; it was much eroded and interspersed, however, with pockets of Stewart and Murray land and the Earls of Atholl held the feudal

Schiehallion, one of the most beautiful mountains in Scotland, rises gracefully above the Robertson lands on the south of Loch Rannoch.

Dunkeld Cathedral. In the fifteenth century the Robertsons were involved in a feud with the Bishop of Dunkeld over their rights to the lands of Little Dunkeld.

superiority of many of the Robertsons' properties in eastern Atholl. Further south, there was a third enclave of Robertson country on the south bank of the Tay, between Grandtully and Dunkeld. The earliest residence of the chief was a castle called Invervack, but the great seat of Robertson of Struan in the days of the clan's prosperity was Dun Alastair, on the north bank of the River Tummel, about 3 miles west of Tummel Bridge (on the B846); this estate passed out of Robertson hands in 1853. A later chiefly residence was Rannoch Barracks, at the western end of Loch Rannoch, built originally by the government to hold down the Jacobite Clan Robertson,

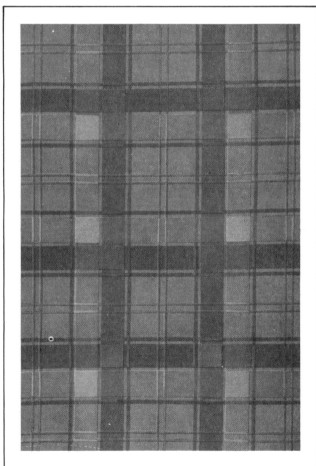

Robertson

MOTTO: *Virtutis gloria merces* (Glory is the reward of valour)
GAELIC NAME: Clann Dhonnachaidh
WARCRY: *Garg'n uair dhuisgear!* (Fierce when roused)
PLANT BADGE: Bracken
PIPE MUSIC: *Teachd Clann Dhonnachaidh*
(The Clan Donnachie has arrived)

A winter scene near Blair Atholl. The ancestors of Clan Robertson were the ancient Celtic Earls of Atholl.

but later acquired by the chief and converted into a private house.

The feud with the Atholl Stewarts proved fatal to William, the 6th Chief, who was killed while trying to recover a large portion of his inheritance which the Earl of Atholl, his kinsman and guardian during his minority, had appropriated in payment of debts owed him. The murdered chief's son and heir, Robert, was faced with another problem — the depredations of the notorious MacGregor clan, who actually took him prisoner in 1545. William, 8th Chief, was confirmed in the barony of Struan

by the Regent, Mary of Guise, in 1546; he too was murdered, in 1587, when his brother Donald inherited the chiefship. Throughout this period, debt, rather than armed aggression, increasingly threatened the Robertsons' tenure of their lands. Things came to a crisis at the end of the sixteenth century when the embarrassed 10th Chief had to be rescued financially by a loyal clansman who had made a fortune as a merchant in Edinburgh — a striking example of the unselfish devotion which Highlanders could exhibit towards their chief, who held his land on behalf of the whole clan. By 1600 the chief's

The Drumochter Pass, now traversed by the main road to Inverness, takes the traveller north from the Robertson lands into the valley of the Spey.

affairs must have improved considerably, for in that year he added the lands of Kinloch, Muirlagen and others to the Struan barony.

When the Civil War broke out in the seventeenth century, Struan Robertson (like Cluny Macpherson, the Robertson chief was customarily described by his estate preceding his surname) was a minor. So the clan was led 'out' to join Montrose in 1644 by the chief's uncle, Donald Robertson, Tutor of Struan; they were the first to rally to the royalist cause. The Tutor particularly distinguished himself at the Battle of Inverlochy and gave all the money he could raise to the king's forces. He was thanked by the exiled Charles II by a letter in the king's own hand, and rose again in 1653 at the time of Glencairn's abortive royalist rebellion, joined this time by the young chief. It was the same story at the Revolution in 1689. Again the Struan Robertson of the day was a young man who had just succeeded to the title, being an undergraduate at St Andrews University. Yet this was no ordinary youth, but the most brilliant of all Robertson chiefs, Alexander, 13th of Struan, known as 'The Poet Chief' because of his literary talent. With 700 clansmen he joined the Jacobite army, just too late to fight at Killiecrankie, but serving the rest of the campaign against Mackay, the Williamite general. For this loyalty to James VII, young Alexander was attainted, his estates were forfeited and he was forced to go into exile in France.

In 1704, however, with the more lenient Queen Anne on the throne, the chief was allowed to return to Scotland, though the formalities for pardoning him were never completed, due to his scrupulous refusal to take any oath to the usurping sovereign. During the 'Fifteen he was again in arms for the Stuart cause, commanding a battalion at the Battle of Sheriffmuir. On this occasion his poetic nature and love of tradition prompted him to carry the *Clach na Brataich* (Ensign Stone), the piece of rock crystal worn in ancient times by Robertson chiefs as a protection in battle. Although he survived Sheriffmuir, Alexander was taken prisoner until rescued by his kinsman Robert Bàn Robertson of Invervack. Later, however, he was again captured, only to escape a second time and find refuge in France. In 1725 he was created a baronet by the exiled James VIII, and the following year he returned to Scotland under remission for treason, though again without taking an oath of allegiance to the Hanoverian dynasty. When Bonnie Prince Charlie set up his standard in 1745, the now aged Struan Robertson joined him and fought at Prestonpans. After the battle, being too old for an extended campaign, he gave command of the clan to Robertson of Woodsheal and returned home triumphantly in General Sir John Cope's captured coach. He died peacefully in 1749 and his poems were published posthumously.

The 13th Chief's heir, Duncan Robertson of Drumachuine, was debarred from inheriting the Struan estate because of his complicity in the 'Forty-five Rebellion. His son Alexander, however, regained it in 1784; at his death in 1822, the chiefship passed to the Woodsheal line where it continues today. The Robertson chiefs did not evict their clansmen during the Highland Clearances, preferring to sell their own land instead. Since the nineteenth century, the chiefs have lived in Jamaica, though carefully retaining links with Scotland; Rannoch Barracks remained their property until 1926. The Robertsons of Inshes, in Inverness-shire, descend from the same stock as the Robertsons of Atholl; the house of Kindeace is in turn a cadet of Inshes. Clansmen who have distinguished themselves include Field-Marshal Sir William Robertson (1860-1933), whose son was created Lord Robertson of Oakridge. Also belonging to Clan Donnachaidh was Admiral Viscount Duncan (1731-1804), a naval hero, whose son was created Earl of Camperdown in 1831.

Struan Robertson's patronymic is Donnachadh reamhar MacAonghais and his heir bears the designation Robertson of Drumachuine. Clan Robertson sept names are Collier, Donachie, Duncan, Duncanson, Dunnachie, Inches, MacDonachie, Macinroy, Maclagan, MacRobbie, MacRobert, Reid, Roy and Stark. The clan plant badge is bracken and its warcry is 'Garg'n uair dhuisgear!' ('Fierce when roused!'). As explained above, its Gaelic name is Clann Dhonnachaidh.

CLAN
ROSS

THE FORTUNES OF THE ROSSES WERE FOUNDED on their ability in different generations to sense the mood of the times and align themselves with the prevailing faction. This adaptability enabled them to weather storms which proved fatal to more conservative clans. They supported successively the extension of the power of the Scots crown to the north, the cause of Bruce, the Reformation, the Covenant, the Revolution and the Hanoverian dynasty.

The clan derives its name from the old Celtic earldom of Ross. Fearchar Mac an t-Sagairt (Farquhar, Son of the Priest) was head of the ancient house of O'Beolain in Wester Ross, hereditary lay lords of the vast lands of the Abbey of Applecross, which had been founded by St Maelrubha in the seventh century. In 1215 a rebellion against the newly-introduced feudal system broke out in Moray and Ross, a formidable challenge to the authority of King Alexander II. Farquhar of Applecross put down the revolt and was knighted as a reward. By 1226 he had been made Earl of Ross, the name coming from the Gaelic word *ros*, meaning a promontory; the headland in question was the peninsula between the Dornoch and Cromarty Firths, which now became the principal land-holding of the O'Beolain earls.

Farquhar, Earl of Ross, founded a Praemonstratensian abbey in the parish of Edderton. Later, in 1338, it moved to Fearn (on the road to Balintore, B9165/6) where, after the Reformation, it became the parish church, now restored after a roof collapse in 1742 which killed 44 people. Patrick Hamilton, the Protestant reformer burnt at the stake in 1528, was titular Abbot of Fearn. An even more sacred place in the Ross country, however, was the chapel of St Duthac at Tain, on the southern shore of the Dornoch Firth, through which the main east coast road (A9) passes. In this chapel, now a ruin, was preserved the sacred shirt of St Duthac, worn for protection in battle by the Earls of Ross. The Scots kings also made regular pilgrimages there — annually in the case of James IV — and it was visited as late as 1527 by James V.

Earl Farquhar died in 1251 and was succeeded by his son William, who conquered Skye and Lewis. His son, also called William, became earl in 1274 and later fought in the Wars of Independence. In 1306, to his mortification, he was forced to violate the shrine of St Duthac by handing over Bruce's wife and daughter, who had sought sanctuary there, to the English. Bruce not only forgave this act of collaboration, but eventually gave his sister, Lady Maud, in marriage to the earl's son Hugh. The earl died in 1322, having fought for Bruce at Bannockburn and been a signatory of the Declaration of Arbroath. His son Hugh, 4th Earl of Ross, was killed at Halidon Hill in 1333, the shirt of St Duthac, which was found on his body, proving inadequate protection.

When Hugh's son William, 5th Earl, died in 1372 he left only a daughter, Euphemia, who brought the earldom of Ross into Clan Leslie by marriage. The Ross chiefship, however, devolved upon William Ross, 2nd of Balnagown, son of the earl's half-brother, Hugh of Rarichies and Balnagown. To advertise their descent from the O'Beolain earls, the house of Balnagown and its dependents assumed the surname Ross. They continued vassals of the successive Leslie and Macdonald Earls of Ross until 1476, when the earldom was forfeited by the crown. The Rosses could not afford to be fastidious about their choice of allies, so that Walter, 3rd of Balnagown, married the daughter of a free-booter named Paul MacTyre who, for a time, was effectively chief. MacTyre, according to a chronicler, 'conquest all that he had through capitanrie and sworde. He reft Strahocill, Stratharron, and Fleschillis, with mekill of Sutherland; caused Cathnes pay him meikill black maill'.

From the fifteenth to the sixteenth century the Rosses were preoccupied with a feud against the Mackays of Strathnaver. This reached a disastrous climax in July 1486, when Alexander, 6th of Balnagown and 17 gentlemen of the clan were among those killed in battle at Allt a'Charrais, on the River Carron. At the Reformation, the clan embraced Protestantism, the chief's kinsman Nicolas Ross, Abbot of Fearn, voting with the reformers in the Parliament of 1560. In the following century, David Ross, 12th of Balnagown, signed the

The Dornoch Firth. *The* ros *or peninsula between the firths of Dornoch and Cromarty gave Clan Ross its name.*

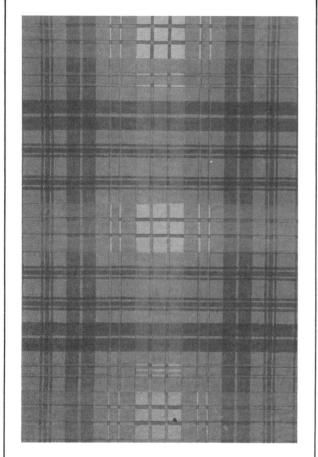

Ross

MOTTO: *Spem successus alit* (Success nourishes hope)
GAELIC NAME: Clann Rois
PLANT BADGE: Juniper
PIPE MUSIC: The Earl of Ross's March

The Cioch of Sgurr a Chaorachain, Applecross. *The ancestors of Clan Ross were hereditary lay lords of the vast lands of the Abbey of Applecross.*

Covenant and was with the force which defeated Montrose at Carbisdale. He later fought for Charles II at Worcester, died a prisoner in London in 1653 and was buried in Westminster Abbey.

His son David, 13th of Balnagown, who supported William and Mary in 1689, was the last of the direct line. At his death in 1711, he settled the Balnagown estate on the Renfrewshire family of Ross of Hawkhead, with whom he had no blood connection whatever. The Munro Rosses of Pitcalnie became the senior representatives of the old line. In both Jacobite rebellions the clan took the Whig side, though Young Pitcalnie was 'out' with the Pretender in 1745. The eighteenth-century Rosses also made a significant contribution to literature: Alexander Ross (1699-1784) was a notable writer of Scots verse, while William Ross (1762-90) was a considerable Gaelic poet, sometimes called 'the Burns of the Highlands'. During the Clearances in the nineteenth century, the clan suffered heavily and the violence used against women by police evicting tenants in Strathcarron in 1854 caused a public outcry.

The Rosses are distinguished by possibly the most important American connections of any Scots clan. As early as 1651 they were settled in Massachusetts. George Ross (of the Balblair family) was a signatory of the Declaration of Independence: 450 years earlier his ancestor had signed the Declaration of Arbroath, asserting Scots independence from England. His nephew's widow, Betsy Ross, made the first Stars-and-Stripes flag for General Washington. Senator James Ross (1762-1847), of Pennsylvania, was another close associate of Washington; Senator Edmund Gibson Ross (1826-1907), of Kansas, cast the deciding vote against impeachment which kept President Andrew Johnson in office. Many Rosses also achieved distinction in Canada, and in Prussia the Counts von Ross were famous soldiers.

Though no longer owned by the Ross chiefs, Balnagown Castle still stands half-way between Alness and Tain (A9). The Rosses of Shandwick appear to be the senior surviving line. Juniper is the clan badge. Its septs are Corbett, Denoon, Fern, MacCulloch, MacTaggart, MacTear, Mitchell, Tarrell and Vass. In Gaelic the name is Clann Rois.

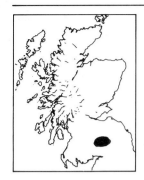

CLAN
SCOTT

THE SCOTTS TAKE THEIR NAME FROM THEIR NATION-
ality, and deservedly so: as guardians of the Middle
March—the central area of the Border—it was they who
repeatedly withstood the main thrust of English invasions
and, in turn, carried fire and sword southwards into the
enemy's country. In early times the name 'Scot' was
almost a title, restricted to men of high birth—a nephew
of King William the Lion, for example, was so styled. It is
from one such distinguished individual that the Clan Scott
descends.

Nothing is known of this shadowy Scot except that he
belonged to a family originally from Galloway, which had
possessed the lands of Scotstoun near Peebles since the
reign of Kenneth III. His son, Uchtred Fitz Scott,
witnessed charters of David I in 1128 and 1130. Richard
Scott, Uchtred's son, was living in 1158 and left two
offspring, Richard of Molle and Sir Michael; the latter
acquired estates in Fife and was ancestor of the Scotts of
Balweary and Ancrum. Richard of Molle, the heir, was
succeeded by his son William, who was mentioned in
many early thirteenth-century charters. It was in the time
of William's sons, Walter and Richard, that the family
emerged as important landowners with a growing
power-base in southern Scotland.

Both Walter and Richard Scott did fealty to Edward I
of England in 1296, their names appearing on the
Ragman Rolls. Walter of Scotstoun was the elder and his
descendants remained the senior line until they died out
50 years later. Richard, the younger brother, born about
1265, married the heiress of Murthockston, in Lanarkshire, and became owner of that estate. Later he was
appointed Ranger of Ettrick Forest, an office which
brought him the additional lands of Rankilburn or
Buccleuch in the county of Selkirk. (Though originally
called Rankilburn, the estate became popularly known as
Buccleuch, from the area where the laird built his
residence.) Richard died in 1320 and his son, Sir Michael
Scott, became 2nd Laird of Buccleuch and Murthockston. Sir Michael reversed his father's cautious policy and
proved a staunch supporter of Bruce and later of David II
against the Balliol faction. He distinguished himself at the

Scott

MOTTO: *Amo* (I love)
WARCRY: *A Bellendaine!, and Alemuir!*
PLANT BADGE: Blaeberry

The High Street of Edinburgh, where Sir Walter Scott of Buccleuch was murdered by his old enemies the Kerrs in 1552.

Abbotsford, the home Sir Walter Scott built himself on the banks of the Tweed.

Battle of Halidon Hill and was killed fighting at Durham in 1346, leaving two sons, Robert and John.

Robert inherited the Buccleuch and Murthockston estates, to which he added Scotstoun on the extinction of the senior line; John, his junior, founded the important cadet house of Synton, from which descended the Lords Polwarth. Robert, 3rd Laird of Buccleuch, died around 1389, possibly from wounds received at the Battle of Otterburn, and was succeeded by his son Sir Walter, 4th of Buccleuch (or Rankilburn, as it was still named in official documents). Sir Walter took part in the negotiations with the English at Haldane, in Roxburghshire, in 1398, when a vain attempt was made to establish peace on the Border. Four years after this effort failed, Sir Walter Scott, with many of his countrymen, fell at the disastrous Battle of Homildon Hill.

Robert, 5th Laird of Buccleuch, consolidated the land-holdings of the expanding Clan Scott. In 1415 he exchanged his lands of Glenkerry with the Abbot of Melrose, in return for the strategically important uplands of Bellenden. Then, in 1420, he acquired half of the lands of Branxholm. After his death in 1426, his son, Sir Walter, 6th of Buccleuch, further enlarged the family estates, notably in 1446 when he exchanged his secure lands of Murthockston for the remaining half of Branxholm, whose laird wished to rid himself of the liability of defending it from English raiders. Royal favour increased Sir Walter's prosperity when, in 1455, he routed the rebel Douglases at Arkinholm (the modern Langholm) and received various tracts of Douglas land as a reward. In 1463, his lands of Branxholm were erected into a feudal barony, held by annual payment to the Crown of a red rose as 'blench farm' on the feast of St John the Baptist. Sir Walter's younger brother founded the cadet house of Haining.

When Sir Walter Scott died in 1469, his son David became Laird of Buccleuch (the name Rankilburn had by then fallen into disuse) and Branxholm; David's younger brothers were ancestors of the Scotts of Howpasley and Hassendean. With the foundation of so many junior branches and such widespread land acquisitions, the

Scotts were now a powerful Border clan. From his castle of Branxholm on the River Teviot, 3 miles south-west of Hawick (on the A7), Scott of Buccleuch commanded a network of dependent lairds. Three miles west of Hawick lay Harden (the seat of Lord Polwarth, still standing) and 12 miles further west was Buccleuch itself. The area between Buccleuch and Hawick (traversed today by the B711 road) was the geographical centre of Scott power; here was Bellenden, the gathering-place of the clan and origin of its warcry 'A Bellendaine!' which was also displayed on Buccleuch's standard. The secondary slogan 'Alemuir!' is the name of a small loch nearby.

Other Scott strongholds were Howpasley (further south, at the head of the Borthwick Water), Hassendean (whose site was near the junction of the B6359 and B6405 roads, 4 miles north-east of Hawick) and Synton, 4 miles south of Selkirk (on the east side of the A7). Further cadet houses of Foulshiels, Tushielaw, Haining, Allanhaugh and many others increased Buccleuch's influence with each generation. This power received recognition in 1470 when the Earl of Angus appointed David Scott of Buccleuch as governor of Hermitage Castle, a great Border fortress whose impressive ruin still stands (west of the B6399 road, about 14 miles south of Hawick). Since Hermitage was situated in Liddesdale, its guardianship signalized the extension of Buccleuch's authority beyond his native Teviotdale. In further testimony to his importance, Buccleuch's son, who predeceased him, married Lady Jane Douglas, sister of Archibald Bell-the-Cat, 5th Earl of Angus. Despite this marriage connection, Buccleuch supported James III throughout his reign, even against Angus and his party.

David Scott died in 1492. His grandson and heir, Sir Walter, 8th Laird, lived partly at Buccleuch, but increasingly favoured Branxholm as his principal seat. Wicked Wat, his son, who became 9th Laird of Buccleuch in 1504, was the most famous chief of Clan Scott. As a young man he was knighted at the Battle of Flodden in 1513, which he survived. Then he was made hereditary Bailie — or protector — of the Abbey of Melrose, an office which was to prove more of a liability than an asset,

Sir Walter Scott with his literary friends at Abbotsford. The great novelist was a descendant of the Scotts of Raeburn.

in view of the increasing incursions by English raiders. The sixteenth century was the worst period of Border warfare, with Scotland weakened by the succession of three consecutive child sovereigns, as well as being torn apart by religious dissension. Clan feuds provided an additional source of discord and none was more bitter than that between the Scotts of Buccleuch and the Kerrs of Cessford. In 1524, therefore, as a precautionary measure, the Queen-Dowager Margaret clapped both Buccleuch and Cessford into prison, explaining to the Duke of Norfolk: 'I thought best to put them both in the Castle of Edinburgh, until that they find a way how the borders may be well ruled, seeing it is in their hands to do and they will, and not to let them break the borders for their evil will among themselves.' A week later Buccleuch escaped and joined the party of nobles opposed to Queen Margaret.

The lawlessness of the Borders, however, was now a major concern of both the Scots and English governments, as well as of the Church. So, in 1524-25, the Archbishop of Glasgow and the Bishop of Durham respectively excommunicated the reivers on each side of the frontier. The Archbishop of Glasgow in particular expressed himself in language the Borderers would understand: 'I curse their head, and all the hairs of their head; I curse their face, their een, their mouth . . . I curse them gangand, I curse them riding; I curse them sitting, and I curse them standing . . . I curse their wives, their bairns, and their servands participant with them in their deeds.' Undeterred, the Scotts and Kerrs continued their feud. On 25th July 1526, at Darnick, just west of Melrose, Buccleuch tried forcibly to liberate the young James V from the custody of the Earl of Angus. He failed, but in the fight one of his men killed Kerr of Cessford, thus aggravating the vendetta between the two families.

The Scott-Kerr feud was so damaging to the interests of both houses that a major effort was made to heal it in 1530 when Buccleuch took as his second wife Janet Kerr of Ferniehirst; at the same time a bond was drawn up whereby both parties agreed to make a pilgrimage to Scotland's four principal devotional centres — Scone,

Dundee, Paisley and Melrose — to pray for the souls of opponents killed at Darnick. Yet Buccleuch had other problems besides the Kerrs. The English burnt Branxholm in 1532, though the Scotts had their revenge in 1544 when they helped Arran defeat an English army at Ancrum Moor. Three years later the fortunes of war changed again and Buccleuch was among the Scots lords routed at Pinkie by the invader Somerset. Faced with increasing aggression from England, the Regent, Mary of Guise, turned to Buccleuch. In 1551 he was appointed Warden of Liddesdale and of the Middle March (i.e. the centre section of the three defensive jurisdictions on the Border). Sir Walter did not live long to enjoy his high office: on the night of 4th October 1552 he was murdered in the High Street of Edinburgh by his old enemies the Kerrs.

While Wicked Wat's grandson and heir — yet another Sir Walter — was still a minor, his guardians took steps to end the feud with the Kerrs in 1565. A complex sequence of marriage contracts was drawn up between the two clans. None of these marriages actually took place, but, ironically, Sir Thomas Kerr of Ferniehirst fell in love with young Walter's sister Janet who became his wife; he was the only Kerr of any importance who had not been involved in the original marriage treaties! So the feud ended, but this did not bring the Scotts peace. That same year they became embroiled in a bitter quarrel with the Eliotts. The English government, seeing a chance of mischief-making, subsidized an Eliott raid into the Scott country. While pursuing the raiders, the Scotts fell into an ambush where they suffered heavy losses. This feud petered out more quickly than the one with the Kerrs had done. As well as these fights with their neighbours north of the Border, the Scotts also had a notable feud with an English clan, the Charltons of Tynedale.

The 10th Laird of Buccleuch was a partisan of Mary Queen of Scots and deeply involved in the politics of her turbulent reign until his early death in 1574. His son, inevitably named Walter, also succeeded as a minor. In adulthood he followed the family tradition of military daring, becoming known to his admirers as 'The Bold

Stobo in the Tweed Valley, at the north-west corner of Scott power.

Buccleuch' and to his enemies as 'The Scourge of God'. Most famous of his exploits was the rescue of one of his henchmen, William Armstrong of Kinmont — the celebrated 'Kinmont Willie' — from Carlisle Castle. Armstrong had been seized by the English on a day of truce, in March 1596. The following month Buccleuch, with a picked band of men, broke into the supposedly impregnable fortress of Carlisle and carried off Kinmont Willie, still in fetters:

> '"And mony a time," quo' Kinmont Willie,
> "I've prick'd a horse out oure the furs,
>   But since the day I back'd a steed
>   I never wore sic cumbrous spurs."'

So the well-known ballad ran. In 1606 Sir Walter Scott was created Lord Scott of Buccleuch and his son, who inherited the title in 1611, was made Earl of Buccleuch in 1619. Both saw military service abroad, in the Dutch army.

From the Union of the Crowns in 1603 the old way of life in the Borders was doomed. Frontier warfare could not be tolerated in what was now the centre of a united realm. Like the other Border families, the Scotts found their clan culture eroded in a way that was not to affect the Highlands until 150 years later. The Highland clans lived in the most remote part of Britain, further isolated by the Gaelic tongue; the Borderers, sandwiched between England and the commercially-minded Scottish Lowlands, were earlier victims of advancing modernity. In blunt terms, the economic basis of the Scotts' existence — like all the Border clans — had been plunder. Though half-hearted attempts were made to grow oats and barley, there was no incentive to serious farming when crops were almost certain to be burned by raiders before they could be harvested. Only cattle and sheep, which could be driven into the hills out of harm's way, represented solid wealth. Border land was incredibly undervalued because of the constant warfare: when the 8th Laird of Buccleuch came into his large estates in 1492, all but the remote lands of Kirkurd, with an annual value of £20 Scots, were waste.

From the seventeenth century, the Buccleuchs were great nobles rather than clan chiefs. The 2nd Earl was a Covenanter and led his clan against Montrose at Philiphaugh, but died at the age of 25. His younger daughter Anne married James, Duke of Monmouth, a bastard son of Charles II. On their wedding day, in 1663, the couple were created Duke and Duchess of Buccleuch. After the failure of Monmouth's rebellion against his uncle, James VII, in 1685, he was executed, but his widow retained the dukedom of Buccleuch which passed to their descendants.

The cadet house of Harden, derived from the Scotts of Synton, inherited the peerage of Polwarth in 1827. Of the Lairds of Harden the most famous was Auld Wat, chief of his house from 1563 to 1631. His wife, Mary Scott of Dryhope, known because of her great beauty as 'The Flower of Yarrow', was renowned for the device whereby she hinted to her husband that it was time to go reiving once more: when the last bullock from the previous raid had been consumed, she set a dish on the table which, when uncovered, revealed a pair of spurs. The Harden line in turn produced an offshoot, the Scotts of Raeburn, from whom descended the greatest figure in Scottish literature, the novelist and poet Sir Walter Scott of Abbotsford. His works are strongly influenced by his clan heritage and contain many references to the history of the Scotts. Another member of the clan notable for scholarly achievement was Michael Scott, 'the Wizard', whose intellectual eminence gained him a European reputation in the thirteenth century, as well as the post of tutor to Emperor Frederick II. It is not certain to which branch of the family he belonged.

The chief of Clan Scott is the Duke of Buccleuch, still resident in his ancestral territory. There is a Scott tartan and the clan's plant badge is the blaeberry; its warcry is 'A Bellendaine!' with 'Alemuir!' as an alternative slogan.

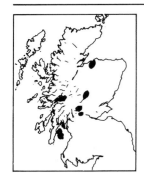

CLAN
STEWART

Stewart, Royal
MOTTO: *Virescit vulnere virtus*
(Courage grows strong at a wound)
PLANT BADGE: Oak, thistle

THE ROYAL STEWARTS MUST SURELY BE ACKNOW-ledged the leading family of Scotland. For the greater part of Scots history they were the reigning dynasty, as they were also of Great Britain for a further century. No foreign royal family can boast better pedigree or marriage alliances and their organization as a Highland and Lowland clan resulted in a significant proportion of the inhabitants of Scotland sharing in this great heritage. So vast and complex were the ramifications of the Stewarts that only a general outline of their main branches can be attempted here.

By origin the Stewarts were Bretons, descended from the hereditary Seneschals of Dol, in Brittany. One of this family, called Alan Fitz Flaald, came to England in the reign of Henry I and became lord of Oswestry. His heir, William, was ancestor of the FitzAlan Earls of Arundel (now Dukes of Norfolk); his second son, Walter, moved north to Scotland, where he was appointed hereditary High Steward of the kingdom by Malcolm IV in 1157. The first High Steward's grandson, another Walter, adopted the title of his office as his family name and so became known as 'Stewart'. His grandson James was fifth High Steward and a supporter of Bruce in the struggle for independence; James's younger brother, Sir John Stewart of Bonkyl, killed in the patriotic cause at the Battle of Falkirk (1298), was ancestor of the Earls of Galloway. In the next generation, Walter, the sixth High Steward, married Marjory, daughter of King Robert Bruce. So, on the extinction of the Bruce dynasty with the death of David II in 1371, the son of Walter Stewart and Marjory Bruce ascended the throne as Robert II.

From then on, the story of the main line of the Stewarts was simply the history of Scotland. Many branches of the clan, however, descended from illegitimate sons of Stewart princes, some of which may briefly be outlined. From King Robert II descended the Marquesses of Bute and the Stewarts of Cardney; from Murdoch, 2nd Duke of Albany (a younger son of Robert II) descended the Earls Castle Stewart, the Earls of Moray and the Stewarts of Balquhidder. The family of Stewart of Ardgowan (now Shaw-Stewart) derived from a natural son of Robert III.

Castle Stalker, *built by Duncan Stewart, 2nd Laird of Appin, in the late fifteenth century.*

Sir John Stewart of Bonkyl, the patriot killed at Falkirk, was also ancestor of the Stewarts of Appin and the house of Traquhair. Rather than try to unravel the complicated genealogies of the founders of each branch, it would be more practical to arrange them into geographical spheres of influence, the first and main division being between Highland and Lowland Stewarts.

There are five main branches of Highland Stewarts: Appin, Atholl, Balquhidder, the Earls of Moray and the Marquesses of Bute. The Stewarts of Appin descended, as has been said, from Sir John Stewart of Bonkyl, through his fourth son, Sir James Stewart of Pierston, in Ayrshire. Sir James fought at Bannockburn and was eventually killed at the Battle of Halidon Hill in 1333. His third son, Sir Robert of Innermeath, died in 1387, leaving two sons: Sir John, his heir, and Sir Robert, ancestor of the Stewarts of Rosyth. The elder, Sir John, exchanged his estate of Durrisdeer with his younger brother for the lordship of Lorn. Of his sons, Robert succeeded him as lord of Lorn, James became known as the 'Black Knight of Lorn' and married the widow of King James I, while Alexander was ancestor of the Steuarts of Grandtully. Robert's heir, Sir John Stewart of Lorn, married a daughter of Maclaren of Ardveich, in Perthshire; their son Dugald had actually been born in 1445, though their marriage did not take place until 1463, for the purpose of legitimizing him. The Maclarens were flattered by this match and their bard saluted the fortunate youth: 'Young Dugald, akin you are to him now wearing the royal crown; and in your pulses is flowing gleefully the blood which makes you of a mighty race.' Unfortunately, the belated bridegroom was fatally stabbed on his way to the wedding at Dunstaffnage Castle by a rebel Macdougall, so that the ceremony had to be completed around his deathbed.

The scheme was successful, however, for young Dugald succeeded to the lordship of Lorn. Yet even with the support of his mother's clan, the Maclarens, he was unable to bring the whole of Lorn under his control. So he came to a compromise arrangement with his uncle and rival, Walter Stewart, in 1469. By this treaty, Dugald ceded his rights to part of his inheritance, but retained Upper Lorn, also known as Appin. Dugald thus became the first Stewart chief of Appin. The country of Appin is a small territory bounded on the west by Loch Linnhe, on the north by Loch Leven and the Macdonald land of Glencoe, with the great Campbell holding of Lorn lying to the south-east, beyond Glen Creran. Castle Shuna, on the island of the same name opposite Portnacroish (on the A828), is the oldest fortress in the area whose ruin survives. Castle Stalker, on an islet in Appin Bay, was built by Duncan Stewart, 2nd of Appin, who succeeded his father in 1497 and was appointed King's Chamberlain of the Isles by James IV. Duncan died unmarried in 1513 and was succeeded by his brother Alan. No sooner had Alan become chief than he and his five sons were required to accompany James IV to the tragic Battle of Flodden. Fortunately they survived and it was from Alan's younger sons that the principal cadet houses of Appin derived; in order of seniority they are: Strathgarry, Achnacone, Fasnacloich and Invernahyle.

Alan's chiefship was bedevilled by constant intrigues by his powerful Campbell neighbours to usurp his land. Furthermore, despite the temporary security of a charter from James V in 1538, by 1547 the Earl of Argyll had contrived to obtain the feudal superiority of part of the Appin lands. Alan Stewart, who had married a daughter of Cameron of Lochiel, died at an advanced age about 1562 and was succeeded by his grandson John, 4th of Appin. This chief joined in the conspiracy to murder the Bonnie Earl of Moray in 1592, in the vain hope of regaining the whole lordship of Lorn. By his second wife, a daughter of Clanranald, he had a son John, 1st of Ardsheal, whose line was destined eventually to inherit the chiefship of Appin. When the 4th Chief died in 1595, however, it was Duncan, the son of his first marriage, who succeeded him. After him came his son, also Duncan, 6th of Appin. He incurred great disgrace as a result of a drunken debauch during which he handed over Castle Stalker to Campbell of Airds in exchange for an eight-oared wherry. When the two parties sobered up, Campbell held the Laird of Appin to his promise, which honour obliged him to fulfil. The furious clansmen did not

Beinn a'Bheithir, the highest point in the Stewart territory of Appin.

depose Duncan from the chiefship, but they declared him disqualified from leading them in war. The disgraced chief's son, yet another Duncan, 7th Laird of Appin, amply compensated for his father's lack of military achievement. He led the clan out under Montrose and fought for Charles I at Inverlochy and Kilsyth, so that after the victory of the Covenanters his estates were forfeited. Charles II restored them in 1660 and appointed Duncan a Commissioner of Supply for Argyllshire. This chief was known as Duncan Mór (the Great) because of his warlike career.

When the Revolution broke out in 1689, Duncan Mór's nephew, Robert Stewart, 8th of Appin, rushed from college to join his clan which was led in the Jacobite cause by Stewart of Ardsheal, Tutor of Appin during the young chief's minority. After Killiecrankie, Ardsheal held Castle Stalker for James VII until October 1690, when he surrendered on honourable terms. During the 'Fifteen, Robert Stewart of Appin commanded 250 men at the Battle of Sheriffmuir and, after the defeat of the Jacobites, was attainted for a second time and fled overseas. In the 'Forty-five, since Robert's heir, Dugald, was only a boy, Charles Stewart, 5th of Ardsheal, led the clan as Tutor of Appin. Of his force of 300 men, almost one-third were killed at Culloden. Yet, even after the rebellion was over, a further misfortune overtook the Stewarts. Colin Roy Campbell of Glenure — The Red Fox — who administered the forfeited Ardsheal estates, was murdered in Appin in 1752. This was the famous Appin Murder on which R. L. Stevenson based his novels *Kidnapped* and *Catriona*. Since the Campbells demanded blood for this outrage, James Stewart of the Glens, the illegitimate half-brother of Ardsheal, was hanged, though clearly innocent of the murder. A cairn on the hillside near Ballachulish Ferry marks the place of his execution, the last death in Scotland resulting from a clan feud. Dugald, 9th Laird, sold Appin in 1765 and, on his death without heirs in 1769, was succeeded by his cousin, Duncan Stewart, 6th of Ardsheal, who became 10th Chief of Appin. The chiefship remains in his line today. Besides the main cadet houses already mentioned, the Stewarts of Ballachulish, Innerhadden, Bunrannoch, Bohallie and Innischaorach also derived from the house of Appin, as did the tribe known as Sliochd Ailein 'Ic Rob (the MacRobs), whose ancestor was an illegitimate grandson of the 1st Chief.

The Stewarts of Atholl were not so much a clan as a confederation. Although they all derived from the main Stewart stock, they consisted of different, unrelated branches whom opportunism had attracted into the same geographical area. Originally, the reason for a Stewart presence in Atholl had been the bestowal of the earldom of Atholl by James II on his half-brother, Sir John Stewart of Balvenie. The Stewart Earls of Atholl flourished from 1457 to 1625, when their heiress carried the title into the house of Murray. Thereafter, the Stewarts living in Atholl generally followed the Chief of Murray, but this was not an absolute rule and there were exceptions. The Steuarts of Grandtully (now Steuart-Fothringham) were a cadet house of the old Stewart earls. In 1745 they were capable of raising 300 men; their seat was Grandtully Castle (still standing) on the south bank of the River Tay, 3 miles north-east of Aberfeldy (on the A827).

The territory in Atholl occupied by the Stewarts was sprawling and irregular. It reached roughly from the northern extremity of Loch Tay, ranging in a north-easterly direction to Geal Charn (2,874ft), about 5 miles south-west of Inverey. This, however, probably gives an exaggerated impression of its size, for it was much broken up and cut into by tracts of Robertson, Menzies and Fergusson land, while the Murrays were in fact the real power in the area. The Stewarts' other principal fortress in Atholl was Garth Castle (just across the Keltney Burn, off the B846 road, about 6 miles south of Tummel Bridge). Garth was originally a stronghold of Alexander, Earl of Buchan — The Wolf of Badenoch — a younger brother of King Robert III. The Wolf's career may be summarized simply by recording that his savagery shocked his contemporaries in fourteenth-century Scotland, who were not noted for their sensitivity. Among his exploits was the destruction of Elgin Cathedral, an expression of his displeasure at being excommunicated.

Loch Lubnaig lies in the pocket of Stewart land north of Callander.

Mary Queen of Scots, the most romantic of the Stuart monarchs.

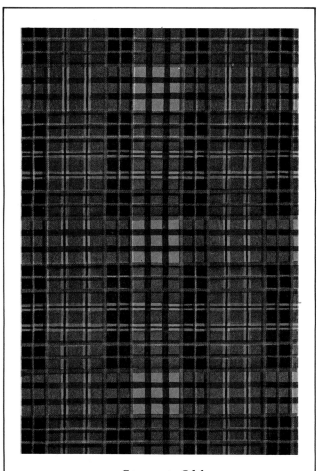

Stewart, Old
ORIGIN OF NAME: From the High Steward of Scotland
GAELIC NAME: Clann Stiubhart

Many of the Atholl Stewarts descended from the Wolf's bastard son James, founder of the Stewarts of Garth. Their chief surviving cadets are the Stewarts of Balnakeilly. The remaining Atholl Stewarts were of mixed extraction. The houses of Strathgarry and Innerhadden were Appin men, as mentioned above, who had migrated to Atholl; the Stewarts of Ballechin derived from a bastard son of James II, the Stewarts of Cardney from an indiscretion of Robert II. The Athollmen were stout Jacobites and rose for their royal kinsmen in 1689, 1715 and 1745; their losses at Culloden were very heavy.

Another area of Stewart settlement was Balquhidder. The Stewarts here descended from Murdoch, 2nd Duke of Albany, grandson of Robert II. Duke Murdoch's own grandson, James Stewart, became Laird of Baldorran in Stirlingshire and his son William, 2nd of Baldorran, had three sons. Walter, the eldest, inherited Baldorran; the two younger sons, John and Andrew, were respectively founders of the houses of Glenbuckie and Gartnafuaran, both in Perthshire. The 4th Laird of Baldorran had two sons: the elder, Alexander, became Laird of Ardvorlich, in Perthshire, about 1580; the younger was ancestor of the Stewarts of Annat. From the late sixteenth century, therefore, this branch of Clan Stewart was settled in the south-western corner of Perthshire, around Loch Katrine, Loch Voil and Loch Earn. The chieftain lived at Ardvorlich, on the southern shore of Loch Earn (on an unclassified road between Edinample and Ardtrostan). James Stewart, 2nd of Ardvorlich, was the character on whom Scott based his *Legend of Montrose*, in which Ardvorlich featured under the name of Darnlinvarach. A

Rothesay Castle, Bute. From 1498 the Stuart Marquesses of Bute were its hereditary Keepers.

Grandtully Castle, near Aberfeldy, the seat of the Steuarts of Grandtully, a cadet house of the Stewart Earls of Atholl.

crystal gemstone kept at Ardvorlich was long regarded as a talisman capable of healing diseased cattle. The Balquhidder Stewarts were Jacobites in 1715 and would have fought for Prince Charlie in the 'Forty-five but for the untimely murder of their commander, the Laird of Glenbuckie.

A notable Jacobite member of the clan was Colonel John Roy Stewart, who belonged to an Inverness-shire branch, the Stewarts of Kinchardine. He was known to Prince Charlie as the 'Body', and gained immortality while hiding from the redcoats after Culloden by composing his famous parody on the 23rd Psalm:

'The Lord's my targe, I will be stout
With dirk and trusty blade,
Though Campbells come in flocks about,
I will not be afraid.'

The Earl of Moray, head of another branch of Clan Stewart, descends both from Robert II through the house of Albany and from James V, whose natural son was 1st Earl. This family had two widely separated areas of influence. The first was in Menteith, on both banks of the River Forth, just south-east of Callander; here their stronghold was Doune Castle, a massive and well-preserved fortress overlooking the confluence of the River Teith and the Ardoch Burn, immediately south of the town of Doune (A820). Their more northerly land was in Elgin, around the mouth of the River Findhorn, where they held Darnaway Castle, about 5 miles south-west of Forres (on an unclassified road branching south off the A96). Nearby stands a more grisly relic of Stewart power — Lochindorb Castle, lair of The Wolf of Badenoch, on the shore of a small loch about 15 miles south of Forres (access by an unclassified road, a short distance south of the junction of the A940 and A939 at Dava). The 2nd Earl was the Bonnie Earl of Moray, murdered by Huntly at Donibristle in 1592; the 5th Earl, who enjoyed the favour of James VII and was a founder Knight of the Thistle, lost all his offices at the Revolution, though his younger brother Archibald was a Whig who held Stirling Castle for William of Orange in 1689.

The Stuarts, Marquesses of Bute, are descended from

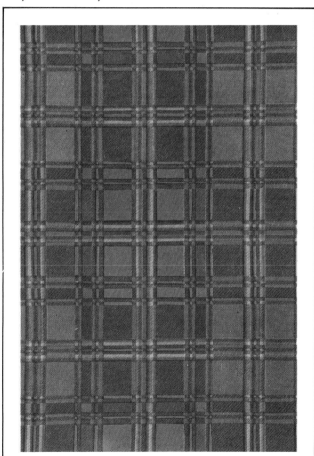

Stewart of Appin

CREST BADGE: A unicorn's head, crined and armed, or
MOTTO: Quidder we'll zje (Whither will ye)
WARCRY: *Creag-an-Sgairbh!* (The Cormorant's Rock)

Sir John Stewart, a natural son of Robert II. Known as 'The Black Stewart', Sir John acquired the hereditary sheriffdom of Bute and Arran in 1385 and these islands were thenceforth the homeland of his offspring. From 1498 the head of the family was also hereditary Keeper of Rothesay Castle. The 10th chieftain of this line was created a baronet in 1627 and fought for Charles I in the Civil War. His grandson, Sir James, was created Earl of Bute in 1703 and was a fierce opponent of the Act of Union. John, 3rd Earl of Bute, was Prime Minister to George III, 1762-63, and his eldest son was promoted in the peerage to be Marquess of Bute in 1796. Since 1805 the family name has been Crichton-Stuart, to commemorate the merging of the Crichton earldom of Dumfries with the Marquessate of Bute, through the marriage of the Crichton heiress to Lord Mount Stuart, father of the 2nd Marquess.

It is in the Lowlands, however, that the senior family of Clan Stewart is to be found. The Earls of Galloway today represent the line of Sir John Stewart of Bonkyl, the thirteenth-century patriot whose elder brother, James, was grandfather of Robert II and so ancestor of the Royal house. In 1623 the head of this branch was created Earl of Galloway, subsequently justifying the honour by his services in the royalist cause during the Civil War. James, 2nd Earl of Galloway, shared his father's politics and was fined £4,000 by Cromwell, though his fortunes prospered again after the Restoration; his second son, Robert, married the sister of David Dunbar of Baldoon, the real-life character on whom Scott based the Master of Ravenswood in *The Bride of Lammermoor*. George, 8th Earl of Galloway, commanded the frigate *Lively* at the Battle of St Vincent (1797), and had the honour of bringing home the news of Nelson's victory.

The various forms of the name — Stewart, Stuart and Steuart — result from random development in different branches of the clan, but since the time of Mary Queen of Scots, it has been conventional to spell the name of the Royal house as 'Stuart'. At the death in 1807 of Prince Charlie's younger brother, Henry, Cardinal York (recognized by Jacobites as Henry IX), the direct descendants of Charles I became extinct and the claim to the British throne passed to the house of Savoy and eventually to the Wittelsbach royal family of Bavaria. Even today the Duke of Bavaria receives loyal greetings on his birthday from many romantic Jacobites in Scotland and England. What is less widely known is the fact that Bonnie Prince Charlie left an authentic but doubly illegitimate grandson who died in Scotland. Charlotte, Duchess of Albany (Burns' 'Bonnie Lass of Albanie'), was Prince Charlie's natural daughter by his mistress, Clementina Walkinshaw. In maturity, Charlotte herself had three illegitimate children as a result of her liaison with a dissolute French archbishop named Prince Ferdinand de Rohan-Guéméné. Little is known of the two daughters (who possibly went to the United States of America and may have descendants living today), but the son, Charles Edward, Baron Roehenstart (his name a combination of Rohan and Stuart) died after a coach accident at Dunkeld on 28th October 1854. His gravestone may be seen in the ruined nave of Dunkeld Cathedral, with the appropriate motto: *Sic Transit Gloria Mundi* (So passes away earthly glory). Thus, although the famous Sobieski-Stuarts were charming impostors, there was a genuine royal Stuart living in nineteenth-century Scotland.

The Chief of Clan Stewart is the Earl of Galloway; Stewart of Appin is styled Mac-Iain Stiubhairt na h-Apunn and the Laird of Ardvorlich is Mac-'ic-Bhaltair. There are many sept names of the various branches. Septs of the royal line are Boyd, France, Garrow, Lennox and Monteith; septs of Appin are Carmichael, Combich, Levack, Livingstone, MacCombich, Mackinlay, MacLay and MacMichael; septs of Atholl are Crookshanks, Duilach, Gray and MacGlashan; the septs of Bute are Bannatyne, Fullarton, Jameson, Jamieson, MacCamie, MacCaw, MacCloy, MacKirdy, MacLewis, MacMunn and MacMutrie. Clan Stewart's plant badges are the oak and the thistle and the Stewarts of Appin have as their warcry '*Creag-an-Sgairbh!*' ('The Cormorant's Rock!'). The Gaelic name is Clann Stiubhart.

CLAN
SUTHERLAND

CLAN SUTHERLAND IS NOTABLE FOR ITS VAST TERRI-tory, the antiquity of its lineage, the royal favour enjoyed by its chiefs since earliest times and its tenure of the premier earldom of Scotland. It has been suggested that the Sutherlands descend from the pre-Christian tribe of the Catti: the modern counties of Caithness and Sutherland were formerly known as the province of Cat, or land of the people of the Cat, and a wild cat is the Sutherland crest.

Whether or not they were intermarried with the original inhabitants, the common ancestor of both the Sutherlands and Murrays appears to have been a Flemish nobleman named Freskin. This incomer received exten-sive land grants from David I in Moray and West Lothian and died before 1172. His grandson, Hugh de Moravia, had acquired considerable lands in Sutherland by 1211 and died within a few years. Hugh's son, William, was created Earl of Sutherland by Alexander II about the year 1235, thus establishing the name of his race, as well as the oldest surviving Scots earldom. Sutherland derives from the Norse *Sudrland* (South Land) which the territory seemed to those living further north in Caithness. The first earl died around 1248 and was succeeded by his son William, whose loyalties are revealed by a letter written to him by Edward I of England in 1304: 'We take it well of you, and we thank you much for the good faith and the good will which you have still borne towards us . . .'

William, the next Earl, however, supported Bruce and signed the Declaration of Arbroath; on his death, some time before 1330, he was succeeded by his brother Kenneth who fell at Halidon Hill (1333). It was Kenneth's son, William, 5th Earl of Sutherland, who did most to enhance the fortunes of the family. A well-known warrior against the English, in 1343 he married Margaret, daughter of the Bruce and sister of David II, who promoted the earldom of Sutherland into a regality two years later. In 1346, as a further mark of favour, the Earl and Countess of Sutherland received a grant of Dunnottar Castle (on the Aberdeenshire coast, just south of Stonehaven), in return for the feudal rendering to the king of a pair of white gloves every Whitsun. By the time the 5th Earl died, *circa* 1370, the Sutherlands were well established as an important clan, taking their surname from their territory.

The clan lands may briefly be described as correspond-ing approximately to the south-eastern half of the county of Sutherland; Strathnaver, the north-western portion, was Mackay country. The most westerly point of Sutherland occupation was around Beinn Leoid, the northern boundary extending eastwards, almost to Loch nan Cuinne, then running in a south-easterly direction along Strath Ullie to Helmsdale (this last part being the route of the A897 road). The southern boundary ran from Glen Cassley (south of Loch Shin) and down the Kyle of Sutherland to the Dornoch Firth. There was a feud between the Sutherlands and their northern neighbours the Mackays, dating from 1372 when Nicolas Sutherland of Duffus treacherously murdered Mackay of Strath-naver and his heir in their beds in Dingwall Castle, where both parties were guests.

The 5th Earl left two sons by a second marriage: Robert, his heir, and Kenneth of Drummoy, ancestor of the house of Forse. Robert, 6th Earl, fought at the Battle of Otterburn in 1388 and built Dunrobin Castle, the magnificent seat of the Sutherland chiefs, 1 mile north-east of Golspie (on the A9). This Earl Robert was chief for about 70 years and his long reign saw peace established with the Mackays, as well as a brief war with MacLeod of Lewis. He died about 1427 and his son John, who married a famous beauty, Margaret Baillie of Lamington, was chief until 1456, when he resigned the earldom to his son, also called John. Both the 8th and 9th Earls were declared incapable of managing their affairs, owing to insanity, so that the 9th Earl's sister, Elizabeth, became Countess of Sutherland in 1514. She married Adam Gordon, second son of the 2nd Earl of Huntly, and henceforth, for almost two centuries, Gordon was the surname of the Earls of Sutherland who thus remained cadets of the house of Huntly, rather than chiefs of Clan Sutherland. The chief cadet was Sutherland of Forse.

The 11th Earl, known as 'the Good Earl John', lost his titles and estates in 1562 after joining in his kinsman

Dunrobin Castle, seat of the Sutherland chiefs. The Victorian exterior encases a much older castle.

Dunnottar Castle, south of Stonehaven, granted to the Earl of Sutherland by David II in 1346 in return for a pair of white gloves every Whitsun.

Huntly's rebellion. He was restored five years later, but met a tragic death soon afterwards. While visiting his uncle's widow, Isabel Sinclair, at Helmsdale Castle, the Earl and his wife were poisoned by the widow, who hoped to secure the succession for her son. Her plans were frustrated since the dying Earl managed to prevent his own heir, Alexander, from eating the poisoned supper; Isabel Sinclair committed suicide in Edinburgh before she could be executed for these murders. Alexander's grandson John, 14th Earl, was a Covenanter who raised a foot regiment and fought against Montrose at Auldearn (1645). His son George, 15th Earl, who had similar religious sympathies, was deprived of his office as Hereditary Sheriff of Sutherland under Charles II. He lived abroad during the reign of James VII, but returned on the accession of William of Orange.

John, 16th Earl, resumed the surname of Sutherland. He supported the Act of Union, was made a Knight of the Thistle and was active on the Hanoverian side in the 'Fifteen, though his kinsman Kenneth Sutherland, Lord Duffus, was 'out' with the Jacobites. His grandson and heir William, 17th Earl, fought in Cumberland's army at Culloden. His granddaughter, Elizabeth, became 19th Countess of Sutherland in 1771 and married George Leveson-Gower, Viscount Trentham, who was created Duke of Sutherland in 1833. The Duke's ill-conceived 'improvements' on his estates caused much misery, but it is only fair to add that they were a genuine effort at philanthropy: they included the building of roads, bridges, harbours, fishing-stations, inns, dwellings, farm-houses, brick-works and a colliery, at a cost of £210,000.

When the 5th Duke of Sutherland died in 1963, the dukedom went to the Egerton Earls of Ellesmere; his niece, however, became 23rd Countess of Sutherland and Morair Chat (the Great One of Cat). The clan's septs are Cheyne, Federeth, Gray, Keith, Mowat and Oliphant. Its warcry is '*Ceann na Drochaide Bige!*' ('The Head of the Little Bridge!'—near Dunrobin), its plant badges are cotton sedge or butcher's broom and its Gaelic name is Clann Sutharlan.

Sutherland, Ancient

MOTTO: *Sans peur* (Without fear)
GAELIC NAME: Clann Sutharlan
WARCRY: *Ceann na Drochaide Bige!*
(The Head of the Little Bridge)
PLANT BADGE: Cotton sedge, butcher's broom

The Clans of Scotland

Pentland Firth

SINCLAIR
CAITHNESS
Wick

MACKAY
SUTHERLAND
KEITH
GUNN
MURRAY
SUTHERLAND

MORRISON

MACLEOD
OF LEWIS
Stornoway

MACAULAY
Lewis
MACIVER

MACLEOD
MACNICOL

L. Shin

1650
Invercarron

MACLEOD
OF HARRIS
Harris

The Minch

MACDONELL
OF GLENGARRY

ROSS

Dornoch Firth

MACQUEEN
MACDONALD

MACDONALD
North Uist

MACLEOD OF LEWIS

L. Maree

MACLEOD
OF LEWIS

MUNRO

URQUHART

Moray Firth

BRODIE
Auldearn

INNES

KEITH
Peterhead

HAY

MACKENZIE

ROSS AND CROMARTY

ROSE
NAIRN

MORAY

GORDON

HAY

MACLEOD
OF LEWIS

MACLEOD
OF HARRIS

MACNICOL

MACKINNON

FRASER

Culloden
1746
Inverness

Spey

GRANT

Harlaw
1411
LESLIE

SKYE

MATHESON

MACDONELL
OF GLENGARRY

MACLENNAN
MACRAE
1719
Glenshiel

CHISHOLM

GRANT

FRASER

MACBEAN

MACINTOSH
MACGILLIVRAY
DAVIDSON

1594
Glenlivet

Cromdale Braes
1690

1645
Alford

ABERDEEN

SKENE

FORBES
Aberdeen

South Uist

MACDONALD
OF CLANRANALD

MACLEOD
OF HARRIS

MACDONALD

MACDONELL OF
GLENGARRY

INVERNESS

L. Arkaig

1544
Blair-na-Leine

COMYN

SHAW

MACPHERSON

FARQUHARSON

KINCARDINE

SEA OF THE HEBRIDES

Rhum

L. Morar

CAMERON

L. Lochy
L. Ness

MACDONELL
OF KEPPOCH

CUMMING

BARCLAY
N. Esk

MACDONALD OF CLANRANALD

MACNEILL

Coll

Inverlochy
1645
Fort
William

MURRAY

LINDSAY

OGILVIE

MENZIES

ROBERTSON

1689
Killiecrankie

GOW

S. Esk

MACLEAN

MACGILLIVRAY
MACKINNON

Tiree

1480
Bloody Bay

MACLEAN

STEWART

1692 Glencoe

HENDERSON

Rannoch

STEWART

1689
Dunkeld

685
Nectansmere

ANGUS

LIVINGSTONE

CAMPBELL

MENZIES

MACINNES
MACMASTER

CAMPBELL

FLETCHER

Tay

DUNCAN

MACQUARRIE

Mull

Pass of Brander
Oban 1308

MACDOUGALL

MACINTYRE

MACGREGOR

MURRAY

OLIPHANT

977
Luncarty

MACALPINE

MACNAB

1306
Methven
1396

HAY

Dundee

Firth of Tay

NORTH
SEA

MACFIE

MACLEAN

MACALLUM

MACNAUGHTON

MACLACHLAN

MACARTHUR

STEWART

GRAHAM

Earn

MACLAREN

DRUMMOND

1644
Tippermuir
Perth

1332
Dupplin

St Andrews

LINDSAY

MACDUFF

Jura

MALCOLM

MACMILLAN

MACCOLL

CAMPBELL

MAC
LACHLAN

MACEWEN

BUCHANAN

STEWART

NAPIER

1488
Sauchieburn

1715
Sheriffmuir

Forth Stirling Br 1297
Stirling

1314
Bannockburn

L. Leven

ERSKINE

CL
KIN

Inverkeithing
1651

BRUCE

Firth of Forth

MACDONALD

Islay

COLQUHOUN
Glenfruin
1603

MACAULAY

LIVINGSTONE

1298 Falkirk
1746

Edinburgh

WEST
LOTHIAN

MID LOTHIAN

Prestonpans
1745

Pinkie
1547

EAST
LOTHIAN

1296
Dunbar

1650

HAY

MACNEILL

MACALISTER

STEWART

ERSKINE

1568
Langside

1679
Bothwell Bridge

Glasgow

HAMILTON

RAMSAY

MELVILLE

LINDSAY

Halidon Hill
1333

CAMPBELL

COOK
BUTE
FULLARTON
Arran
HAMILTON
STEWART

MONTGOMERY

1263
Largs

CUNNINGHAM

1679
Drumclog

WALLACE

BAIRD

LANARK

Clyde

1018
Carham

SCOTT

SELKIRK

1645
Selkirk
Philiphaugh

PEEBLES

BERWICK

Berwick-
upon-Tweed

1513
Flodden

MACDONALD

Firth of Clyde

KENNEDY

Ayr

DOUGLAS

Tweed

ELLIOT
ROXBURGH
KERR

Teviot

ATLANTIC
OCEAN

Firth of Lorn

FERGUSON

Dumfries

BRUCE
DUMFRIES

JOHNSTON

1542
Solway Moss

ARMSTRONG

Cree

KIRKCUDBRIGHT

Dee

WIGTOWN
Stranraer

Annan

Solway Firth

North Channel

CL   CLACKMANNAN
DUN DUNBARTON
KIN KINROSS

This map gives the approximate
location of the most prominent
Clans and Families of Scotland.
Absence of any Clan or Family
does not mean that they were
landless.

0   10   20   30   40 miles

CLANS, SEPTS AND RELATED NAMES

NAMES RELATED TO CLANS DISCUSSED IN THE TEXT

Details of the relationship will be found in the relevant chapter (indicated by italics).
This is a complex and controversial area, and this list is by no means exhaustive.

Adam, *Gordon*
Adamson, *Chattan*
Adie, *Gordon*
Aird, *Chisholm*
Alanach, *Grant*
Alderston, *Hay*
Alexander, *Donald*
Allan, *Donald*
Allanson, *Donald*
Allardice, *Graham*
Allat, *Eliott*
Ayer, *Hay*
Aylewood, *Eliott*
Ayson, *Chattan*

Bain, *Mackay*
Bannatyne, *Stewart*
Baxter, *MacMillan*
Bayne, *Mackay*
Beagrie, *Hay*
Bean, *Chattan*
Beath, *Donald*
Beaton, *Donald*
Bell, *MacMillan*
Bethune, *Donald*
Blue, *MacMillan*
Bontein, *Graham*
Bontine, *Graham*
Bowie, *Donald*
Boyd, *Stewart*
Brieve, *Morrison*
Brown, *MacMillan* (if connected
    with Kintyre)
Burnhouse, *Campbell*
Burns, *Campbell*

Caddell, *Campbell*
Cadzow, *Hamilton*
Callum, *MacLeod* (where there is
    a Raasay connection)
Carmichael, *Stewart*

Cattanach, *Chattan*
Chalmers, *Cameron*
Charleson, *Mackenzie*
Cheyne, *Sutherland*
Clanachan, *Maclean*
Clark, *Cameron* (where
    Lochaber connection is
    established), *Chattan*
Clarkson, *Chattan*
Collier, *Robertson*
Colson, *Donald*
Combich, *Stewart*
Combie, *Chattan*
Comrie, *MacGregor*
Connall, *Donald*
Connochie, *Campbell*
Corbett, *Ross*
Coutts, *Chattan*
Crerar, *Chattan*
Crombie, *Gordon*
Crookshanks, *Stewart*
Croser, *Eliott*
Crosier, *Eliott*
Crowther, *MacGregor*
Currie, *Chattan*

Dalgety, *Hay*
Dallas, *Chattan*
Dalliot, *Eliott*
Dalserf, *Hamilton*
Darroch, *Donald*
Davidson, *Chattan*
Davie, *Chattan*
Davis, *Chattan*
Dawson, *Chattan*
De La Haye, *Hay*
Denoon, *Campbell*, *Ross*
Doles, *Chattan*
Donachie, *Robertson*
Donaldson, *Donald*
Drain, *Donald*

Drysdale, *Douglas*
Duilach, *Stewart*
Duncan, *Robertson*
Duncanson, *Robertson*
Dunnachie, *Robertson*

Edie, *Gordon*
Elder, *Chattan*
Eliot, *Eliott*
Ellat, *Eliott*
Elliot, *Eliott*
Elliswood, *Eliott*
Ellot, *Eliott*
Ellwood, *Eliott*
Elwaird, *Eliott*
Elwald, *Eliott*
Erroll, *Hay*
Esson, *Chattan*

Farquhar, *Chattan*
Farquharson, *Chattan*
Federeth, *Stewart*
Fergie, *Fergusson*
Fergus, *Fergusson*
Ferguson, *Fergusson*
Fern, *Ross*
Ferrie, *Fergusson*
Ferries, *Fergusson*
Ferris, *Fergusson*
Fersen, *Chattan*
Findlay, *Chattan*
Findlayson, *Chattan*
Fletcher, *MacGregor*
France, *Stewart*
Frizell, *Fraser*
Fullarton, *Stewart*

Galbraith, *Donald*
Garrow, *Stewart*
Garvie, *Maclean*
Gifford, *Hay*

Gilbride, *Donald*
Gillan, *Maclean*
Gillespie, *Chattan*
Gillies, *Chattan*
Gilmore, *Morrison*
Gilroy, *Grant*
Gilzean, *Maclean*
Glen, *Chattan*
Glendinning, *Eliott*
Glennie, *Chattan*
Gorrie, *Donald*
Gow, *Chattan*
Gray, *Stewart*
Gregor, *MacGregor*
Gregorson, *MacGregor*
Gregory, *MacGregor*
Gregson, *MacGregor*
Greig, *MacGregor*
Grier, *MacGregor*
Grierson, *MacGregor*
Grigor, *MacGregor*

Hardie, *Chattan*
Hawthorn, *Donald*
Hayburn, *Hay*
Hayes, *Hay*
Hayfield, *Hay*
Haynes, *Hay*
Haystoun, *Hay*
Henderson, *Donald*
Hewison, *Donald*
Houston, *Donald*
Howison, *Donald*
Hughson, *Donald*
Hunter, *Eliott* (where there is a
    Liddesdale connection)
Huntly, *Gordon*
Hutcheson, *Donald*
Hutchinson, *Donald*

Inches, *Robertson*

Isles, *Donald*

Jameson, *Stewart*
Jamieson, *Stewart*

Kay, *Chattan*
Kean, *Donald*
Kearns, *Grant*
Keith, *Stewart*
Kellie, *Donald*
Kenneth, *Mackenzie*
Kennethson, *Mackenzie*
Kerrons, *Grant*
King, *MacGregor*
Kinnell, *Donald*
Kinnoull, *Hay*

Laxfrith, *Hay*
Lean, *Maclean*
Leask, *Hay*
Leckie, *MacGregor*
Lees, *Chattan*
Leith, *Hay*
Lennox, *Stewart*
Levack, *Stewart*
Lewis, *MacLeod*
Livingstone, *Stewart*
Lockerwort, *Hay*

MacAdam, *MacGregor*
MacAdie, *Fergusson*
MacAllan, *Donald*
MacAndrew, *Chattan*
MacAra, *MacGregor*
Macaree, *MacGregor*
MacAskill, *MacLeod*
MacAulay, *MacLeod* (where
    there is a Lewis connection)
MacAy, *Chattan*
MacBain, *Chattan, Mackay*
MacBaxter, *MacMillan*

MacBeath, *Chattan*
MacBeolain, *Mackenzie*
Macbeth, *Chattan*
MacBride, *Donald*
MacBrieve, *Morrison*
MacCaig, *Chattan, MacLeod*
MacCaishe, *Donald*
MacCamie, *Stewart*
MacCardney, *Chattan*
MacCash, *Donald*
MacCaw, *Stewart*
MacCay, *Mackay*
MacChlerich, *Chattan*
MacChlery, *Cameron, Chattan*
MacChoiter, *MacGregor*
MacCloy, *Stewart*
MacClure, *MacLeod*
MacCodrum, *Donald*
MacCombich, *Stewart*
MacCombie, *Chattan*
MacConnach, *Mackenzie*
MacConnell, *Donald*
MacConnochie, *Campbell*
MacCook, *Donald*
MacCormick, *Maclean*
MacCrain, *Donald*
MacCrie, *Mackay*
MacCrimmon, *MacLeod*
MacCuaig, *MacLeod*
MacCuish, *Donald*
MacCulloch, *Ross*
MacCunn, *Chattan*
Macdaid, *Chattan*
MacDaniell, *Donald*
MacDavid, *Chattan*
MacDermid, *Campbell*
MacDiarmid, *Campbell*
MacDonachie, *Robertson*
Macdonald, *Donald*
Macdrain, *Donald*
MacEachern, *Donald*

MacEachin, *Donald*
MacEaracher, *Chattan*
MacElfrish, *Donald*
MacElheran, *Donald*
MacElmail, *MacMillan*
MacFadyen, *Maclean*
MacFadzean, *Maclean*
MacFall, *Chattan*
MacFarquhar, *Chattan*
MacGaradh, *Hay*
MacGeachie, *Donald*
MacGibbon, *Campbell*
MacGillivray, *Chattan*
MacGillonie, *Cameron*
MacGilroy, *Grant*
MacGilvernock, *Graham*
MacGilvra, *Maclean* (where
　　there is a Mull connection)
MacGlashan, *Stewart*
MacGorry, *Donald*
MacGowan, *Chattan*
MacGrime, *Graham*
Macgruder, *MacGregor*
MacGruer, *Fraser*
MacHardie, *Chattan*
MacHarold, *MacLeod*
MacHenry, *Donald*
MacHugh, *Donald*
MacHutcheon, *Donald*
MacIan, *Donald*
Macilduy, *Maclean*
Macilreach, *Donald*
Macilrevie, *Donald*
MacIlroy, *Grant*
MacIlvain, *Chattan*
MacIlvora, *Maclean*
Macilvrae, *Chattan*
Macilvride, *Donald*
Macilwraith, *Donald*
Macinroy, *Robertson*
Macintyre (of Badenoch),

Chattan
MacIsaac, *Campbell*
MacIver, *Mackenzie* (where
　　there is a connection with
　　Ullapool and district)
MacIvor, *Mackenzie* (where
　　there is a connection with
　　Ullapool and district)
MacKeachan, *Donald*
MacKean, *Donald*
Mackechnie, *Donald*
MacKee, *Mackay*
MacKeggie, *Chattan*
MacKellachie, *Donald*
MacKellar, *Campbell*
MacKelloch, *Donald*
MacKeochan, *Donald*
MacKerlich, *Mackenzie*
MacKerracher, *Chattan*
MacKerras, *Fergusson*
MacKerron, *Grant*
MacKersey, *Fergusson*
MacKessock, *Campbell*
MacKiaran, *Grant*
MacKichan, *Donald*
Mackie, *Mackay*
MacKillican, *Chattan*
Mackinlay, *Stewart*
Mackintosh, *Chattan*
MacKirdy, *Stewart*
MacKuer, *Donald*
Maclagan, *Robertson*
Maclaine, *Maclean*
MacLardie, *Donald*
MacLay, *Stewart*
Maclean (of the North), *Chattan*
MacLeish, *Chattan*
Maclennan, *Mackenzie*
MacLergain, *Maclean*
MacLewis, *Stewart*
MacLise, *Chattan*

MacLiver, *MacGregor*
MacMartin, *Cameron*
MacMichael, *Stewart*
MacMoil, *MacMillan*
MacMunn, *Stewart*
MacMurchie, *Mackenzie*
MacMurray, *Murray*
MacMurrich, *Chattan*
MacMutrie, *Stewart*
MacNee, *MacGregor*
MacNeish, *MacGregor*
MacNicol, *MacLeod*
MacNiven, *Chattan*
MacNucator, *MacMillan*
MacOran, *Campbell*
MacPeter, *MacGregor*
MacPhadden, *Maclean*
MacPhail, *Cameron, Mackay*
　　(where there is a Sutherland
　　connection)
Macphail, *Chattan*
MacPhedran, *Campbell*
Macpherson, *Chattan*
MacPhun, *Campbell*
Macqueen, *Chattan*
MacQuey, *Mackay*
MacQuistan, *Donald*
MacQuoid, *Mackay*
Macrae, *Mackenzie*
Macraild, *MacLeod*
Macritchie, *Chattan*
MacRobbie, *Robertson*
MacRobert, *Robertson*
MacRory, *Donald*
MacRuer, *Donald*
MacSorley, *Cameron*
MacSporran, *Donald*
MacSwan, *Chattan*
MacSween, *Chattan*
MacTaggart, *Ross*
MacTause, *Campbell*

MacTear, *Ross*
MacThomas (of Glenshee), *Chattan*
MacUlric, *Cameron*
MacUre, *Campbell*
Macvail, *Chattan*
MacVanish, *Mackenzie*
MacVeagh, *Maclean*
MacVean, *Chattan*
MacVey, *Maclean*
MacVinish, *Mackenzie*
MacVurrich, *Chattan*
MacWhannell, *Donald*
Malloch, *MacGregor*
Matheson, *Mackenzie*
May, *Donald*
Milne, *Gordon*
Mitchell, *Ross*
Monteith, *Graham, Stewart*
Moray, *Murray*
Morton, *Douglas*
Mowat, *Stewart*
Murchie, *Mackenzie*
Murchison, *Mackenzie*
Murison, *Morrison*

Neilson, *Mackay*
Nicolson, *MacLeod*
Nixon, *Eliott*
Noble, *Chattan*
Norman, *MacLeod*

O'Drain, *Donald*
Oliphant, *Stewart*
O'May, *David*

Patrick, *Grant*
Patten, *Maclean*
Paul, *Cameron* (where Lochaber connection is established)
Peter, *MacGregor*

Petrie, *MacGregor*
Polson, *Mackay*
Purcell, *Donald*

Rattray, *Murray*
Reay, *Mackay*
Reid, *Robertson*
Reoch, *Chattan*
Revie, *Donald*
Riach, *Chattan*
Ritchie, *Chattan*
Roy, *Robertson*

Sanderson, *Donald*
Scobie, *Mackay*
Shannon, *Donald*
Shaw, *Chattan*
Simon (and most surnames derived therefrom, e.g., Sime, Simpson), *Fraser*
Slains, *Hay*
Small, *Murray*
Smith, *Chattan* (if there is ancestral connection in Clan Chattan territory), *Morrison* (if deriving from Harris)
Spalding, *Murray*
Stark, *Robertson*
Stuart, *Stewart*
Swan, *Chattan*

Tarrell, *Chattan, Ross*
Tarrill, *Chattan*
Tawesson, *Campbell*
Taylor, *Cameron* (where Lochaber connection is established)
Thomson, *Eliott*
Todd, *Gordon*
Tolmie, *MacLeod*
Tosh, *Chattan*

Toshach, *Chattan*
Train, *Donald*
Turriff, *Hay*
Tweedie, *Fraser*

Ure, *Campbell*

Walker, *MacMillan*
Whannell, *Donald*
Williamson, *Mackay*

Vass, *Ross*

Yester, *Hay*

ILLUSTRATION ACKNOWLEDGEMENTS

The letters a, b, c following the page numbers indicate the order on pages with more than one illustration (not counting tartans); the illustrations are ordered from the top of the left hand column to the bottom of the right hand column.

British Tourist Authority: 116
Colour Library International: 64a
David Gowans: 80b
Dennis Hardley: 21, 24b, 39c, 41b, 68a, 77, 88, 89b, 90, 117a, 117b, 120b, back cover
David Kilpatrick: 114
Laing Art Gallery and Museum, Newcastle upon Tyne: 12
The Mansell Collection: 67b, 78
By courtesy of the Manx Museum: 102a, 102b
Mitchell Library, Glasgow: 29a, 55a, 59a, 67c
George Morice: 18, 19, 22, 35, 37a, 89a, 92a
Michael Murphy: 31, 37b, 38, 52, 76, 80a, 81, 82, 84, 85, 96b, 101a, 108a, 115, 116a
National Galleries of Scotland: 11a, 13, 17, 39a, 39b, 43b, 46, 49a, 51a, 55a, 57a, 66, 70, 74, 86b, 110a, 110b, 111, 116b
National Museum of Antiquities of Scotland: 24a
National Portrait Gallery, London: 47a, 47b, 51b, 59b, 67a, 118b, 118c
Henry Nivet: 45
David Paterson: 53
R.J. Pearce: 36a
Reproduced by gracious permission of Her Majesty the Queen: 33
Tony Ridge: 92b, 93b
Scottish Tourist Board: front cover, 15a, 15b, 15c, 23a, 23b, 41a, 43a, 49b, 56, 57, 63, 64b, 64c, 68b, 68c, 73, 86a, 89c, 100, 101b, 112, 118
D. Sim: 120a
Eric Thorburn (copyright Highlands and Islands Development Board): 25
Vista of Glasgow: 28, 108b
Tom Weir: 27, 29b, 42, 60a, 60b, 61a, 61b, 72, 93a, 94, 96a, 98, 104a, 104b, 105, 106